D1513525

Some Effects of Participative Budgeting on Managerial Behavior

by

Robert J. Swieringa

Graduate School of Business and
Public Administration
Cornell University

and

Robert H. Moncur

School of Business
Queen's University

National Association of Accountants

New York, N.Y.

Published by

National Association of Accountants

919 Third Avenue, New York, N.Y. 10022

Copyright by National Association of Accountants © 1975

Library of Congress Catalog Card Number 74-28619

NAA Publication Number 74-75

Foreword

In recent years we have witnessed increased interest by management accountants and others in the relationships between behavioral science and accounting. In part, this increased interest has reflected the realization by these individuals that accounting has a behavioral impact and that appropriate attention should be given to behavioral considerations in designing and implementing management accounting systems.

The National Association of Accountants also has become increasingly aware of the potential significance of behavioral science to accounting and of the need for more and better research in this area. In January 1970, the Association sponsored a Behavioral Science Symposium at the University of North Carolina to explore opportunities for research. As a result of the discussions at this Symposium, an Advisory Committee on Applications of Behavioral Science to Accounting was formed to assist the Association in the development of a conceptual framework for research in this area and to identify projects and to select qualified researchers.

This monograph is the first in a new Association research series which will comprise studies dealing with applications of behavioral science to accounting. The research presented in this monograph was undertaken by Professors Robert J. Swieringa and Robert H. Moncur. They conceived the need for research on the effects of participative budgeting on managerial behavior and submitted a research proposal to the Association's Advisory Committee. This Committee reviewed their proposal and their report of a pilot study and made suggestions about the design of the research. The members of this Committee were: William J. Bruns, Jr., Edwin H. Caplan, Homer R. Figler, Henry A. Schwartz, Arthur B. Toan, Jr. and John T. Wheeler.

Guidance in the preparation of this monograph was provided by a Project Subcommittee of the Association's Committee on Research:

Homer R. Figler (Chairman)
Ernst & Ernst
New York, New York

Henry A. Schwartz
IBM Corporation
Armonk, New York

Henry L. Clayton, Sr.
Corning Glass Works
Corning, New York

Arthur B. Toan, Jr.
Price Waterhouse & Co.
New York, New York

It is my pleasure to express the Association's appreciation to the members of the Advisory Committee and Project Subcommittee who kindly and generously contributed their time and talents. Their suggestions and comments were extremely valuable to the researchers. However, this monograph reflects the views of the researchers and not necessarily those of the Association, the Committee on Research, the Advisory Committee or the Project Subcommittee.

STEPHEN LANDEKICH
Research Director
National Association of Accountants

July 1974

Preface

This research monograph focuses primarily on some effects of participative budgeting on managerial behavior. It presents a theoretical model that indicates some key variables and relationships among them that may be important in linking a company's use of participative budgeting with the behavior of its managers and ultimately with some effects which may be associated with this behavior. It also presents relevant empirical data about some of these variables, relationships and effects. Thus, the approach of the monograph is neither strictly theoretical nor purely empirical. Rather, it endeavors to bring to bear both theory and empirical data to provide insights into the nature and extent of these effects.

This monograph is an outgrowth of our conviction that a company's use of budgeting should be described in behavioral terms. We propose "managers' budget-oriented behavior" as a key concept for doing this and argue that from this concept stems a new view of budgeting, a fuller appreciation of its inherent structure and a broader conception of its role and likely effects. Accordingly, the primary thrust of the monograph is on describing this behavior, the process through which it is defined, and the broader context in which it occurs.

In addition, we obtain measures of this behavior from a relatively large sample of operating managers, identify and describe several dimensions of this behavior, and indicate the relative importance of these dimensions for explaining differences among managers. We also analyze the relationships between various predictor variables and dimensions of this behavior as well as the relationships between these dimensions and managers' attitudes about their positions.

The research reported in this monograph is part of a research program we launched while affiliated with the Graduate School of Business at Stanford University. The principal aims of this program were to develop research methods, theory and substantive findings that would provide insights into the behavioral effects of budgeting. Two studies were completed prior to the research reported in this monograph. An initial study (Swieringa and Moncur, 1972) focused on the budget-oriented behavior of a sample of branch bank managers and on the relationships between this behavior and various attitude, position, size and performance measures. A second study (Moncur and Swieringa, 1973), which was a pilot study for the present research, focused on the budget-oriented behavior of managers in companies that differed in their use of participative budgeting.

Subsequent to our initial drafting of the manuscript for this monograph, Moncur (1975) has reported the results of some additional analysis of the personality data collected as part of this research, and Swieringa (1974) has presented some additional thoughts about the choice of an optimal participative budgeting system.

We hope that this monograph will be useful to both researchers and practitioners. The theoretical model and research findings provide a framework which can be used to organize some of the diverse literature relating to the behavioral effects of budgeting, and we hope that they will stimulate our academic colleagues to undertake further, more refined studies in this area. We also hope that the model and findings will raise some relevant issues for practitioners to consider in designing and redesigning participative budgeting systems. Although the formulation of prescriptions for practice was not a major stimulus for our research, some potential implications for practice do follow from it. These implications are discussed in the final chapter.

We are pleased to acknowledge the generosity of the National Association of Accountants and the Graduate School of Business at Stanford University in providing financial and institutional support for our research. We also acknowledge with gratitude the hospitality of the four companies that served as our research sites. To name them or the executives and managers with whom we dealt would risk their anonymity; nevertheless, we appreciate their invaluable assistance.

We are indebted to Stephen Landekich, Research Director for the National Association of Accountants, for his advice, counsel and patience during the course of our research. We also are indebted to the members of the Association's Advisory Committee for their help in formulating the research design and to members of its Committee on Research Project Subcommittee for their careful reading of our earlier manuscript drafts and for their helpful suggestions.

Finally, we are happy to acknowledge the support and encouragement of our wives, Pamela and Reggie, who not only assisted us in coding and key-punching data and in typing and proofreading drafts of this manuscript, but also tried to motivate us by subtly, but persistently, asking us "Are you finished yet?"

ROBERT J. SWIERINGA
ROBERT H. MONCUR

June 1974

Table of Contents

Chapter 1

Introduction

This monograph reports the results of an exploratory investigation into some effects of participative budgeting on managerial behavior. This introductory chapter describes briefly the general setting of the research problem and outlines the overall nature of the study.

The Setting of the Problem

The participation of operating managers in the decisions by which budgets are established to measure and evaluate their performance has long been one of the most controversial issues in the budgeting and management accounting literature. Early models of the budget-or target-setting process were autocratic in nature.[1] A company's top management was viewed as having the responsibility for setting operating budgets, issuing them to operating managers, and then holding these managers accountable for performance in accordance with these imposed budgets.

In some respects, early models of the budget-setting process thus reflected traditional models of the managerial process in which managers were viewed as making decisions on matters within their areas of freedom, issuing orders or directives to their subordinates, and then monitoring their performance to ensure conformity with these directives.[2] Early developments in budgeting, as well as in scientific management generally, contributed to the centralization of important decision making in organizations by focusing on the development of methods by which managers could make more rational decisions by substituting objective measurements and empirical validated methods for casual judgments.

---

[1] Becker and Green (1962: 393), for example, state that "early business budgeting largely imitated governmental practice and technique. It began with 'imposed' budgets and the obvious controls — limit, restraint, clerical and communicative."

[2] Koontz and O'Donnell (1964) summarize these traditional models by suggesting four principal functions which the manager must perform — (1) plan; (2) organize; (3) motivate; and (4) control.

1

Pointing to evidence of restriction of output and lack of involvement under traditional managerial systems, several social psychologists, most notably Mayo (1945), McGregor (1960), Argyris (1957, 1964), and Likert (1961, 1967), argued for greater influence in decision making on the part of those who are held responsible for decision implementation and execution. Similarly, several individuals, including Argyris (1952), Becker and Green (1962), Wallace (1966), and Hofstede (1967), called for greater participation by operating managers in the budget-setting process. Pointing to evidence of operating manager resistance and hostility under early models of the budget-setting process, these individuals suggested that top management share budget-setting responsibility with operating managers.

The term "participative budgeting" is used to refer to the practice of "allowing individuals who will be responsible for performance under a budget to participate in the decisions by which that budget is established" (Caplan, 1971: 85). The two primary advantages usually associated with participative budgeting are summarized by Caplan (1971: 85) as follows: (1) it helps to provide operating managers with a sense of challenge and sense of responsibility, and (2) it increases the probability that the goals of the budget will be internalized by the managers involved — that is, that they will accept these goals as their own.

Companies differ dramatically in both the amount and form of participation and influence they afford their operating managers in the budget-setting process. First, near the low end of the participation scale are the so-called autocratic methods in which the top management of a company sets operating budgets by itself, using information generally available to it at that time. Second, there are methods in which top management affords operating managers some limited participation in budget setting. For example, even though it maintains ultimate budget-setting responsibility, top management may obtain information from operating managers, solicit their ideas and suggestions, and/or even ask them to generate and evaluate alternatives in the process of setting operating budgets. Top management may, of course, vary the extent to which it obtains these inputs from these managers and also the extent to which it allows these inputs to influence the budgets it sets. Finally, near the high end of the participation scale are the so-called group decision methods in which top management shares budget-setting responsibility with operating managers; that is, they generate and evaluate alternatives together and attempt to reach agreement and consensus on the budgets set.

In designing and redesigning budgeting systems, management accountants and others are often faced with the problem of choosing from among alternative amounts and forms of participation by operating managers in setting budgets. In doing so, they must deal with a variety of questions.

How much participation is appropriate for a given budgeting situation? In what budgeting situations is more participation by operating managers in the budget-setting process to be preferred to less, or vice versa? The answers to these questions are both complex and variable.

In general, the choice of how much participation is appropriate for a given budgeting situation should be made on the basis of an evaluation of the consequences associated with alternative amounts and forms of participation. Greater participation in the budget-setting process is often associated with the benefits of increasing the likelihood of high-quality budgets, greater acceptance of these budgets by operating managers, and better management team development. However, other consequences are also likely to be associated with greater participation. For example, greater participation is likely to require more time and effort (e.g., man-hours) in order to set operating budgets. In addition, Schiff and Lewin (1968, 1970) have suggested that greater participation may result in operating managers building "organizational slack" into their budgets by underestimating revenues and overestimating costs.

How much participation is appropriate for a given budgeting situation will depend on the weights assigned to various consequences such as budget quality, acceptance, team development, and the time and effort required to set budgets; and these weights are likely to vary from one situation to another. In the short run, for example, the managers of a company might seek to minimize the time and effort required to set budgets, subject to minimal quality and acceptance constraints. That is, they might seek to sacrifice the quality of the budgets set, and their acceptability, in order to expend the least amount of time and effort in the process. In the long run, however, they might place less weight on the amount of time and effort required to set budgets as the basis for choice. Rather, they might be more interested in the trade-offs between time and effort and other consequences such as team development, both of which may increase with greater participation.

How much participation is appropriate for a given budgeting situation also will depend on the likelihood of different amounts of these consequences obtaining under each alternative. Empirical evidence suggests that this likelihood is also apt to vary from one situation to another.[3] While greater participation in budget setting may increase the likelihood of higher budget quality and greater acceptance in some situations, it may, in fact, decrease this likelihood in other situations. The reason for this variation appears to lie in the context within which participative budgeting is used — namely, within an organizational setting. This set-

---

[3] This empirical evidence is summarized in Becker and Green (1962), Stedry (1960) and Hofstede (1967). See also Vroom (1969), and Campbell *et al.,* (1970) for excellent summaries of empirical evidence on the efficacy of participation in decision making.

ting is complex and the interrelationships and interdependencies among organization members are both potent and subtle. The personalities of these members must be considered, as must be patterns of social relations and the processes of communication and social influence.

Given the potential importance of organizational, personality, and interpersonal variables for the effectiveness of participative budgeting, we think it is critical that the consequences or effects of participative budgeting be investigated so that situational definitions can be developed of the circumstances under which participation in the budget-setting process may contribute to, or hinder, a company's ability to achieve its goals. These situational definitions could then be translated into guidelines of potential value to management accountants and others in choosing the appropriate amount and form of participation to fit the situation they encounter.

Identification of situations and circumstances under which different amounts and forms of participative budgeting are effective, however, requires systematic investigation of a wide assortment of variables over a variety of situations so that we can state with confidence which variables are likely to impinge on their success. In the next section of this chapter we describe the nature of a research study designed to identify a number of these variables, specify their impact in selected organizational settings, and suggest how they might be considered in designing and redesigning budgeting systems.

The Nature of the Study

A Theoretical Model

The objective of our investigation was to study some effects of participative budgeting on managerial behavior. At the start of the investigation there was no body of theory sufficiently well developed to guide us in specifying the nature and extent of these effects. Particularly lacking were empirical data on these effects and a conceptual model of these effects. Because of these deficiencies, we found it necessary to develop a conceptual framework to guide our thinking. The result was a theoretical model, presented in Chapter 2, that relates participative budgeting, the behavior of individual managers, and other key variables.

At the core of this model is a set of variables, termed "managers' budget-oriented behavior," which includes the various actions and interactions of company management personnel which are brought about by a company's use of budgeting. Because we were interested in investigating some effects of participative budgeting on managerial behavior, we sought to develop a way of linking the properties of a company's use of budgeting with the behavior of its managers. Most budgeting and managerial textbooks tend to describe budgeting in terms of the sets of technical

4

methods and procedures these systems typically encompass. Even though the objective of these methods and procedures is to influence managerial behavior — how managers plan, coordinate, and control the activities of the company — we know very little about the mechanism through which or by which these methods and procedures in fact influence that behavior. The concept of managers' budget-oriented behavior provides us with a way of describing a company's use of budgeting in behavioral terms. Rather than describe budgeting in terms of technical methods and procedures, we describe it in terms of the behavior of individual managers, and this provides a way of linking the properties of a company's use of budgeting with the behavior of its managers.

The model also includes two other sets of variables. One set, termed "participative budgeting variables," includes the structural properties of a company's use of participative budgeting. This set includes alternative amounts and forms of participation afforded operating managers in the budget-setting process, and a causal relationship is asserted to exist between the participative budgeting variables and managers' budget-oriented behavior. The other set, termed "mediating variables," includes three additional classes of variables — organizational, interpersonal, and personality — which taken in combination represent the context within which participative budgeting is used and within which managers' budget-oriented behavior occurs.

The model focuses on these three sets of variables and the relationships that are hypothesized to exist between them. The major implications of the model are the potential importance of (1) the concept of managers' budget-oriented behavior both as a way for describing budgeting in behavioral terms and as a way for linking budgeting with the behavior of individual managers, (2) the participative budgeting and mediating variables for understanding the context of managers' budget-oriented behavior, and (3) the recognition that different effects may be associated with managers' budget-oriented behavior.

An Empirical Study

In order to obtain measures of some of the variables contained in the theoretical model and to determine what gross relationships may exist among them, we conducted a field study in four production companies. The overall research design of this study and the research methods used to implement that design are described in Chapter 3. The four companies used as research sites were similar in that they were in the same industry and had similar production processes and markets; however, they were different in both the amount and form of participation they afforded operating managers in the budget-setting process. Interviews were conducted with the top financial executives of each company, and a complete description of each company's use of participative budgeting was developed. Two samples of operating managers were drawn from each company; and a survey research questionnaire was used to obtain data from these managers about their budget-oriented behavior, about various organizational, personality, and interpersonal variables, and about their attitudes and opinions concerning their jobs.

Our analysis of the data obtained in the empirical study is presented in Chapters 4-10. In Chapter 4, we report the results of our analysis of managers' budget-oriented behavior. Forty-four descriptive items were used to obtain measures of managers' budget-oriented behavior. Descriptive, normative and evaluative measures of all items were obtained by asking each manager to indicate how frequently each item described takes place, should take place, and how important the item is to him. Our analysis of these items results in the substantive identification and description of 13 descriptive and 14 normative budget factors which are capable of providing both an economical and yet reasonably complete description of managers' budget-oriented behavior.

The most important descriptive budget factors reflect budget-oriented behavior that is evaluative in nature and reflect the extent to which managers have positive attitudes about budgeting and are influential in budget setting. The next most important descriptive budget factors reflect how managers cope with large budget variances, how acceptable their methods for achieving budgeted performance are, and how expressive they are about budgeting. The least important descriptive budget factors reflect general evaluative behavior, interactions with superiors, subordinates and others, level of involvement in budgeting, and the time pressures experienced because of budgeting.

The most important normative budget factors reflect managers' attitudes about performing various activities brought about by budget variances, their use of the budget to evaluate subordinates, their taking an influential role in improving budgeting systems, and their level of involvement in the budgeting process. The next most important normative budget factors reflect managers' attitudes about having their methods of achieving budgets accepted by others, working with others in preparing operating budgets, the usefulness of budgeting to them, and taking an active and expressive role in the budgeting process. The least important normative budget factors reflect managers' attitudes about their having difficulty meeting operating budgets and their starting to prepare operating budgets before being asked.

Our comparison of the descriptive and normative budget factor structures reveals that these two structures are similar in that specific items have the highest loadings on similar descriptive and normative budget factors and that similar factors are most important in both structures. However, these two structures are different in that the relative loadings of items on similar factors differ in their relative importance in the two

6

structures. Finally, an intercorrelation analysis reveals that the descriptive and normative budget factors are not highly intercorrelated.

In Chapters 5-7, we report the results of our analysis of the relationships between the predictor variables measured as part of the study and the measures of managers' budget-oriented behavior developed in Chapter 4. We describe in detail the 17 predictor variables that were measured as part of the study in Chapter 5. Two of these variables are categorical in nature, reflecting the fact that our total sample was drawn from four different companies and from different management levels within each company. The other predictor variables include four demographic variables, three attitudinal variables, and eight personality variables.

Because there was little in the way of either theory or empirical evidence that could help us specify how these predictor variables might be related to any particular measure of managers' budget-oriented behavior, we used an analysis strategy which allowed us to observe which predictor variables and combinations within them produced the greatest discrimination in explaining differences in our measures of managers' budget-oriented behavior.

The results of our analysis of the relationships between the predictor variables and the descriptive budget factors are reported in Chapter 6. These results reveal that different variables may be important for predicting different dimensions of managers' budget-oriented behavior.

For example, these results reveal (1) that a company's use of participative budgeting and the organizational context within which it is used are the most important predictors of the extent to which managers engage in various budget-related coping behaviors, to be personally involved in budgeting, to be shown comparisons of actual and budgeted performance for other units, and to experience intensive time demands from budgeting; (2) that the personality variables of emotional stability, ascendency, and the interpersonal variable of internal-external control are the most important predictors of the extent to which managers' methods of achieving their budgets are accepted by others and the extent to which managers are influential in the budgeting process, expressive about budgeting, and have positive attitudes about budgeting; (3) that the demographic variables of managers' time in company, time in position, and time spent on budgeting are the most important predictors of the extent to which managers use budgets as evaluative devices, to perform various budget variance-related activities, and to be involved in the budgeting process; and (4) that managers' levels in their companies is the most important predictor of the extent to which managers work with their superiors and others in preparing their operating budgets.

In Chapter 7 we report the results of our analysis of the relationships between the predictor variables and the normative budget factors. These results also reveal that different variables may be important for predicting different aspects of what managers think about their budget-oriented behavior. For example, these results suggest (1) that a company's use of participative budgeting and the organizational context within which it is used are the most important predictors of managers' attitudes about the extent to which they think they should perform certain budget-variance-related activities, work with their superiors and others, suggest changes or improvements in the budgeting system, be expressive about budgeting, and have positive attitudes about the usefulness of budgeting; (2) that a manager's level in his company is the most important predictor of his attitudes about budget-oriented interaction with his superiors; (3) that the demographic variables of a manager's time in company, time in position, and time spent budgeting are the most important predictors of his attitudes about the extent to which he thinks he should offer suggestions for the improvement of budgeting systems, interact with his superiors, have difficulty meeting his budgets, and be involved in the budgeting process; and (4) that the personality variables of emotional stability and cautiousness are the most important predictors of managers' attitudes about the extent to which they think they should work with others in preparing their budgets, perform various budget-oriented activities, have positive attitudes about the usefulness of budgeting and be influential in budgeting.

In Chapters 8-10, we report the results of our analysis of the relationships between the measures of managers' budget-oriented behavior and managers' attitudes about their positions. The results of our analysis of managers' attitudes about their positions are reported in Chapter 8. Twenty attitudinal items were used to measure managers' attitudes about their positions. These items were drawn from questionnaires developed and used by Porter (1964), Haire, Ghiselli, and Porter (1966), and Porter and Lawler (1968) to measure managers' job attitudes and by Kahn *et al.* (1964) to measure job-related tension, satisfaction and ambiguity. Descriptive, normative, and evaluative measures of each of these items were obtained by asking managers to indicate how frequently each item described takes place, should take place, and how important it is to him. Our analysis of these measures results in the identification and description of five descriptive and five normative position factors.

The results of our analysis of the relationships between the descriptive budget factors and managers' attitudes about their positions are reported in Chapter 9. These results suggest (1) that how often managers experience job-related tension may be related to how often they experience time pressure from budgeting; (2) that how often they experience job-related self-actualization may be related to how often they are influential in budgeting; (3) that how often they experience job-related ambiguity may be related to how often they have positive attitudes about the usefulness of budgeting; (4) that managers' attitudes about how often they think they should experience job-related tension may be related to how much time pressure they experience from budgeting and how involved they are in budgeting; and (5) that managers' attitudes about how much job-related tension they think they should experience may be related to how much time pressure they experience from budgeting, how expressive they are about budgeting, and how involved they are in the budgeting process.

The results of our analysis of the relationships between the normative budget factors and managers' attitudes about their positions are presented in Chapter 10. These results suggest (1) that how often managers think that they engage in meaningful social interaction may be related to how often they think that they should be influential in budgeting; (2) that how often managers experience job-related ambiguity may be related to how often they think that their methods of achieving their budgets should be accepted by others; (3) that managers' attitudes about experiencing job-related ambiguity may be related to their attitudes about being influential in budgeting; (4) that their attitudes about having job-related influence may be related to their attitudes about the usefulness of budgeting; (5) that their attitudes about experiencing job-related tension may be related to their attitudes about going to and working with their superiors; and (6) that their attitudes about experiencing meaningful job-related social interaction may be related to their attitudes about being expressive about budgeting.

Finally, in Chapter 11, we present a speculative discussion of the implications of our research for the development of a behavioral approach to participative budgeting and discuss some limitations and extensions of our research.

Chapter 2

The Theoretical Model

In designing a study to investigate some effects of participative budgeting on managerial behavior, we found it necessary to develop a conceptual scheme to guide our thinking. The result was a theoretical model, outlined in this chapter, that attempts to relate participative budgeting to the behavior of individual managers and ultimately to some consequences which may result because of that behavior. We developed this model to help determine what data to obtain as part of our empirical investigation, to help integrate the findings from our empirical investigation, and to provide a theoretical orientation that we hoped would stimulate future research. Our intention was to indicate at least some of the important variables and to hypothesize some of the relationships between them. Thus, we hoped that this model would provide a way of thinking about the relationships between a large number of variables, some of which previously had not been combined in a meaningful manner.

We do not claim that this model totally explains all of the relationships that may exist between participative budgeting and managerial behavior. Future empirical research may uncover evidence that some of the relationships do not exist in the manner depicted in our model and also may indicate that other important variables should be included in the model. However, if the variables and relationships included in the model lend themselves to specific disproof, and consequently to specific improvement as a means of explanation, then the development of this model will have served a useful purpose.

In this chapter, we define the variables contained in our theoretical model and discuss the relationships hypothesized to exist between them. The chapter consists of four sections. The first three sections will focus on the three sets of variables contained in the model — managers' budget-oriented behavior, participative budgeting, and mediating variables.

The managers' budget-oriented behavior variables include various actions and interactions of managers which are brought about by a company's use of budgeting. These variables describe a company's use of budgeting in behavioral terms — in terms of the behavior of individual

11

managers. A role model describes how budgeting may be reflected in the content of some of the roles and how role relationships may be defined for the managers who occupy these positions.

The participative budgeting variables include alternative amounts and forms of participation in budget setting. A causal relationship is asserted to exist between these variables and managers' budget-oriented behavior. Companies differ dramatically in how they allow managers to participate in the budget-setting process, and these differences may be reflected in managers holding different expectations about their budget-oriented behavior.

The mediating variables include several organizational factors, personality factors, and interpersonal relationships which may affect the relationship between participative budgeting and managers' budget-oriented behavior.

Finally, in the fourth section we discuss some implications of our theoretical model for our empirical investigation of some effects of participative budgeting on managerial behavior.

The Managers' Budget-Oriented Behavior Variables

Budgeting usually is viewed as encompassing the preparation and adoption of a detailed financial operating plan, the comparison of the results of actual operations with those set forth in the plan, and an analysis and evaluation of the reasons for deviations from the plan. The objective of budgeting is to successfully influence how managers plan, coordinate, and control the activities of the company so that better managerial performance may result. Bacon (1970: 3), for example, suggests that the planning that goes into the preparation of the budget may yield several important advantages for the company and its management:

- *Sets goals* (People perform better when they have definite objectives to work toward.)
- *Establishes limits* within which managers understand they are expected to operate.
- *Increases flexibility* (This appears to be a paradox, but it is not; often the company that has considered alternatives beforehand is in a position to make better-informed decisions when the need for change arises than the company that must react without benefit of prior consideration.)

Horngren (1972: 24) suggests that budgets may help management in several ways:

1. The existence of a well-laid plan is the major step toward achieving coordination. Executives are forced to think of the relationship of individual operations, other operations, and the company as a whole.

2. Budgets help to restrain the empire-building efforts of executives. Budgets broaden individual thinking by helping to remove unconscious biases on the part of engineering, sales, and production officers.
3. Budgets help to search out weaknesses in the organizational structure. The administration of budgets isolates problems of communication, of fixing responsibility, and of working relationships.

Vatter (1969: 16) suggests that budgeting may help managers control their activities:

> Budgeting is a kind of "future tense" accounting, in which the problems of the future are met on paper before the transactions actually occur. This approach makes it possible to compare actual events with the planned ones, to establish a feedback control arrangement which makes management more systematic and more effective.

Even though the objective of budgeting is to influence managerial behavior — how managers plan, coordinate, and control the activities of the company — our present knowledge of the mechanism through which or by which budgeting influences that behavior is at best incomplete. There have been few, if any, attempts to describe budgeting in behavioral terms. Most budgeting and managerial accounting textbooks describe budgeting in terms of a relatively well-defined set of technical methods and procedures.[1] In addition, many companies describe their use of budgeting in terms of these methods and procedures in their budget and procedure manuals, job descriptions, flow charts, memoranda, and so forth. Yet, how do these methods and procedures influence managerial behavior?

Because we wanted to investigate some effects of participative budgeting on managerial behavior, we were faced with the problem of developing a model of the mechanism through which and by which budgeting may influence this behavior. To do this, we sought to develop a way of describing budgeting, not in terms of technical methods and procedures, but in terms of the behavior of individual managers. We found that a natural and both immediate and practical way of doing this was to describe budgeting in terms of the set of activities or potential behaviors of company management personnel that are brought about by a company's use of budgeting.

Various actions and interactions which occur as part of the normal routine of company management personnel can be associated primarily, if not solely, with the company's use of budgeting. For example, a department manager may spend considerable time with his superiors, his

---

[1] See, for example, Horngren (1970; 1972), Vatter (1969), and Welsch (1971).

subordinates, and his fellow department managers in formulating and preparing the operating budgets for his department. In addition, he may work closely with accounting and budgeting personnel so that those factors and problems he would like to have considered in his operating budget receive special treatment. In administering the budget and using it to monitor and evaluate his department's performance, he may receive inquiries from his superiors and others about his department's performance, he may make personal investigations of variances in his department, and he may work closely with his subordinates and others in taking corrective action. Also, he may express his opinions on budget matters, offer suggestions for improving the budgeting system, and discuss specific budget items in informal conversations with superiors, subordinates, other department managers, and accounting and budgeting personnel.

We use the term "managers' budget-oriented behavior" to refer to the actions and interactions of company management personnel which presumably are precipitated by a company's use of budgeting. The concept of managers' budget-oriented behavior provides us with a way of describing budgeting in behavioral terms — in terms of the behavior of individual managers. Moreover, this concept provides a way of describing how a company's use of budgeting may influence managerial behavior. For example, it suggests that a company's use of budgeting may influence managerial behavior by bringing about and requiring the performance of budget-oriented actions and interactions.

A Role Model

In order to be more precise about how a company's use of budgeting may be related to the behavior of individual managers, we must be able to locate each manager within the total set of ongoing relationships and behaviors comprised by an organization. To do this requires a concept or model of organization. An organization can be viewed as a system of interrelated parts, where the parts are not individual members as such but are *roles* (Kahn *et al.*, 1964; Katz and Kahn, 1966; McGrath, 1966). To explain this way of viewing or conceptualizing organizations, we must introduce and define several related concepts: positions, roles, role relationships, and role set.

The individual members of an organization can be viewed as occupying different *positions* or of having different niches or jobs in an organization. Associated with each position is a set of potential behaviors which constitute the *roles* to be performed, at least approximately, by any individual who occupies that position. Also associated with each position is a set of certain other positions and, further, a set of *role relationships* between the individual who occupies that position and the individuals who occupy the other, related positions. For example, any individual who occupies a given position is likely to be related to certain other individuals who

14

depend on his performance of the potential behaviors associated with his position in some fashion — they may be rewarded by it or require it in order to perform their own tasks. These other individuals with whom a given individual is connected constitute his *role set*. This set usually includes an individual's superiors, subordinates, peers, and others.

An example of how the concepts of position, role, role relationships, and role set can be used to describe and analyze the location of an individual in an organization may be useful at this point. Bacon (1970: 70) notes that the organization chart of the International Textbook Company includes a *position* entitled "Corporate Budget Director." Some of the *roles* associated with this position, as described in the position's job description, include the major activities of "preparation, consolidation, and distribution of the corporate profit and loss and capital expenditure budgets, analysis and interpretation of results, and preparation of financial and operating statistical reports to provide a basis for management planning, operating controls, and performance appraisal," and they include the minor activities of "develop methods and procedures for the preparation of the budgets, recommend budgetary policies and practices, (and) . . . perform . . . special studies." Some of the *role relationships* associated with this position are also described in the position's job description. For example, the position is responsible to the position of "Manager — Financial Planning" and also "is so located in the organizational structure of the Corporation that the individual (who occupies this position) will be required to maintain contact with division heads and their staffs on a daily basis." The Manager — Financial Planning and the division heads and members of their staffs are members of the Corporate Budget Director's *role set*.

Any individual who occupies the position of Corporate Budget Director is expected to perform the roles and engage in the role relationships associated with that position. However, it is important at this point to distinguish between the roles and role relationships associated with a particular position and the actions and interactions actually performed and engaged in by an individual who occupies that position. For example, the roles and role relationships associated with the position of Corporate Budget Director may not be descriptive of how the indiviual occupying that position actually behaves. To understand why this is so, we must now introduce and define the additional concepts of role expectations, sent role, received role, and role behavior.

The members of an individual's role set develop beliefs and attitudes about what he should or should not do in performing the activities and behaviors associated with his position. These prescriptions and proscriptions are designated as *role expectations* and are used as standards in terms of which they evaluate his performance. The members of the

15

individual's role set perceive the way in which an individual actually performs these behaviors associated with his position and communicate their expectations to him. These communications are described as the *sent role*. The purpose of their communicating their expectations to him is not merely informational; rather, it is to exert pressure, to influence him so that his behavior will be congruent with their expectations. The individual experiences this pressure, termed the *received role,* and it arouses in him psychological forces of some magnitude and direction. The individual then acts or responds, exhibiting *role behavior* which shows some combination of compliance or noncompliance with the expectations of these other persons.

Consider again the position of Corporate Budget Director described above. The actual behavior of the individual who occupies this position can be viewed as being a complex outcome of the various pressures to which he is exposed. The Manager — Financial Planning and the division heads and members of their staffs have expectations (role expectations) about what this individual, as Corporate Budget Director, should or should not do; and they communicate these expectations to him by exerting pressure on him (sent role). The individual experiences this pressure (received role) and exhibits behavior (role behavior) which is then observed and evaluated by these other individuals.

A Role Episode Model

The four concepts of role expectations, sent role, received role, and role behavior can be thought of as constituting a sequence or *role episode* (Kahn *et al.,* 1964; Katz and Kahn, 1966). Figure 2-1 presents a model of the role episode. Arrow 1 in Figure 2-1 represents the communication of role expectations from members of the role set *(Other Managers)* to an individual occupying a particular position *(Focal Manager).* As discussed above, these Other Managers have expectations about the way in which the Focal Manager performs the roles associated with his position, they perceive the way in which he is actually performing these roles, and they exert pressure on him to make his performance congruent with their expectations. The Focal Manager receives the expectations sent to him and then acts or responds. Arrow 2 in Figure 2-1 is a feedback loop. The Other Managers observe and evaluate the Focal Manager's behavior, and the degree to which his behavior conforms to the expectations they hold for him at one point in time will affect the state of those expectations at the next moment. The cycle then moves into another episode.

The role episode model described above is, of course, an abstraction from the context in which it occurs. That context can be thought of as consisting of all the relatively stable, enduring properties of the situation within which a role episode takes place. The recurring actions and

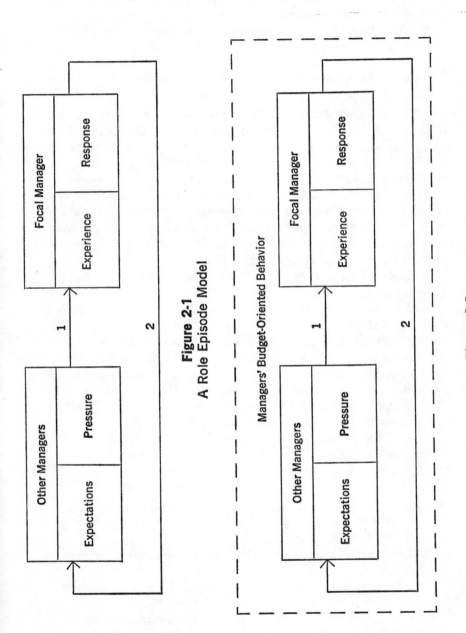

Figure 2-1
A Role Episode Model

Figure 2-2
A Role Episode Model of Managers' Budget-Oriented Behavior

interactions that may be brought about by a company's use of budgeting provide the basis for, and the context within which, each new occurrence of the role episode can be understood. Accordingly, managers' budget-oriented behavior can be conveniently represented in an enlargement and extension of Figure 2-1. That figure and the sequence it represents now form the core of Figure 2-2.

The Relationship Between Expectations and Response (Arrow 1)

Arrow 1 in Figure 2-2 suggests that a Focal Manager's budget-oriented behavior may be affected by the demands and requirements placed on him by the Other Managers. In effect, a company's use of budgeting can be viewed as superimposing a set of potential budget-oriented behaviors, actions and interactions on a company's management positions. The managers who occupy these positions have expectations about how and to what extent they think that they should perform the potential budget-oriented behaviors associated with their positions. The content of these expectations may include preferences with respect to specific acts and personal characteristics and styles; they may deal with what a manager should be, what he should think or believe, what he should do, and how he should relate to others.

Some of the expectations held for a Focal Manager may be reflected in the job description for his position. For example, the job description for the position of Corporate Budget Director described earlier specified in a general way what the individual who occupies this position should do, e.g., prepare, consolidate, and distribute the corporate profit and loss and capital expenditure budgets, analyze and interpret the results, etc., and how he should relate to others, e.g., to the Manager — Financial Planning and to the division heads and the members of their staffs.

Some of the expectations held for a Focal Manager may also be reflected in the company's budget manual. The following excerpts are taken from the budget manual of an office equipment company:

The following basic principles should be adhered to by all personnel participating in the budget process in order to maximize the effectiveness of the Profit Plan:

- All activities within each Division must be represented in the Division's operating budget.

- All budgeted figures should be compiled in such a way as to clearly identify the persons responsible for their attainment.

- Actual performance is to be reported in such a manner that it can be related to the specific budget controlling the measured activity.

- Budgeted figures should represent reasonable but not easily attainable goals.

18

- Management personnel responsible for achieving segments of Division operating budgets should participate in the development of those budgets, and agree that the goals set for the activities for which they are responsible are reasonable.
- Divisional One-Year Operating Budgets should be congruent with the Company's long-range and Five-Year Budget and make identifiable contributions towards the attainment of those long-range goals.
- Division Operating Budgets should not be submitted with the expectation that they will be "cut." Rather, they should be prepared as final plans, supported by adequate justifying data, representing each Division's best judgment as to how its contributions to the Company can be maximized in the forthcoming year (Bacon, 1970: 17).

These excerpts reveal how a company's budget manual also may specify in a general way what individuals who occupy specific management positions should or should not do; e.g., management personnel responsible for achieving segments of division operating budgets should participate in the development of those budgets; division operating budgets should not be submitted with the expectations that they will be cut.

Of course, the expectations held for a Focal Manager are by no means limited to those reflected in his position's job description or the company's budget manual. The Other Managers develop their own expectations about what they think the Focal Manager should or should not do, they perceive and evaluate the way in which he performs and behaves, and they exert pressure on him by communicating their expectations to him so that his behavior may conform more closely to their expectations.

The Other Managers may use various ways to communicate their expectations to a Focal Manager. Sometimes an Other Manager may use direct, overt ways to communicate his expectations to a Focal Manager:

> I go to the office and check that budget every day. I can then see how we're meeting the budget. If it's O.K., I don't say anything. But, if it's no good, then I come back here (smiles) and give the boys a little . . . Well, you know. I needle them a bit. I give them the old . . . hm . . . well . . . you know what . . . the old needle (Argyris, 1952: 24).

> I make it a policy to have close contact, human contact, with all the people in my department.
> If I see we're not hitting the budget, I go out and tell them I have $40,000 on the order.
> Well, they don't know what that $40,000 means. They think it's a lot of money so they get to work.
> Human factor, that's important. If you treat a human being like a human being, you can use them better and get more out of them (Argyris, 1952: 24).

Sometimes an Other Manager may use indirect, covert ways to communicate his expectations to a Focal Manager:

> You know it's a funny thing. If I want my people to read the budget, I don't shove it under their nose. I just lay it on my desk and leave it alone. They'll pick it up without a doubt (Argyris, 1952: 24).

These examples reflect the fact that the Other Managers communicate their expectations to the Focal Manager for the purpose of influencing him so that his behavior may more closely conform to their expectations. Occasionally, however, a Focal Manager's response may not be the one that was either intended or desired. Consider the following situation in which a division general manager tried to influence the budget-oriented behavior of his subordinates:

> The general manager of one division of a food distribution company sent a memo to his immediate subordinates warning that any manager who was over his budget two months in a row would have "his management abilities seriously questioned." This memo was copied and sent down to each successive level of management, in some cases with additional comments in a covering memo. In order to avoid being caught in this unfavorable budget situation and still meet sales targets and production quotas, the managers resorted to a very common ruse. At budget proposal preparation time, each manager, from the bottom management level up the line, simply added his own "fudge factor," thereby inflating the total budget (Hughes, 1965: 20).

The Relationship Between Response and Expectations (Arrow 2)

Arrow 2 in Figure 2-2 suggests that the expectations Other Managers hold for a Focal Manager may be affected by his actual behavior. The extent to which a Focal Manager's budget-oriented behavior conforms to the expectations held for him by the Other Managers at one point in time may affect the state of those expectations at the next moment. If a Focal Manager's response is essentially a hostile counterattack, the Other Managers may be apt to think of him and behave toward him differently than if he were submissively compliant. If he complies better under pressure, they may increase the pressure; if he is adversely affected by pressure, they may reduce the pressure.

In sum, the behavior of a Focal Manager in response to the communications and pressures sent to and exerted on him by Other Managers feeds back to each of these Other Managers in ways that either alter or reinforce these communications and pressures. Consider the following example in which a division manager's behavior clearly affected his superior's expectations and subsequent response:

> Finding himself with surplus funds at the end of the year, the manager of a major division of a large publishing company thought he would become a "fiscal hero" by announcing to his boss that he was giving back the dollars he had not spent. To his surprise, he was told

that he must be either a "poor planner" (over-budgeted), "incompetent organizer" (insufficient activity), or "not-growth oriented" (bigger and better budgets). In view of his unspent dollars, his request for funds for the following year was cut back. Belatedly he learned that what he considered to be smart money management was regarded as unprogressive and almost un-American. And naturally, the next time he was able to save the company money, he found other ways to spend the savings (Hughes, 1965: 21).

The Participative Budgeting Variables

Alternative Amounts and Forms of Participation

"Participative budgeting" refers to the application of participative management techniques to budgeting; it refers to the practice of allowing managers to participate in the decisions by which budgets are established to measure and evaluate their performance. Participative budgeting is not an all or nothing proposition; rather, companies can and do differ dramatically in both the amount and form of participation and influence they afford their operating managers in the budget- or target-setting process.

Near the low end of the participation scale are the so-called autocratic methods in which a company's top management sets operating budgets by itself, issues them to operating managers and then uses them to monitor and evaluate their performance. Consider the following situation:

> The top management of a large technical instruments and components manufacturing company sets earnings targets for the company's operating divisions without obtaining additional information from or consulting with the general managers of these divisions. These earnings targets are then translated into aggregate divisional sales and work estimates. Division general managers, working with their marketing, finance, and production managers, use these estimates to formulate an orders forecast, a cost of goods sold schedule, and forecasts of other expected operating costs. These forecasts and schedules are then used to prepare each division's detailed operating plan (Moncur and Swieringa, 1973).

Note that, in this company, division general managers and their subordinates do not participate in the setting of divisional earnings targets. The company's top management sets these targets and then imposes them on division managers. Moreover, note that in the process of setting these budgets, top management does not obtain additional information from or consult with divisional operating managers. Autocratic methods of budget setting essentially reflect decision-making processes which may involve little or no interaction between top management and operating managers prior to budget setting.

21

In other companies, top management may afford operating managers limited participation in budget setting. For example, even though it retains complete budget-setting responsibility, top management may obtain additional information from operating managers, solicit their ideas and suggestions, and/or even ask them to generate and evaluate alternatives in the process of setting operating budgets. In these situations, operating managers essentially perform an information-providing or consultative role in the budget-setting process. However, top management can not only vary the extent to which it obtains information from and consults with these managers, but also the extent to which it allows the information and advice obtained from these managers to influence the budgets it sets. Consider the following situation:

> The general manager of an ordnance engineering division of a company which manufactures heavy equipment sets operating budgets for his division. However, before setting these budgets, his operations manager obtains detailed forecasts of direct labor hours and non-labor direct costs for each program from program managers. These forecasts are used to generate complete forecast reports for each program. These reports are then reviewed by the program managers who assign a probability of success factor to reflect the likelihood that the program will be successfully completed in the next budget period. These probability factors are then used in generating a set of adjusted forecast reports which are again reviewed by program managers and then are submitted to the division's general manager for his consideration and use in setting operating budgets for the division (Moncur and Swieringa, 1973).

Note that, in this company, the program managers do not participate directly in the budget-setting process; rather, their role in this process is effectively limited to that of providing information which can be considered and used by the division's general manager in setting operating budgets for the division. Also note that the information these program managers provide in the budget-setting process is limited to estimates of direct labor hours, non-labor direct costs, and probability of success factors only. Specifying the minimum information inputs required from program managers in order to generate complete forecast reports at the division level may reduce the time and effort these managers have to devote to the budget-setting process, but it may also serve to limit the participation of these managers in that process.

Finally, near the high end of the participation scale are the so-called group decision methods in which top management shares budget-setting responsibility with operating managers; together they generate and evaluate alternatives and attempt to reach agreement and consensus on the budgets set. Consider the following situation:

> In a large institutional food services company, top management shares budget-setting responsibility with operating managers. First, service

unit managers work closely with account directors in preparing initial forecasts for their service units for the coming year. Next, district managers bring their unit managers and account directors together for a week-long series of group meetings. The sole purpose of these meetings is to set operating targets for each service unit. The initial forecasts for each unit are presented and then evaluated jointly by the district managers and all of the unit managers and account directors present. Group target-setting meetings are also held at the regional and national levels. For example, regional operations directors hold group target-setting meetings with their district managers and a marketing vice-president holds group target-setting meetings with his regional operations directors. Finally, the targets set in these meetings are compiled into an overall operating plan which is used to evaluate the year's actual operating results (Moncur and Swieringa, 1973).

Note that, in this company, operating managers at each level of management participate in setting the operating targets and budgets used to monitor and evaluate their performance. Essentially, this company uses an approach to budget setting in which all planning, including the preparation of annual forecasts and the setting of goals and targets, originates at the lowest levels of managerial responsibility. Note also that extensive use is made of group decision methods in setting these operating targets. Group target-setting meetings are held at each level of management so that managers may reach agreement and consensus on the targets set.

The Relationship Between Participative Budgeting and Managers' Budget-Oriented Behavior (Arrow 3)

The situations described above reveal how companies can differ in their use of participative budgeting. Yet, to what extent are these differences likely to be reflected in differences in managers' budget-oriented behavior? The relationship asserted to exist between participative budgeting and managers' budget-oriented behavior is depicted in Figure 2-3. The "participative budgeting variables" in Figure 2-3 refer to the structural properties of a company's use of participative budgeting. These properties include both the amount and form of participation afforded operating managers in the budget-setting process. Arrow 3 in Figure 2-3 suggests that the content of the expectations Other Managers hold for a Focal Manager's budget-oriented behavior may be determined in part by these structural properties. What a Focal Manager is supposed to do, with and for whom, may be given by these properties. Although these expectations exist in the minds of the Other Managers, these properties may be sufficiently stable so that they can be treated as independent of these Other Managers.

The Mediating Variables

Participative budgeting is used, and managers' budget-oriented behavior occurs, in a broader context. In order to understand more fully

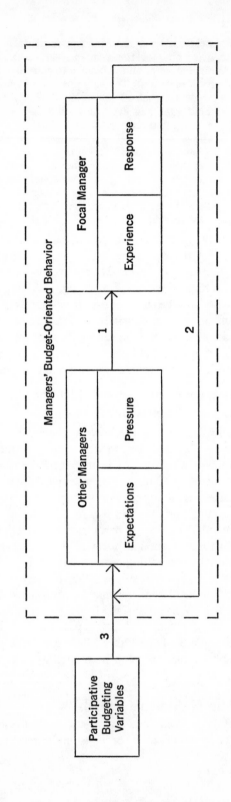

Figure 2-3

The Relationship Between Participative Budgeting Variables
and Managers' Budget-Oriented Behavior

the relationship between participative budgeting and managers' budget-oriented behavior, we must now extend our analysis to include three additional sets of variables which, taken in combination, represent this broader context. These additional sets of variables include the more enduring states or characteristics of the organization, of the individual members of the organization, and of the interpersonal relationships between them. These variables, which we term "mediating variables," can be conveniently represented as an enlargement or extension of Figure 2-3. That figure now forms the core of Figure 2-4.

The Significance of Organizational Variables (Arrow 4)

The "organizational variables" in Figure 2-4 refer to characteristics of the company in which participative budgeting is used and in which managers' budget-oriented behavior occurs. Some of the variables included in this set characterize the company as a whole, for example, its size, its number of management levels, its products and services, and its financial base. Other variables included in this set have to do with the relationship of a certain manager to the company, for example, his level in the company, or the number and positions of others who are directly concerned with and affected by his performance.

Arrow 4 in Figure 2-4 suggests that a causal relationship may exist between these organizational variables and the structural properties of a company's use of participative budgeting. How much participation and influence are afforded operating managers in the budget-setting process may differ significantly from company to company, and even from level to level or from position to position within a given company. These differences are far from random events. Within the context of each company's unique operating environment, the structural properties of a company's use of participative budgeting may be shaped by systematic organizational variables.

For example, Moncur and Swieringa (1973) observed that a company's use of participative budgeting may reflect the relative stability of its operating environment. They observed that an equipment manufacturing company which operated in a relatively stable and predictable environment was able to carefully plan its responses to changing operating conditions, and that this was reflected in the company's use of limited amounts and forms of participative budgeting to facilitate the setting of long-term targets. Because of the relative stability of the company's operating environment, its top management relied heavily on a centralized data processing system in setting long-term targets and obtained only selected information inputs from operating managers prior to setting those targets.

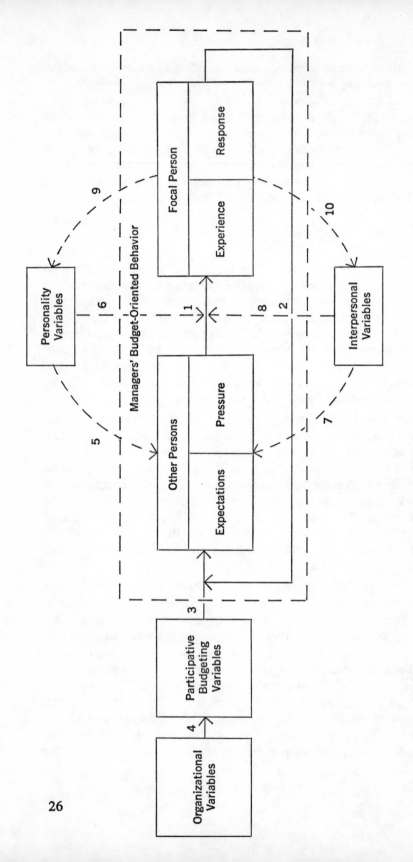

Figure 2-4

A Theoretical Model of Relationships among Participative Budgeting
Variables, Managers' Budget-Oriented Behavior and Mediating Variables

Moncur and Swieringa (1973) further observed that an institutional food services company which operated in a relatively unstable and highly volatile environment was not able to carefully plan its responses to changing operating conditions, and that this was reflected in the company's use of extensive amounts and forms of participative budgeting to facilitate the setting of near-term targets. Because of the instability and volatility of the company's operating environment, top management shared target-setting responsibility with operating managers, in part because they either possessed or had access to the information required to set these targets.

Moncur and Swieringa (1973) also observed that how participative budgeting is used within a company may differ from level to level and from position to position. They noted that two line managers who occupied positions in different levels of the organization of an institutional food services company performed different roles in the company's use of participative budgeting. Where a district manager spent most of his time working closely with his unit managers in preparing their operating budgets, his superior, a regional operations director, spent most of his time explaining and correcting budget variances, tracing the causes of these variances to districts and units, submitting explanations about the causes of these variances to corporate management, reporting actions taken, and revising budgets for the coming periods.

Similarly, they noted that two managers who occupied different positions in an equipment manufacturing company performed different roles in that company's use of participative budgeting. Where one manager, an operations manager in an ordnance engineering division, was an active participant in the company's budget-setting process, performing essentially a controllership role or function, another manager, a director of engineering in an equipment division, was relatively uninvolved in the company's budget-setting process.

The Significance of Personality Variables (Arrows 5, 6 and 9)

The "personality variables" in Figure 2-4 refer to the enduring properties of the managers who exhibit budget-oriented behavior. The variables included in this set characterize a manager's propensities to behave in certain ways, his motives and values, his sensitivities and fears, his habits, etc. The personality predispositions of managers may lead to, and may in fact account for, differences in their budget-oriented behavior. For example, a volatile, aggressive Focal Manager may elicit strong reactions and pressures from Other Managers because only strong reactions have a lasting effect on him. Similarly, a very rigid Focal Manager may successfully resist attempts by Other Managers to influence him.

Arrows 5, 6 and 9 in Figure 2-4 suggest that personality characteristics of a Focal Manager and of the Other Managers may mediate the relationship between expectations and response. Consideration of the personality characteristics is important for several reasons. First, these characteristics may affect the expectations Other Managers hold for a Focal Manager and also the kinds of pressures they are likely to exert on him (arrow 5). Where some Focal Managers may elicit strong and conflicting pressures from Other Managers, and their reactions to these pressures may serve to intensify them, other Focal Managers may perform their jobs in ways which seldom evoke pressures of any magnitude. Similarly, where some Focal Managers may encourage free and open communications with Other Managers, other Focal Managers may, in fact, discourage it.

Second, personality characteristics also may mediate the relationship between pressures and experience (arrow 6). Some Focal Managers may be able to tolerate stressful conditions without visible signs of discomfort and with relatively little disruption of their normal behavior. Other Focal Managers may be overwhelmed with tension and anxiety when faced with even relatively moderate levels of stress.

Third, personality characteristics may affect the Focal Managers' responses. Argyris (1952: 19), for example, describes how two supervisors can differ in their responses to pressure:

> (i) Supervisor A is quiet, relatively non-emotional, seldom expresses his negative feelings to anyone, but at the same time he works excessively. Supervisor A can be found working at his desk long after the others have gone home. As one supervisor expressed it, "That guy works himself to death."
>
> (ii) Supervisor B is nervous, always running around "checking up" on all his employees. He usually talks fast, gives one the impression that he is "selling" himself and his job when interviewed. He is forever picking up the phone, barking commands and requesting prompt action.

Finally, the personality characteristics of a Focal Manager may, in turn, be affected by his experience and response (arrow 9). Even though psychologists usually view personality characteristics as being relatively fixed, having been formed during earlier years of life and by earlier experiences, the process of personality formation continues throughout life. A Focal Manager's experiences may lead to some modifications in his personality characteristics. For example, a Focal Manager's ability to handle the pressures exerted on him by the Other Managers may be reflected in changes in his self-esteem or levels of aspiration.

The Significance of Interpersonal Variables
(Arrows 7, 8 and 10)

The "interpersonal variables" in Figure 2-4 refer to the characteristics of the interpersonal relationships between a Focal Manager and Other

28

Managers. These relationships include the relatively stable patterns of interaction which may result from the formal organizational structure of the company, from informal interaction, and from sharing common experiences. The factors included in this set have to do with the power and ability of managers to influence others, the affective bonds of respect and trust between managers, the dependence of one manager on another, the style of communication between managers and so on.

Arrows 7, 8 and 10 in Figure 2-4 suggest that interpersonal variables may mediate the relationships between expectations and responses. Arrow 7 suggests that the expectations Other Managers hold for a Focal Manager as well as the kind of pressure they exert on him may be affected by the nature of the interpersonal relationships between them. A Focal Manager's superiors may hold expectations that differ from those held by his subordinates. Further, his superiors may exert pressure in a different manner from his subordinates.

Arrow 8 suggests that the relationship between pressure and experience also may be affected by interpersonal variables. A Focal Manager may interpret pressures differently depending on the nature of the relationships he has with Other Managers. For example, pressures exerted by relatively powerful superiors may arouse in him more tension than similar pressures exerted by others.

Finally, arrow 10 suggests that a Focal Manager's response may, in turn, affect the nature of his interpersonal relationships with Other Managers. For example, a Focal Manager's loss of respect for an Other Manager may affect the pattern of relationships between them in the future.

The following example reveals how the nature of interpersonal relationships may mediate the relationships between expectations and response:

Each fall the corporate management of an oil company requested its various divisions to submit their budget proposals for the coming year for review. In one division, the manager and his immediate subordinates referred to this fall event as the "silly season." A department head, going one better, described his own department's efforts at forecasting dollar outlays in such terms as "playing Monopoly" and "Chinese money." His subordinates took their cue from him, with the result that budgets in the department were unusually unrelated to actual expenditures and could serve no control function. Record keeping became a kind of numbers game, with funds gaily shifted from one account to another, and expenses charged off whenever it seemed most convenient. In short, budgeting among this group was simply, a "fun type" of activity, yielding figures that were quite useless as performance measures. (Hughes, 1965: 21).

Note that the expectations held by a division manager and his subordinates about their budget-oriented behavior affected the expectations they held for department managers as well as the process of communicating these expectations to these managers. The department managers received these expectations, and their behavior, in turn, affected the expectations held by the division manager and his subordinates.

Discussion

Up to this point, we have described a theoretical model which relates a company's use of participative budgeting to the behavior of individual managers. We have described a company's use of budgeting in terms of a set of potential managers' budget-oriented behaviors and have suggested that the amount and form of participation afforded managers in the budget-setting process may be an important antecedent of this behavior. We also have suggested that the relationship between participative budgeting and managers' budget-oriented behavior may be mediated by several organizational, personality, and interpersonal variables.

One broad implication of the model is the potential importance of the concept of managers' budget-oriented behavior both as a way for describing budgeting in behavioral terms and as a way for linking a company's use of budgeting with the behavior of individual managers. The specific implications of this concept are both immediate and practical:

1. In order to describe a company's use of budgeting, we must attempt to determine what behavior of managers is brought about by its use. Many actions and interactions which occur as part of the normal routine of a company's management personnel can be associated primarily, if not solely, with the operation of its budgeting system. A manager may spend considerable time with his superiors, subordinates, and peers in formulating and preparing his operating budgets and may work closely with budgeting personnel so that factors and problems he would like to have considered receive special treatment. Moreover, he may receive inquiries from his superiors and others about his unit's performance, he may make personal investigations of variances, he may work closely with his subordinates and others in taking corrective action, and he may express his opinions and offer suggestions on budget matters. These actions and interactions are precipitated by a company's budgeting system and represent the basic defining characteristics of that system. Thus, we must attempt to determine what behavior of managers is brought about by a company's use of budgeting.

2. In order to understand, describe, or predict a Focal Manager's budget-oriented behavior, we must determine to what other jobs or positions his is connected and what the nature of the connecting bonds is. We have viewed each manager as occupying a different position in a company and as being expected to perform and engage in the budget-oriented behaviors and relationships associated with that position. More-

over, we have viewed the actual budget-oriented behavior of the Focal Manager who occupies a given position as being a complex outcome of a definitional process between the Focal Manager and the Other Managers who occupy other related positions. Because these Other Managers have expectations about the Focal Manager's budget-oriented behavior and attempt to influence his behavior by exerting pressure on him, it would be almost impossible for us to fully understand, describe, or predict a Focal Manager's budget-oriented behavior without determining what Other Managers are attempting to influence him and without determining why and to what extent they are attempting to do so.

3. In order to change a Focal Manager's budget-oriented behavior, we must attempt to bring about complementary changes on the part of all the Other Managers to whom the manager is connected. As discussed above, the budget-oriented behavior of a Focal Manager is of direct concern to Other Managers and is substantially determined by the behavior of these Other Managers toward him. Any change in the Focal Manager's behavior will not only require complementary changes on their part, but also the success of such a change will in large part depend upon their acceptance and reinforcement of this change. Thus, the expectations of these Other Managers have to be taken into account in any process of evaluating and attempting to change the budget-oriented behavior of a Focal Manager.

A second broad implication of the model is the potential importance of other variables and combinations of them for understanding managers' budget-oriented behavior. Some forces must be overcome, at least partially, in order for managers to perform budget-oriented behavior. The participative budgeting and mediating variables reflect the potential importance of surrounding conditions for understanding managers' budget-oriented behavior. These conditions inhere in the structural properties of a company's use of participative budgeting, in the organizational setting in which it is used, in the personalities of the managers performing managers' budget-oriented behavior, and in the nature of the interpersonal relationships between these managers.

A third broad implication of the model is that different effects may be associated with managers' budget-oriented behavior. The model takes into account the fact that Other Managers may hold quite different expectations toward a given Focal Manager and that at any given time, these Other Managers may impose pressures on him for different kinds of behavior. To the extent that these pressures give rise to conflicting forces within him, a Focal Manager may experience psychological conflict. A Focal Manager may receive incompatible pressures from different Other Managers — for example, from his superiors and his subordinates, from the same Other Manager at different times or in different circumstances — or he may receive pressures for behavior which are incompatible with his own needs and values. These kinds of conflict may come about because a lack of agreement or coordination among managers may produce mutually contradictory sets of expectations and pressures or because these expectations and pressures may take an inadequate account of the needs and abilities of a given Focal Manager.

This conception of managers' budget-oriented behavior also takes into account the fact that certain information is required for adequate performance of the behaviors associated with a position. In order for a Focal Manager to conform to the expectations held by Other Managers, he must know what these expectations are — he must know what rights, duties, and responsibilities are associated with his position. The Focal Manager must also know something about what activities will fulfill these responsibilities and how these activities can best be performed. A lack of information can result from many causes. The required information may not exist or may exist but not be available to him. In any event, to the extent to which information may be lacking, a Focal Manager may experience ambivalence.

In general, we expect that a manager's experience in a budgeting situation is likely to be a function of the objective demands and pressures to which he is subjected in that situation. When Other Managers are generally supportive of a Focal Manager's present behavior and performance, we expect that fact to be so perceived and the Focal Manager's response to be primarily one of satisfaction and confidence. When pressures from Other Managers are particularly strong and directed toward changes in the behavior of a given Focal Manager, or when they are contradictory to one another, the experience may be fraught with conflict and ambiguity, and evoke responses of tension, anger, or indecision.

Finally, the model provides an overall framework for our empirical study of the effects of participative budgeting on managerial behavior. First, we are interested in measuring managers' budget-oriented behavior and in identifying different dimensions of that behavior. Second, we are interested in identifying and measuring some of the variables which may influence that behavior. These variables may include differences in how companies use participative budgeting as well as some organizational, personality, and interpersonal variables which may mediate the relationship between participative budgeting and managers' budget-oriented behavior. Third, we are interested in identifying and measuring some of the effects of managers' budget-oriented behavior on managers' attitudes about their positions. The research design and methods used in our empirical study are described in Chapter 3.

Chapter 3

Research Design and Methods

The theoretical model presented in Chapter 2 identified a number of variables which may be important in investigating some effects of participative budgeting on managerial behavior. The model focused on a set of budget-oriented actions and interactions exhibited by company management personnel and suggested that these actions and interactions may be affected by the structural properties of a company's use of participative budgeting as well as by several organizational, personality, and interpersonal variables. The model also suggested that these actions and interactions may, in turn, affect managers' attitudes about their positions, including the extent to which managers may experience job-related influence, satisfaction, and self-actualization as well as job-related tension, ambiguity, and conflict.

In this chapter, we describe the empirical study we conducted to obtain measures of some of the variables contained in the theoretical model and to determine what gross relationships may exist among them.

The first section describes the overall research design of this study. To obtain measures of managers' budget-oriented behavior, of several factors which may influence this behavior, and of managers' attitudes about their positions, a field study was conducted in four production companies. These companies were similar in that they were in the same industry and had similar production processes and markets. However, these companies were different in that they afforded their operating managers different amounts and forms of participative budgeting.

The second section describes the research methods that were used to implement the overall research design. Interviews were conducted with the top financial executives of each company, and a complete description of each company's use of participative budgeting was developed. Two samples of operating managers were drawn from each company, and a survey research questionnaire was used to obtain data from these managers. The research findings of our empirical study are reported in the next eight chapters.

The Research Design

A distinction sometimes is made between experimental and nonexperimental research designs. Experimental designs involve investigator-produced changes in some variables in order to observe their effects on other variables. An investigator creates conditions and studies their effects on the people exposed to them. Subjects usually are recruited for the experiment and are assigned to conditions in such a way as to minimize or eliminate any confounding of subjects with conditions. Experimental designs can be used in either laboratory or field settings. For example, laboratory experiments have been used by Stedry (1960) to examine the relationships between performance, aspiration levels, and externally imposed budgets, and by Cyert *et al.* (1961) and Pondy and Birnberg (1969) to examine the systematic distortion of information resulting from the use of budgets for both resource allocation and performance evaluation purposes. In addition, a field experiment was used by Stedry and Kay (1966) to investigate the effects of budget levels on the performance of foremen.

Experimental designs are particularly suited to the determination of causality. They permit precision of measurement, control of variables, and considerable freedom to manipulate variables of central concern. The major disadvantage of these designs is that they often lack realism because their use is effectively limited to either artificially created or highly penetrable natural settings. Further, these designs are often limited in the number of variables they can consider. They can be expanded somewhat by adding more conditions and subjects. However, although this may be possible in a laboratory setting, it is rarely possible in a field setting.

Nonexperimental research designs focus on the relationships between variables without any of the variables being altered by the investigator. Observations relevant to two or more variables are made for each sample of persons or groups. The degree and direction of the relationships among these observations are then determined by the use of statistical methods. Nonexperimental research designs include intensive non-quantitative studies of single settings as well as statistical analyses of relationships among variables in a larger number of settings. For example, these designs have been used by Argyris (1952) to study the effects of budgets on people, by Fertakis (1967) to examine the relationship between felt budget-induced pressure and supervisory leadership behavior, by Hofstede (1967) to study the effects on managerial motivation of various control aspects of budgeting, by Schiff and Lewin (1968, 1970) to study how managers build slack into their budgets, by Onsi (1973) to study behavioral variables affecting budgetary slack, and by Hopwood (1972) to study the relationships between styles of evaluation and various consequences.

Nonexperimental designs are particularly valuable in the initial exploration of a problem area. A large number of variables can be studied simultaneously and, with new data-processing methods, extremely complex statistical analyses can be performed quickly and economically. Many variables which would be difficult or impossible to manipulate experimentally can be measured and related statistically to hypothetical determinants or consequences. The major disadvantage of the nonexperimental designs stems from the fact that they do not permit conclusive inferences about causal relations among variables. It is almost impossible to determine conclusively from these designs whether a statistical association between two variables, X and Y, is attributable to the fact that X causes Y, Y causes X, or whether X and Y are caused by some third variable Z. However, these designs are useful inasmuch as they expose causal hypotheses to disconfirmation. If no statistical association exists between two variables, the credibility of a causal hypothesis is lessened. If a statistical association exists, the credibility of a causal hypothesis is strengthened in that it has survived a chance of disconfirmation. But a rigorous testing of the hypothesis requires the use of an experimental design.

After considering the relative advantages and disadvantages of the experimental and nonexperimental designs, we decided that our purposes could best be served by a nonexperimental design. A field study was the specific type of nonexperimental design we decided to use. The reasons for choosing this type of nonexperimental design stem directly from the theoretical model presented in Chapter 2.

First, we wanted to conduct our empirical study in natural rather than created settings. A major implication of the model was the potential importance of surrounding conditions for understanding the effects of participative budgeting on managerial behavior. These conditions inhere in the organization setting in which participative budgeting is used, in the personalities of the managers in that setting, and in the nature of the interpersonal relationships between them. Because these effects are highly interactive and inherently contextual, we believed that it was important to conduct our study in natural settings.

Second, this study is by necessity an exploratory one. It focuses on an area where little previous research has been done. Even though the model identified some of the conditions surrounding the use of participative budgeting, it did not assess the relative importance of these conditions for understanding the effects of its use on managerial behavior. The field study is particularly suited for exploratory work. It can be used to find out which are the major variables in a situation and what gross relationships exist among them.

Third, we wanted our empirical study to be extensive rather than intensive in scope. We wanted to consider the possible significance of a large number of variables and to consider their possible effects. A field study design makes it possible to look at a large number of variables. Looking at all the variables and relationships specified in the model with an experimental approach would require many studies. We believed that an intensive and definitive study of these variables and relationships could be attacked more profitably after an exploratory study had provided a framework and hypotheses.

The Research Methods

Selection of Research Sites

A number of criteria guided our search for and selection of research sites. First, because we wanted to maintain relatively close personal contact with the companies to be used as research sites, we decided to confine our search for research sites to the Greater San Francisco Bay Area. Second, in order to obtain a relatively large sample of managers from each site, we further restricted our search to only the medium and large companies in the area. Third, because we wanted to delimit the diversity of our research sites, we decided to restrict our search to production companies which were either in the same industry or had similar production processes and markets. Finally, because we wanted to isolate some effects of participative budgeting, we restricted our search to companies which tended to view their use of budgeting as an important planning and control device, but which tended to use different amounts and forms of participative budgeting.

Using a directory of San Francisco Bay Area companies, we listed the available companies by industry. Only the electronics industry provided a sufficient number of companies that met the criteria described above. In all, we selected and were given access to four production companies in the electronics industry.

One company, Company A, is a data systems company; it conceives data systems, analyzes data from them — systems analysis and data analysis, and builds them — data receiving systems, data communication systems, and data processing systems. The company was established in the early 1960's. It was initially owned by its employees and became publicly held in 1970. Its major products include the technical analysis of data collected by reconnaissance systems, programs concerned with conceiving and evaluating solutions to data systems problems, the design and development of remotely controlled receiving systems, data communications systems and data processing systems. Annual sales are about $18 million, and the company has about 550 employees.

The second company, designated Company B, is a major producer of communications transmission equipment. The company was established in the early 1940's and in 1959 became a subsidiary of the major communications equipment manufacturing subsidiary of a large independent telephone holding company. Company B's products include microwave radio equipment, multiplex equipment, data transmission equipment, and complex specialized military communications equipment. Its sales are primarily to the telephone industry, Government, railroads, electric utilities, and for export. Annual sales are about $100 million, and the company has about 3,500 employees.

The third company, designated Company C, is a major producer of measuring instruments and sensing devices. It was established in the early 1950's and consists of two operating groups which each account for about one-half of the company's total sales. One group produces measuring instruments, signal analyzers, signal sources, and recording devices; the other produces sensing devices which are designed to detect minute changes in such physical parameters as motion, force, temperature, flow, and position and to translate this information into electrical signals. Annual sales are about $40 million, and the company has about 1,500 employees.

Finally, the fourth company, designated Company D, is a major electronics manufacturing company. It was established in the early 1940's; major products include electronic instruments, computers, calculators, and telecommunications equipment. Annual sales are about $600 million, employees about 15,000.

Sample Selection

We made an initial decision to limit the number of Focal Managers in the study to about 50. This number represented a compromise between aspirations and resources but was large enough to permit statistical anaysis. In each company, we selected for study 14 managers from the table of organization after some consultation within the company. The criteria of both homogeneity and diversity guided our selection of Focal Managers. To control for the effects of different management levels, all of the Focal Managers were drawn from the same level in each company.

All Focal Managers selected were department managers. This was the level of management which had a sufficient number of managers from which to choose in each company. However, in order to allow for some purposive diversity in our sample of Focal Managers, we selected managers from various functions, including production, marketing, development, and finance. Moreover, when possible, we selected managers who were not in close personal contact with each other. In all, 14 Focal Managers were selected from each company.

The sample of Other Managers included in our study was selected as follows. Each Focal Manager was asked to list the names of the members of his company with whom he spent the most time in drafting and using budgets. He was asked to list first the members under his supervision and then the members not under his supervision. The second list included members in positions above his own, those at the same level, and those in positions below his own. A master list of Other Managers was compiled for each company from these lists. These master lists constituted our sample of Other Managers to be initially included in the study. In all, 188 Other Managers were initially included in our study.

Data Collection

The data on which the study is based were collected in the following manner. First, the senior financial executive of each company was interviewed to obtain a description of the company's budgeting system and to select the Focal Managers to be included in the study. Next, the senior financial executive sent a letter to each Focal Manager informing him that he had been chosen to participate in a research study on budgeting and that he would be receiving materials which would explain the nature of the study and the rather limited involvement requested of him. This letter also stated that his participation in the study was earnestly needed to make the research successful and useful, that his responses would be held in complete confidence by the researchers, and that he would be sent a summary of the final report.

A survey research questionnaire was then sent to each Focal Manager along with a cover letter from the researchers. This letter asked the manager, as one of a small number of selected managers from his company, to complete the enclosed questionnaire and to return it directly to the researchers in an accompanying postpaid envelope. In addition, each manager was told that pretesting indicated that the questionnaire could be completed in a relatively short period of time, that the researchers would be the only persons to see his completed questionnaire, and that he was not to discuss the questionnaire with his colleagues because they may or may not be participating in the study. The questionnaire, which is presented in Appendix B, was 28 pages in length and consisted of the following nine parts:[1]

PART I: This part used the following four questions to obtain data on four demographic variables: How long have you worked since leaving school? How long have you worked for this company? How long have you worked in your present position? Consider the last month; what percentage of your time was spent on budget-related activities?

PART II: This part listed 44 descriptive characteristics relating to a

---

[1] Each part is described in greater detail in later chapters.

manager's use of budgeting. For each characteristic, managers were asked to give three ratings:

a. How frequently does the characteristic take place?
b. How frequently do you think the characteristic should take place?
c. How important is the characteristic to you?

Each rating was made on a line which looked like this:
minimum_____maximum

The managers were asked to put a mark (x) on the lines at a point that approximated how frequently the characteristic takes place, how frequently it should take place, and how important it is to them. This part was included to obtain measures of managers' budget-oriented behavior.

PART III: This part listed 20 characteristics or qualities relating to managers' positions in their companies. As in Part II, managers were asked to put a mark (x) on the lines at a point that approximated (a) how frequently the characteristic takes place, (b) how frequently it should take place, and (c) how important it is to them. This part was included to obtain measures of managers' attitudes about their positions.

PART IV: This part used the "Least-Preferred Co-worker" (LPC) index developed by Fiedler (1967) to obtain a measure of managers' leadership style. The index consists of a 16-item scale modeled after the Semantic Differential (Osgood *et. al.,* 1957).

PART V: This part used a version of the "Machiavellianism" test developed by Christie (1970) to obtain a measure of managers' attitudes about their interpersonal relationships. The test consists of 10 statements which tend to reflect or support a Machiavellian viewpoint. Managers were asked to indicate the extent to which they agreed or disagreed with each item.

PART VI: This part used the "Internal versus External Feelings of Control" test developed by Rotter (1966) to obtain a measure of managers' attitudes about the causes of major events in their lives. This test consists of 29 forced-choice items.

PART VII: This part employed the "Personality Profile" and "Personality Inventory" developed by Gordon (1963) to obtain measures on eight personality dimensions. Thirty-eight sets of four descriptive phrases were used to obtain measures of these personality dimensions. For each set, managers were asked to select which phrase was most like them and which phrase was least like them.

Table 3-1

SUMMARY DATA ABOUT QUESTIONNAIRES DISTRIBUTED
AND RETURNED BY FOCAL AND OTHER MANAGERS

| Company | Focal Managers | | | Others | | | | | |
	Distributed	Returned	%	Distributed	Returned	%	Distributed	Total Returned	%
A	14	13	93	41	30	73	55	43	78
B	14	11	79	42	17	40	56	28	50
C	14	9	64	34	8	24	48	17	35
D	14	13	93	71	36	51	85	49	58
Total	56	46	82%	188	91	48%	244	137	56%

Table 3-2

SUMMARY DATA ABOUT RELATIONSHIPS OF OTHER
MANAGERS TO THE FOCAL MANAGERS

Company	Superior	Subordinate	Budget Staff	Others	Total
A	4	19	3	4	30
B	2	12	2	1	17
C	1	4	3	0	8
D	3	27	3	3	36
Total	10	62	11	8	91

PART VIII: This part employed a questionnaire developed by Stogdill and Shartle (1955) to obtain a list of Other Managers from each Focal Manager. The names listed by each Focal Manager were used to select our sample of Other Managers.

PART IX: This part employed a "Test of Imagination" to obtain information about managers' motivational structures — their need for achievement. Managers were asked to look at a series of three pictures and then to write stories about what was suggested by the pictures. This part was included to obtain data for a related study (Moncur, 1975).

A follow-up card was mailed to the Focal Managers two weeks later thanking those who had completed and returned their questionnaires and urging those who had not to do so at their earliest convenience.

Another survey research questionnaire then was sent to each of the Other Managers listed by the Focal Managers. This questionnaire consisted of Parts I-VIII of the questionnaire sent to the Focal Managers and described above. A cover letter from the researchers was again included with this questionnaire; however, the Other Managers did not receive an introductory letter from their companies' senior financial executive. A follow-up card was mailed to the Other Managers two weeks later.

Table 3-1 summarizes the data about the number of questionnaires distributed and returned by both the Focal and Other Managers. Forty-six, or 82 percent, of the Focal Managers returned their questionnaires. Ninety-two, or 48 percent, of the Other Managers returned their questionnaires. Table 3-2 summarizes the data about the relationships of the Other Managers to the Focal Managers. About 68 percent of the Other Managers included in the study are subordinates of the Focal Managers included in the study.

Chapter 4

Measures of Managers' Budget-Oriented Behavior

In Chapter 2 we used the term "managers' budget-oriented behavior" to refer to the various actions and interactions which are brought about by a company's use of budgeting and which are descriptive of how managers use budgeting in carrying out their management functions. It has been suggested that how managers use budgeting may affect its effectiveness. Argyris (1952), for example, observed that the ways in which people expressed their interest in budgets and the ways in which they described and used them were directly related to the pattern of leadership they used in their daily life — a rather domineering, aggressive, "go-getting" top executive tended to use budgeting in a rather domineering manner. Argyris concluded that supervisors' use of budgeting as a way of expressing their own patterns of leadership often resulted in people getting hurt and budgeting, in itself a neutral thing, often getting blamed. Similarly, Hofstede (1967) concluded that one of the most powerful determinants of the effects of budgeting on managerial motivation was the way in which budget problems were handled by superiors in the hierarchy. And similar observations and findings have been reported by Hughes (1965) and Fertakis (1967).

Even though it has been suggested that how managers use budgeting may influence its effectiveness, we know relatively little about how they use budgeting, what factors or variables are likely to affect how they use budgeting, or what consequences or outcomes are likely to be associated with how they use budgeting. In part, the incompleteness of our knowledge of either the determinants of, or consequences associated with, managers' budget-oriented behavior can be attributed to the fact that no thorough or systematic attempt has been made to measure this behavior and to relate it to other factors or variables in complex organizational settings.

A major part of our research was aimed at measuring managers' budget-oriented behavior and at identifying different dimensions of that behavior. In this chapter, we will report the results of this intensive effort.

The first section describes the form and content of the questionnaire used to measure managers' budget-oriented behavior and describes the measures it was designed to obtain. Forty-four descriptive items were used to obtain measures of how managers actually use budgeting, what they think about their use of budgeting, and how concerned they are about their use of budgeting.

The second section reports the results of our analysis of the measures of how managers actually use budgeting. This analysis results in the substantive identification and description of 13 summary descriptive budget factors which are capable of providing both an economical and yet reasonably complete description of managers' budget-oriented behavior. The most important budget factors reflect budget-oriented behavior that is evaluative in nature and reflect the extent to which managers tend to have positive attitudes about budgeting and tend to be influential in budget-setting. The next most important descriptive budget factors reflect how managers cope with large budget variances, how acceptable their methods for achieving budgeted performance are, and how expressive they are about budgeting. The least important descriptive budget factors reflect general evaluative behavior, interactions with superiors, subordinates, and others, level of involvement in budgeting, and the time pressures experienced because of budgeting.

The third section reports the results of our analysis of the measures of what managers think about how they use budgeting. This analysis results in the identification and description of 14 summary normative budget factors. The most important normative budget factors reflect managers' attitudes about their performing various activities brought about by budget variances, their use of the budget to evaluate their subordinates, their taking an influential role in improving budgeting systems, and their level of involvement in the budgeting process. The next most important normative budget factors reflect managers' attitudes about having their methods of achieving their budgets accepted by others, their working with others in preparing their operating budgets, the usefulness of budgeting to them, and their taking an active and expressive role in the budgeting process. The least important normative budget factors reflect managers' attitudes about their having difficulty meeting their operating budgets and their starting to prepare their operating budgets before being asked to.

The chapter will conclude with a comparison of the descriptive and normative budget factor structures. This comparison reveals several striking similarities and differences in these two structures. In general, these two structures are similar in that specific items have the highest loadings on similar descriptive and normative budget factors and that similar factors are most important in both structures. However, these two structures are different in that the relative loadings of items on similar factors differ in their relative importance in the two structures. Finally, an intercorrelation analysis will reveal that the descriptive and normative budget factors are not highly intercorrelated.

Method

The words that make up the term "managers' budget-oriented behavior" suggest that we should expect to deal with matters that are: first, related to budgeting, and second, observable, at least to the extent this word can be applied to self-reports of overt behavior. In the present research we limited ourselves to the study of overt behavior based on measures of managers' budget-oriented behavior obtained by using a survey research questionnaire. Because we wished to obtain measures of this behavior from a relatively large and heterogeneous sample of managers functioning in their normal organizational settings, a questionnaire approach seemed desirable. Moreover, using this approach, each manager could serve as both an observer and evaluator of his own budget-oriented behavior.

This approach, however, also has a number of limitations associated with it. Among these limitations are the following: (1) questionnaire items may be interpreted in an entirely different manner by two individuals; (2) individuals' responses may be, at least in part, a function of the way questionnaire items are worded; (3) an individual may not possess sufficient information to respond to questionnaire items; and (4) there may be reasons that prompt an individual to give a response which he knows to be inaccurate — for example, he may give what he considers to be a socially acceptable rather than an accurate response.

These limitations may be overcome to a considerable extent by formulating the questionnaire after a thorough preliminary investigation, including the pretesting of trial questionnaires on samples of respondents similar to those from whom the information is desired. The questionnaire used to obtain measures of managers' budget-oriented behavior in the present study was constructed with the limitations of the method in mind.

Questionnaire Construction

In shaping the general form of the questionnaire, it was believed that the descriptive items used to obtain measures of managers' budget-oriented behavior should be broadly based in the sense that they should be able to provide as complete a description of this behavior as possible. In addition, it was believed that these items should be flexible in the sense that they should be able to be used to obtain measures of the budget-oriented behavior of almost any manager. Experience gained from studies by Fertakis (1967), Swieringa and Moncur (1972), and

Moncur and Swieringa (1973) guided development of the descriptive items used in the questionnaire. These studies are described briefly below.

Fertakis (1967) hypothesized that a supervisor's leadership behavior was related to the amount of felt budget-induced pressure he experienced. To test this hypothesis, Fertakis used various sources to develop a questionnaire to measure felt budget-induced pressure. The questionnaire consisted of 97 descriptions of supervisory activities, events and interrelationships which occurred on a regular basis and which supervisors could relate to the use of budgeting in their departments. Thirty-one supervisors in eight companies indicated (on a six-point scale) how frequently each described activity or event occurred. The descriptive items were scored on the basis of whether high or low frequency of occurrence represented high or low felt budget-induced pressure. A total felt budget-induced pressure score was derived for each supervisor by simply summing his scores on each descriptive item. This total score was then correlated with two measures of each supervisor's leadership behavior obtained by administering the Leadership Behavior Description Questionnaire (Halpin, 1957) to a sample of each supervisor's subordinates. Fertakis found that a supervisor, when subjected to higher felt budget-induced pressure, tended to exhibit both more structuring and more considerate leadership behavior toward his subordinates.

Swieringa and Moncur (1972) hypothesized that how managers used budgeting was related to various selected attitude, position, size and performance measures. To test this hypothesis, they measured the budget-oriented behavior of a sample of 26 managers drawn from the branch organization of a large international bank. The branch managers headed relatively autonomous units of organization and used essentially the same highly decentralized, participative budgeting system. Each manager had almost complete operating responsibility for his branch, and the primary instrument for setting performance goals for each branch and planning for their achievement was the annual budget or operating plan prepared by each branch manager.

To measure the branch managers' budget-oriented behavior, Swieringa and Moncur modified both the nature and the scoring of the descriptive items developed by Fertakis. Because the sample for their study consisted of branch bank managers rather than supervisors in an industrial setting, the questionnaire items used by Fertakis were rewritten so that they were descriptive of a branch bank manager's budget-oriented behavior. Moreover, because Swieringa and Moncur were interested in studying the relationship between this behavior and other variables measured as part of their study, rather than the relationship between felt budget-induced pressure and these other variables, the descriptive items were scored on the basis of frequency of occurrence only, and no attempt was made to transform these scores into measures of felt budget-induced pressure.

Managers indicated (on a five-point scale) how frequently each item occurred. An item-by-item analysis revealed that some sets of responses on individual items had low standard deviations and thus failed to differentiate among respondents. Elimination of these items reduced the total set to 65 items. These remaining items were then intercorrelated, and the intercorrelations were factor analyzed, yielding four independent facets of managers' budget-oriented behavior which could be meaningfully identified and described:

Active Participant Behavior — This facet reflected behavior that was active and influential in the budgeting process. This behavior reflected participation with other branch managers and home office budget people in preparing budgets and the use of carefully planned programs to introduce them. Moreover, it reflected situations in which special problems that were mentioned to budget people received special treatment in budgets and in which supervisors listened to problems in budget matters, gave assistance and support in accomplishing budget changes, talked about budget variances in branches, and listened to opinions on budget matters.

Involved Exponent Behavior — This facet reflected behavior brought about by the need to explain and correct budget variances. This behavior reflected tracing the causes of budget variances to groups or individuals in their branches, submitting explanations about these causes in writing to home office budgeting personnel, and reporting the actions taken to correct the causes of these variances. Moreover, budget variances were mentioned by superiors during performance evaluation interviews and as factors considered in evaluations for promotion and pay raises.

Reluctant Victim Behavior — This facet reflected behavior which diverted managers from what were for them more important activities. This behavior reflected attendance at meetings on the meaning and importance of the budget and bringing managers together for "pep talks" in connection with budget requirements. This behavior reflected situations in which budgets required extra paperwork and in which it was necessary to stop activities or change other accounts when budgeted funds for these activities were used up. Moreover, it reflected situations in which budgets for branches were not changed to meet changes in operating conditions.

Unconcerned Recipient Behavior — This facet reflected behavior that was essentially passive and which lacked concern over the use of the budget as an evaluative mechanism. This behavior reflected situations in which superiors did not express dissatisfaction about the results of a branch when the budget was not met and in which they did not mention budgets while talking about managerial efficiency or visiting a branch. This behavior reflected situations in which managers did not express their opinions on budgeting matters to home office budgeting personnel or offer suggestions to their superiors for the improvement of budgeting systems.

Swieringa and Moncur found that each of these four facets of managers' budget-oriented behavior was differentially related to various other variables measured as part of their study. For example, they found that managers exhibiting more active participant behavior tended to have higher confidence in their company; managers exhibiting more involved exponent, reluctant victim, and unconcerned recipient behavior tended to have lower confidence in their company. Similarly, managers exhibiting more active participant behavior tended to have longer tenure in their positions, to spend more time with subordinates and other managers, and to spend less time with customers than those who exhibited more involved exponent behavior. These findings suggested that the behavioral effects of managers' budget-oriented behavior may differ dramatically depending on what facets of that behavior are considered.

Moncur and Swieringa (1973) hypothesized that how managers used budgeting was related to the nature and content of a company's use of participative budgeting. To test this hypothesis, they measured and analyzed the budget-oriented behavior of six managers in three companies which differed in both the amount and form of participation they afforded operating managers in the budget-setting process. One company, an institutional food services company, allowed operating managers at each level of management to participate in the setting of operating targets and budgets used to monitor and evaluate their performance. The second company, a heavy equipment manufacturing company, limited participation of operating managers to the role of providing information that could be considered and used by top management in setting operating targets and budgets. The third company, a technical instruments and components manufacturing company, did not allow operating managers to participate in setting operating targets and budgets; rather top management set operating targets and budgets and imposed them on operating managers.

A 79-item questionnaire was used to measure each manager's budget-oriented behavior. The items included in this questionnaire consisted of 65 rewritten versions of the items used in the earlier study (Swieringa and Moncur, 1972) and 14 new items written especially for this study. The questionnaire was administered in an interview with each manager. Each manager indicated (on a seven-point scale) how frequently each budget-related activity or event occurred. Also, in completing the questionnaire, each manager was asked to point out any ambiguities in the descriptive items and to indicate any other difficulties he encountered. After completing the questionnaire, each manager was asked to describe the budgeting process in his company and to describe his role in it. Finally, each manager was asked to provide a list of the names of other individuals with whom he worked in drafting and using budgets and to indicate how much time was spent with them. In each case, the list included the names of superiors, subordinates, fellow managers, and others.

Several shorter questionnaires were used to obtain data about each manager's budget-oriented behavior from these other individuals. The descriptive items included in each questionnaire generally matched those included in the questionnaire administered to each manager. However, the items included in each of these questionnaires differed depending on whether the individual completing the questionnaire was the manager's superior, peer, or subordinate or whether he was a budget officer. Each individual indicated (on a seven-point scale) how frequently the manager exhibited the budget-oriented behavior item described.

The responses of each manager on each item were compared with those of the other individuals on comparable items and also with each manager's description of the budgeting process and his role in it. These comparisons provided the basis for developing capsule descriptions of how each manager used budgeting in carrying out his management functions and how his use of budgeting was related to the amount and form of participation afforded him in budget setting. Moreover, these comparisons provided considerable insight into the face validity and reliability of the descriptive items used to measure managers' budget-oriented behavior. Based on these comparisons and the information obtained from the managers about item ambiguities and other difficulties, some descriptive items were again reworded and some items were discarded.

Sufficient information was obtained in these studies to permit construction of the final form of the questionnaire used to measure managers' budget-oriented behavior in the present study. The questionnaire consisted of the 44 items presented in Table 4-1. Note that the items presented in Table 4-1 do not describe momentary events, activities, or interactions; rather they are descriptive of enduring properties of managers' budget-oriented behavior. Note further that these items are representative of a cross section of this behavior. For example, some items relate to the preparation of an operating budget, others relate to administration of this budget, and still others relate to the use of this budget as an evaluative device.

The Sets of Measures Obtained

For each item presented in Table 4-1, managers were asked to give three ratings:

    a. How often does it take place?   (Descriptive)
    b. How often should it take place?   (Normative)
    c. How important is it to me?   (Evaluative)

Each rating was made on a line which looked like this:

(min)_____(max)

Each rating was scored on a five-point scale by placing a clear plastic template divided into five equally spaced intervals over the line. A score of 1 on a given rating meant that the item "never" takes place and a score of 5 meant that the item "always" takes place.

These ratings were designed to obtain three sets of measures of managers' budget-oriented behavior. First, we wanted to measure how managers actually use budgeting in carrying out their management functions. The first question asked each manager to indicate how often each item *takes place*. Managers' responses to this question for each item were used as *descriptive* measures of their budget-oriented behavior. Second, we wanted to measure what managers think about their use of budgeting. The second question asked each manager to indicate how often he thought each item *should take place*. Managers' responses to this question were used as *normative* measures of this behavior. Finally, we wanted to measure how concerned managers were about their use of budgeting. The third question asked each manager to indicate how important each item was to him. Managers' responses to this question were used as *evaluative* measures of this behavior.

Thus, these three ratings were designed to obtain one set of descriptive measures and two sets of attitudinal measures for each item presented in Table 4-1. The remaining sections of this chapter present the results of our analysis of the data obtained from our sample of managers for the descriptive and normative sets of measures for each item. The results of our analysis of the data obtained for the evaluative set of measures for these items are presented elsewhere.[1]

Table 4-1

LIST OF BUDGET-ORIENTED BEHAVIOR ITEMS

1. I start preparing the budget for my unit before I am asked to.
2. I spend time outside of normal working hours preparing the budget for my unit.
3. I am not able to spend as much time as I would like preparing the budget for my unit.
4. I work with my superior in preparing the budget for my unit.
5. I work with my subordinates in preparing the budget for my unit.
6. I work with other unit heads in preparing the budget for my unit.
7. I work with financial staff people in preparing the budget for my unit.

---

[1] See Moncur (1975) for an analysis of the data obtained from our sample of managers for the evaluative set of measures for each item.

50

8. I am consulted about special factors I would like to have included in the budget being prepared.
9. New budgets include changes I have suggested.
10. The budget is not finalized until I am satisfied with it.
11. Preparing the budget for my unit requires my attention to a great number of details.
12. I am reminded of the importance of meeting the budget for my unit.
13. I am evaluated on my ability to meet the budget for my unit.
14. I have difficulty meeting the budget for my unit.
15. I am shown comparisons of actual and budgeted performance for other units.
16. My explanation of budget variances is included in performance reports.
17. I investigate favorable as well as unfavorable budget variances for my unit.
18. I go to my superior for advice on how to achieve my budget.
19. I am required to prepare reports comparing actual results with budget.
20. My methods of reaching budgeted performance are accepted without question by my superior.
21. My methods of reaching budgeted performance are accepted without question by my subordinates.
22. My superior calls me in to discuss variations from the budget.
23. My superior accepts my explanation of budget variances in my unit.
24. My superior expresses dissatisfaction to me about results in my unit when the budget has not been met.
25. My superior mentions budgets when talking to me about my efficiency as a manager.
26. I ask for assistance from staff departments concerned with budgeting.
27. I am required to submit an explanation in writing about causes of large budget variances.
28. I use the budget to plan activities in my unit.
29. I am required to trace the cause of budget variances to groups or individuals within my unit.
30. I personally investigate budget variances in my unit.
31. I evaluate my subordinates by means of the budget.
32. I am required to report actions I take to correct causes of budget variances.
33. I find it necessary to stop some activities in my unit when budgeted funds are used up.
34. I find it necessary to charge some activities to other accounts when budgeted funds for these activities have been used up.
35. I have to shift figures relating to operations to reduce budget variances.
36. Budget matters are mentioned in informal conversations.
37. I express my opinions on budget matters.
38. I offer suggestions for the improvement of budget systems.
39. The budgeting system is changed in accordance with my suggestions.
40. I discuss budget items when problems occur.
41. The budget enables me to be more flexible.
42. The budget enables me to be more innovative.
43. The budget enables me to keep track of my success as a manager.
44. The budget enables me to be a better manager.

Table 4-2
MEANS AND STANDARD DEVIATIONS OF OCCURRENCE FOR DESCRIPTIVE MEASURES OF FORTY-FOUR BUDGET-ORIENTED BEHAVIOR ITEMS
(N = 137)

Item No.	Means	Standard Deviations
1	2.93	1.52
2	2.60	1.46
3	2.13	1.44
4	2.60	1.54
5	3.74	1.41
6	2.55	1.44
7	3.34	1.49
8	3.20	1.51
9	3.36	1.27
10	3.20	1.59
11	3.45	1.38
12	2.91	1.43
13	2.94	1.36
14	2.34	1.27
15	2.68	1.77
16	2.43	1.45
17	3.55	1.31
18	2.15	1.34
19	2.14	1.55
20	3.22	1.32
21	3.30	1.31
22	2.31	1.32
23	4.16	1.18
24	2.35	1.37
25	2.10	1.27
26	3.10	1.49
27	2.07	1.47
28	3.47	1.34
29	2.32	1.43
30	3.78	1.23
31	2.35	1.30
32	1.97	1.22
33	2.08	1.22
34	1.81	1.06
35	1.43	0.90
36	2.94	1.33
37	3.70	1.15
38	2.90	1.37
39	2.13	1.12
40	3.42	1.27
41	2.27	1.33
42	2.30	1.34
43	2.84	1.41
44	3.19	1.32

Analysis of Descriptive Measures of Managers' Budget-Oriented Behavior

Marginal Distributions of the Measures

Table 4-2 presents the means and standard deviations of occurrence (How often does it take place?) for these measures based on data obtained from our total sample. From inspection of Table 4-2 we can obtain a general notion of the budget-oriented behavior of our sample of managers. The items managers indicate occur most frequently suggest that, in general, our sample of managers experiences a relatively high degree of personal involvement in budgeting. For example, these items include the following: my superior accepts my explanation of budget variances in my unit (Item 23), I personally investigate budget variances in my unit (Item 30), I express my opinions on budget matters (Item 37), and I investigate favorable as well as unfavorable budget variances for my unit (Item 17). The items managers indicate occur least frequently suggest generally that the personal involvement of these managers in budgeting may be of relatively high quality. For example, these items include their having to shift figures relating to operations to reduce budget variances (Item 35) and their finding it necessary to charge some activities to other accounts when budgeted funds for these activities have been used up (Item 34).

Correlations Among the Measures

The simple correlation coefficients for pairs of the descriptive measures of the 44 budget-oriented behavior items are presented in Table 4-3. Inspection of this table reveals that, in general, these coefficients are relatively low, suggesting that these items are not highly intercorrelated. For example, only nine of the coefficients presented in Table 4-3 are above .50, and the highest coefficient is .72. However, a closer inspection of this table reveals that a number of dimensions or patterns of relations can be observed.

For example, note that the following items are intercorrelated: I work with financial staff people in preparing the budget for my unit (Item 7), I am consulted about special factors I would like to have included in the budget being prepared (Item 8), new budgets include changes I have suggested (Item 9), and the budget is not finalized until I am satisfied with it (Item 10).

Another grouping of interrelated items includes the following: I find it necessary to stop some activities in my unit when budgeted funds are used up (Item 33), I find it necessary to charge some activities to other accounts when budgeted funds for these activities have been used up (Item 34), and I have to shift figures related to operations to reduce budget variances (Item 35).

Table 4-3

CORRELATIONS AMONG DESCRIPTIVE MEASURES OF FORTY-FOUR BUDGET-ORIENTED BEHAVIOR ITEMS

(N = 137)

	1	2	3	4	5	6	7	8	9	10	11	12	13	14	15	16	17	18	19	20	21	22
1		.24	.03	.08	.35	.08	.21	.24	.26	.34	.27	.10	.25	.00	.27	.38	.29	.04	.36	.15	-.07	.14
2			.21	.15	.32	.18	.16	.15	.12	.17	.19	.22	.00	.15	.23	.19	.18	.16	.31	.00	-.07	.25
3				.07	.01	-.01	.08	.05	.11	.00	.00	.06	-.01	.14	.03	-.10	-.01	.07	-.09	-.20	.11	-.05
4					.15	.29	.26	.25	-.01	.14	.16	.18	.05	.09	.17	-.02	.31	.04	.21	-.19	-.04	.15
5						.22	.31	.29	.23	.23	.19	.19	.22	.10	.32	.22	.31	.04	.21	.19	-.04	.15
6							.34	.15	.06	.12	.08	.28	.25	.20	.11	.12	.11	.17	.23	-.04	-.06	.17
7								.43	.38	.29	.12	.12	.14	-.03	.26	.18	.25	.18	.34	.11	.12	.20
8									.54	.36	.22	.12	.21	-.02	.24	.29	.21	.04	.17	.03	-.03	.13
9										.41	.26	.03	-.01	.12	.15	-.02	.15	-.02	.24	.13	-.02	.20
10											.20	.22	.32	.00	-.09	-.27	.15	.06	.20	-.01	.12	.18
11												.13	.08	.16	-.04	.10	.26	.10	.11	.05	.08	.12
12													.46	.29	.16	.19	.16	.22	.14	-.08	-.13	.28
13														.19	-.02	-.28	.29	.24	.10	.10	.01	.04
14															-.05	-.06	.04	.23	.09	-.27	-.32	.10
15																.24	.24	.10	.28	-.07	-.12	.43
16																	.35	.20	.51	.14	.12	.36
17																		.20	.19	.20	.19	.25
18																			.14	-.13	-.06	.48
19																				-.03	-.02	.41
20																					.53	-.07
21																						.01
22																						
23																						
24																						
25																						
26																						
27																						
28																						
29																						
30																						
31 through 43																						
44																						

	23	24	25	26	27	28	29	30	31	32	33	34	35	36	37	38	39	40	41	42	43	44
1	.10	.14	.21	.35	.33	.24	.23	.23	.36	.25	-.08	-.12	-.10	.07	.26	.33	.35	.13	.24	.25	.16	.12
2	.01	.22	.17	.04	.08	.10	.13	.16	.06	.02	.13	.07	-.03	.06	.15	.30	.17	.28	.13	.15	.01	.14
3	.05	.05	.05	-.05	-.02	-.06	.08	-.01	.01	.00	.20	.17	.10	.12	.08	.19	.04	.09	.03	.15	-.01	.14
4	.08	.23	.17	.23	.09	.08	.19	-.07	-.07	-.13	.11	-.06	-.10	.10	-.03	.22	.24	.09	.07	.06	-.08	-.07
5	-.02	.27	.13	.29	.07	.14	.31	.27	.29	.04	.09	-.17	-.22	.17	.22	.17	.20	.22	.17	.13	-.05	.23
6	.23	.17	.13	.28	.22	.17	.27	.04	.08	.15	.21	-.07	.04	.03	.17	.25	.17	.21	.12	.18	.14	.16
7	.07	.04	.11	.52	.12	.34	.25	.23	.06	.02	.12	-.13	-.05	.17	.22	.30	.31	.12	.15	.17	.15	.26
8	.18	.05	.06	.30	.14	.27	.22	.13	.09	.05	-.03	-.20	-.05	.15	.18	.11	.33	.32	.10	.16	.11	.18
9	.21	.10	.02	.27	.04	.20	.16	.30	-.11	.00	-.09	-.08	-.10	.05	.31	.19	.24	.20	.22	.18	.04	.14
10	.06	.35	.00	.30	.10	.17	-.04	.14	.12	.07	-.05	-.06	-.06	.09	.12	.07	.19	.17	.16	.23	.10	.13
11	.02	.28	.07	.08	.07	.19	.08	.20	-.12	.08	.01	.02	.05	-.03	.16	-.11	.04	.17	.06	.16	.05	.16
12	-.08	.14	.24	.14	.24	.16	.16	.04	.38	.24	-.18	.17	.04	.19	.14	-.09	.15	.10	.23	.21	.11	.03
13	-.42	.19	.34	.20	.24	.21	.13	-.10	-.02	.23	.17	.08	.16	-.04	-.11	.40	.04	.13	.16	-.07	.36	.33
14	-.04	.17	-.01	.00	.00	.20	-.16	-.12	.08	.10	.16	.09	-.04	.16	-.05	.21	-.04	.10	.09	.07	-.13	-.11
15	.20	.13	.26	.29	.22	.02	.15	.07	.25	-.31	.09	-.05	-.11	.13	.20	.17	.45	.24	.18	.10	.00	.02
16	.23	.26	.31	.09	.46	.34	.24	.19	.21	.15	-.08	-.07	-.08	.14	.32	.11	.27	.21	.26	.19	.22	.25
17	.01	.12	.22	.27	.21	.31	.13	.41	.06	.26	-.17	.02	.38	.11	.26	.27	.15	.16	.11	.20	.25	.29
18	.04	-.04	.29	.06	.19	.17	.31	.06	.06	.19	.23	.26	.00	.09	.06	.08	.17	-.06	.10	.14	.07	.07
19	.36	.21	.14	-.17	-.46	.14	.37	.11	-.21	.02	.00	-.03	-.12	.05	.21	.20	.40	-.03	.16	.06	.00	.14
20	.36	.10	.12	.15	.11	.21	-.05	.23	.02	-.03	-.06	-.13	-.04	.17	.17	.20	.03	.22	.15	.07	.08	.15
21	.03		.48	.05	.00	.25	.08	.19	.04	.19	-.11	.00	.12	.25	.07	.35	.14	.15	.01	.10	.17	-.01
22				-.13	.30	.10	.36	.15	.14	.07	-.05	-.11	-.11	.05	.23	.14	.39	.29	.18	.19	-.08	.27
23				.23	.13	.32	-.01	-.25	.34	.27	-.13	-.05	.03	.10	.21	.19	.10	.21	.19	.25	.13	.26
24				.25	.27	.23	.36	-.01	.40	.36	.16	.10	.09	.16	.06	.15	.17	.18	.26	.22	.31	.37
25				.29	.34	.33	.26	-.14	.17	.02	.01	-.22	-.06	-.01	.18	.12	.15	.15	.21	.16	.46	.25
26					.10	.23	.04	.21	.37	.61	.13	.02	-.05	.19	.14	.26	.22	.27	.26	.33	.20	.31
27						.30	.42	.16	.29	.26	-.03	-.02	.07	.17	.25	.00	.08	.26	.36	.22	.26	.41
28							.20	.37	.26	.39	.08	-.06	.03	.23	.30	-.14	.35	.29	.06	.24	.46	.26
29								.22	.29	.21	.05	.14	.01	.10	.29	-.12	.14	.21	.09	.06	.17	.26
30									.29	.39	.04	.09	.19	-.06	.41	.20	.06	.24	.26	.25	.24	.41
31												.13	.36	.15	.14	.48	.16	.17	.21	.23	.33	.22
32												.40	.59	.05	.22		-.02	-.01	.20	.29	.37	.10
33														.09	-.02		.14	.33	.05	.09	.09	.05
34															-.05		.14	.48	.02	.11	.12	-.02
35															.59		.26	.39	.01	.02	.08	.23
36																	.55	.29	.15	.17	.16	.35
37																			.27	.28	.27	.21
38																			.20	.26	-.10	.23
39																			.18	.15	.08	.25
40																				.72	.22	.40
41																					.38	.42
42																					.14	.66
43																						
44																						

55

Still other groupings of intercorrelated items include the following: budget matters are mentioned in informal conversations (Item 36), I express my opinions on budget matters (Item 37), I offer suggestions for the improvement of budgeting systems (Item 38), and I discuss budget items when problems occur (Item 40); and the budget enables me to be more flexible (Item 41), innovative (Item 42), to keep track of my success as a manager (Item 43), and to be a better manager (Item 44).

Finally, note that the following items are interrelated: my explanation of budget variances is included in performance reports (Item 16), I am required to prepare reports comparing actual results with budget (Item 19), and I am required to submit an explanation in writing about causes of large budget variances (Item 27).

These groupings of interrelated items suggest that the data do not include anything like 44 separate dimensions of managers' budget-oriented behavior. Moreover, even though these correlation coefficients suggest that patterns of relations exist, they do not take multivariate interconnections among them into account.

Factor Analysis of Intercorrelations

A statistical procedure known as "factor analysis" is designed to help unravel problems of this sort by identifying the major dimensions or "factors" that exist in a given set of intercorrelated data.[2] Factor analysis is essentially a generic term for a variety of procedures which have been developed for the purpose of analyzing the intercorrelations within a set of variables. Several advantages are associated with the use of this procedure.

First, the procedure can be used to reduce the dimensionality of a set of items by taking advantage of their intercorrelations. The procedure involves finding a way of linearly transforming an original set of items into a new and smaller set of independent factors which, when multiplied together in a specified manner, will produce the original correlation matrix as closely as possible. A principal components analysis is typically used to determine the minimum number of independent dimensions needed to account for most of the variance in the original set of variables.[3] This analysis determines an initial axis in the n-dimensional item space along which the variance is a maximum; then a second axis, orthogonal to the first, which accounts for as much of the remaining variance as possible; a third axis, orthogonal to the first two; etc. Each new orthogonal axis accounts for a smaller proportion of the original variance, and at some point in the sequence of locating new axes, an insignificant

---

[2] Harman (1967) provides a comprehensive and thorough discussion of factor analysis.
[3] See Harman (1967) for a discussion of principal components analysis.

amount of variance is found in the remaining dimensions, thus reducing the number of dimensions required.

Second, the procedure can be used to help seek new "dimensions" or "constructs." As indicated above, a principal components analysis is used to obtain an initial factor solution. However, this solution may not be acceptable from the point of view of interpreting the new variates. To facilitate interpretation, a new set of axes can be formed by rotating the derived principal components axes. Rotation of the axes yields new factors which also have the property of reproducing the original correlation matrix in exactly the same way as did the original factors.

Third, the procedure can be used to obtain factor scores for each manager on each dimension. Factor scores have the advantages of being normally distributed and of being uncorrelated, thus giving maximum information for a space of a given dimensionality.

To identify the principal descriptive dimensions of managers' budget-oriented behavior, the intercorrelations in Table 4-3 were factor analyzed. First, a principal components analysis was conducted. So that the total 44-item variance would be factor analyzed, unities were used in the principal diagonal of the correlation matrix.[4] The criterion used to determine how many factors should be extracted was the size of the successive characteristic roots of the correlation matrix. These roots are equal to the variances of their respective factors and therefore represent the explanatory power of the factors. The first principal component always has the largest root, the second the next largest, and so on. When the roots have dropped to less than one, it means that all of the subsequent factors account for a smaller proportion of the pooled variance of the sample than do any of the individual variables. This provides a rational criterion for when to stop factoring.

The principal components analysis yielded 13 characteristic roots that were greater than one. These roots are presented in Table 4-4. The 13 factors corresponding to these roots were the only ones preserved for further analysis. As shown in Table 4-4, these 13 factors account for over two-thirds of the total variance (68 percent). The relatively low correlations in the raw data are emphasized by the fact that 13 factors are required to account for this percentage of the total variance.

The 13 factors were then rotated using Kaiser's normal orthogonal varimax criterion (Kaiser, 1960). The results of this analysis are presented in Table 4-5. The first 13 columns in Table 4-5 list the rotated factor loading coefficients for the 13 factors. A loading coefficient is

---

[4] This was done on the basis of the recommendations of Kaiser (1960). It should be noted, however, that there is considerable controversy about what ought to be placed in the diagonals of the matrix to be factored. See Harman (1967) for discussion of this issue.

Table 4-4

CHARACTERISTIC ROOTS FOR PRINCIPAL COMPONENTS ANALYSIS FOR DESCRIPTIVE MEASURES OF BUDGET-ORIENTED BEHAVIOR ITEMS

Root Number	Characteristic Root	Cumulative Proportion of Total Variance
1	8.224	.1869
2	3.320	.2624
3	3.118	.3332
4	2.118	.3814
5	1.993	.4266
6	1.726	.4659
7	1.695	.5044
8	1.548	.5396
9	1.394	.5712
10	1.334	.6016
11	1.167	.6281
12	1.160	.6545
13	1.039	.6781
Total	29.836	

defined as the correlation between the descriptive item and the factor in question. That is, a loading coefficient of .64 for item x on factor y means that the correlation coefficient between item x and factor y is .64.

The last column in Table 4-5 lists the communalities of each descriptive item. The total communality of an item is defined as the proportion of the variance of that item that is associated with (explained by) the rotated factors. Since the loading coefficients are correlation coefficients between the items and factors, and the factors are independent of each other, the communality of an item can be calculated by summing the squares of its loading coefficients on all factors. In Table 4-5, these communalities range from .51 to .77. If all the 44 possible factors had been used, these communalities would have been 1.0.

The contribution of each factor and its percent of the total communality are reported in the last two rows of Table 4-5. The contribution of each factor is defined as the proportion of total variance explained which is associated with (explained by) each factor. The contribution of a factor is calculated by summing the squares of the loading coefficients on all items on that factor. In Table 4-5, the contributions of the factors range from 1.652 to 3.008 and the percent of communality ranges from 5.6 to 10.1 percent.

The rotated factor loading coefficients presented in Table 4-5 were used to develop substantive descriptions of each factor. These descriptions were developed by considering only the items which were highly correlated with each factor. The following paragraphs provide for each factor a substantive identification of the factor, the items highly correlated with it, and the loading of these items on the particular factor.

Descriptive Budget Factor I:
Evaluation by Superiors and of Subordinates

A higher score on this factor indicates budget-oriented behavior that is strongly evaluation-oriented. The items that have the highest loadings on this factor are Item 31, I evaluate my subordinates by means of the budget (.75); Item 25, My superior mentions budgets when talking to me about my efficiency as a manager (.63); and Item 24, My superior expresses dissatisfaction to me about results in my unit when the budget has not been met (.58). What these items have in common is their reference, either directly or indirectly, to the use of the budget as an evaluative device. Managers' superiors use the budget to evaluate the managers' performances — they mention budgets when talking to the managers about their efficiency and they express dissatisfaction when the budget has not been met. The managers, in turn, use the budget to evaluate their subordinates. This factor accounts for about 10 percent of the combined variance of all the descriptive items.

Descriptive Budget Factor II:
Actions Brought About by Expected Budget Overruns

Managers having higher scores on this factor more often exhibit budget-oriented manipulative behavior. The items which have the highest loadings on this factor are Item 34, I find it necessary to charge some activities to other accounts when budgeted funds for these activities have been used up (.81); Item 35, I have to shift figures relating to operations to reduce budget variances (.80); and Item 33, I find it necessary to stop some activities in my unit when budgeted funds are used up (.59). This factor reflects managers' efforts to cope with overspent budgeted funds and large budget variances by charging some activities to other accounts, shifting figures, and stopping some activities. Table 4.2 indicated that these activities do not occur very frequently, relative to the other descriptive items included in our questionnaire. However, this factor does identify this particular dimension of managers' budget-oriented behavior. This factor accounts for 8 percent of the combined variance for all the descriptive items.

Table 4-5
ROTATED FACTOR LOADINGS FOR DESCRIPTIVE MEASURES OF FORTY-FOUR BUDGET-ORIENTED BEHAVIOR ITEMS
(N = 137)

Item No.	I	II	III	IV	V	VI	VII	VIII	IX	X	XI	XII	XIII	Communality
1	.30	−.16	.04	.31	−.13	.21	−.06	.35	.33	.28	−.03	−.09	.04	.60
2	−.01	−.02	.14	.15	.11	.11	−.03	−.02	.43	.17	.07	.09	.49	.53
3	.03	.24	−.02	−.07	−.05	.05	−.12	.09	−.06	.01	.10	.02	.63	.51
4	.02	−.05	.03	−.05	.76	.03	−.10	.14	.01	.16	−.04	.20	.01	.68
5	.23	−.24	.12	.02	−.07	−.03	.02	.19	.50	.30	.08	.33	.17	.65
6	.06	−.06	.21	.16	.20	.15	−.07	.06	−.03	−.03	.07	.69	.04	.63
7	.01	.03	−.06	.10	.16	.04	.20	.55	.06	.23	.13	.53	−.05	.73
8	.01	−.13	.03	.14	.15	.09	−.05	.68	.10	.12	.10	.13	−.09	.59
9	.03	−.05	−.06	.09	−.05	−.00	.09	.77	.12	−.07	.15	.00	.24	.72
10	−.05	−.06	.47	.08	.04	.15	.02	.66	.04	.04	.00	−.14	.05	.72
11	−.04	−.10	−.00	.00	.31	.23	−.04	.24	.63	−.28	.01	−.11	.07	.71
12	.13	.07	.72	.14	.20	.00	−.09	.00	.06	.02	.15	.12	.13	.70
13	.34	.09	.67	.06	−.09	.15	−.03	.17	.10	−.05	.05	.16	−.22	.73
14	.05	.14	.25	.06	.06	−.18	−.57	−.06	.29	−.19	−.10	.28	.15	.68
15	.06	.01	−.02	.24	.14	−.00	−.06	.06	.08	.79	.11	−.01	.10	.74
16	.11	−.08	.28	.67	−.03	.10	.16	.11	.19	.14	.12	−.09	−.19	.71
17	.08	.08	.13	.16	.01	.15	.20	.08	.61	.20	.18	.04	−.15	.59
18	.14	.41	.13	.23	.59	−.00	−.05	−.01	.11	−.01	.07	.07	−.01	.62
19	−.06	.02	.03	.76	−.05	.03	−.03	.18	.12	.18	.03	.22	.07	.72
20	.16	−.14	−.01	.02	−.21	−.02	.72	.01	.16	−.02	.00	.07	.06	.64
21	−.09	.07	−.09	.01	.01	.09	.76	−.15	.18	−.10	.00	.12	−.24	.73
22	−.02	.20	.14	.50	.47	−.16	.04	.05	.14	.30	.17	−.01	.11	.71
23	.08	−.07	.08	.03	.06	.14	.72	.22	−.08	.03	.10	−.11	.07	.65
24	.58	−.02	.30	.00	.30	.11	.05	−.06	−.00	.11	.01	.24	.18	.63

Item No.	I	II	III	IV	V	VI	VII	VIII	IX	X	XI	XII	XIII	Communality
25	.63	.13	.16	.06	.27	.17	.13	−.09	.08	.27	.12	−.04	−.07	.68
26	.20	.06	.08	−.14	.08	.10	.16	.47	.08	.47	.03	.31	−.12	.67
27	.41	−.01	.05	.70	.07	.24	.06	.00	−.06	−.01	.01	.04	.00	.73
28	.26	.11	.04	.13	.14	.33	.34	.24	.15	−.12	.26	.09	−.23	.57
29	.45	−.03	−.19	.47	.21	−.06	−.14	.07	.07	−.09	.20	.35	.08	.71
30	.25	.22	−.16	.09	−.13	−.10	.28	.27	.46	−.04	.36	−.08	−.02	.68
31	.75	.04	.11	.10	−.23	.11	.10	.09	.11	.06	.01	−.00	.05	.68
32	.56	.12	.03	.45	.18	.16	−.05	−.02	−.05	−.16	.13	−.10	−.01	.64
33	−.09	.59	.13	−.12	.01	.26	.03	−.15	.12	.14	.07	.39	.15	.70
34	.12	.81	.09	−.07	−.00	.03	−.04	−.09	.04	.06	−.00	−.17	.10	.74
35	.05	.80	−.05	.07	.10	.03	−.12	−.02	−.13	−.12	−.00	.01	.01	.72
36	.01	.11	.17	−.03	.00	−.07	−.00	.03	−.01	.19	.80	.06	−.06	.73
37	.06	−.06	.00	.24	−.06	.11	.10	.12	.13	.02	.82	.01	.08	.80
38	.07	−.22	−.21	.28	.17	.32	.02	.16	.03	.29	.36	−.05	.41	.72
39	.03	−.19	−.09	.40	.22	.22	−.09	.23	−.09	.43	.20	.07	.16	.63
40	.20	−.04	.04	.02	.20	.11	.08	.14	.12	−.05	.59	.10	.32	.59
41	.11	.04	.07	.06	.02	.82	.15	.05	.10	.08	−.03	.02	.05	.74
42	.12	.11	.07	.16	.04	.81	.06	.09	.05	−.01	−.02	.09	.19	.77
43	.47	.09	.05	−.03	−.07	.51	.04	.03	.02	−.04	.31	.05	−.38	.74
44	.41	.01	−.04	.06	−.17	.52	.08	.14	.15	.03	.31	.16	−.18	.67
Contribution of Factor	3.008	2.389	1.804	2.951	2.005	2.693	2.414	2.751	1.980	1.947	2.514	1.728	1.652	29.836
Percent of Communality	10.1	8.0	6.0	9.9	6.7	9.0	8.1	9.2	6.6	6.5	8.4	5.8	5.6	

Descriptive Budget Factor III:
Responsibility for Meeting Budget

This factor reflects responsibility for meeting an operating budget. The two items with the highest loadings on this factor are Item 12, I am reminded of the importance of meeting the budget for my unit (.72); and Item 13, I am evaluated on my ability to meet the budget for my unit (.67). This factor suggests that being reminded of the importance of the budget and being evaluated on one's ability to meet it may be interrelated. This factor accounts for 6 percent of the combined variance for all the descriptive items.

Descriptive Budget Factor IV:
Required Explanations of Budget Variances

Managers with higher scores on this factor more often exhibit various required activities which are either brought about by or related to the existence of budget variances. The six items with the highest loadings on this factor are Item 19, I am required to prepare reports comparing actual results with budget (.76); Item 27, I am required to submit an explanation in writing about causes of large budget variances (.70); Item 16, My explanation of budget variances is included in performance reports (.67); Item 22, My superior calls me in to discuss variations from the budget (.49); Item 29, I am required to trace the causes of budget variances to groups or individuals within my unit (.47); and Item 32, I am required to report actions I take to correct causes of budget variances (.45). Note that many of these items describe activities which are "required." For example, managers *are required* to prepare reports, submit explanations, trace the causes of budget variances, and report the actions they take to correct these variances. Note further that many of the activities described by these items are either brought about or related to the existence of *budget variances*. In fact, these items provide a relatively complete description of budget-oriented behavior that may be required because of budget variances. This is a relatively important factor, accounting for 9.9 percent of the combined variance for all items.

Descriptive Budget Factor V:
Interactions with Superiors

A higher score on this factor indicates budget-oriented behavior that is *superior-oriented*. The two items with the highest loadings on this factor are Item 4, I work with my superior in preparing the budget for my unit (.76); and Item 18, I go to my superior for advice on how to achieve my budget (.59). Note that both of these items describe a manager's interaction with his superior. Note further that these items describe the manager as the initiator of these interactions. For example, he works with his superior; he goes to his superior. This factor accounts for 6.7 percent of the combined variance for all items.

Descriptive Budget Factor VI:
Usefulness of Budgeting

This factor is essentially an attitudinal factor. Managers with higher scores on this factor more often view budgeting as a useful and worthwhile process. The items with the highest loadings on the factor are Item 41, The budget enables me to be more flexible (.82); Item 42, The budget enables me to be more innovative (.81); Item 44, The budget enables me to be a better manager (.52); and Item 43, The budget enables me to keep track of my success as a manager (.51). Managers who think that the budget enables them to be more flexible and innovative, to keep track of their success as a manager, and to be a better manager have a relatively positive view of budgeting. Also, note that Item 28, I use the budget to plan activities in my unit, has the next-highest loading on this factor. This suggests that those managers who more often think that budgets are useful and helpful to them also may be more likely to use them to plan activities in their units. Because the loading of Item 28 on this factor is only .33, the relationship between having a positive attitude about budgeting and using the budget in planning activities is not a strong one. This factor is a relatively important one, accounting for 9 percent of the combined variance for all items.

Descriptive Budget Factor VII:
Acceptability of Methods

This factor reflects primarily the extent to which managers' methods of achieving budget targets are accepted by both their superiors and their subordinates. The items with the highest loading on this factor are Item 21, My methods of reaching budgeted performance are accepted without question by my subordinates (.76); Item 23, My superior accepts my explanation of budget variances in my unit (.72); Item 20, My methods of reaching budgeted performance are accepted without question by my superiors (.72); and Item 14, I have difficulty meeting the budget for my unit (−57). The first three items refer to the acceptability of a manager's methods and explanations by his superiors and subordinates. The last item, Item 14, refers to how often a manager has difficulty meeting his operating budget. Note that the loading for the last item is negative. This suggests that a relationship may exist between the acceptability of a manager's methods and the difficulty he has meeting his budget. Managers whose methods and explanations are accepted and who also do not have difficulty meeting the budgets for their units have higher scores on this factor. This is a relatively important factor, accounting for 8.1 percent of the combined variance on all items.

Descriptive Budget Factor VIII:
Influence in Budget Setting

This factor reflects budget-oriented behavior that is influential in budget setting. The items with the highest loadings on this factor are Item 9, New budgets include changes I have suggested (.77); Item 8, I am consulted about special factors I would like to have included in the budget being prepared (.68); Item 10, The budget is not finalized until I am satisfied with it (.66); Item 7, I work with financial staff people in preparing the budget for my unit (.55); and Item 26, I ask for assistance from staff departments concerned with budgeting (.46). Managers with higher scores on this factor more often have an influential role in the budget-setting process. Their budgets include changes they have suggested, they are consulted about special factors they would like to have included in the budget being prepared, and their budgets are not finalized until they are satisfied with them. Moreover, they work with financial staff people in preparing their operating budgets and ask for assistance from these staff people. This is a relatively important factor, accounting for 9.2 percent of the combined variance on all items.

Descriptive Budget Factor IX:
Personal Attention to Budgeting

A higher score on this factor indicates budget-oriented behavior that is self- and subordinate-oriented. The items with the highest loadings on this factor are Item 11, Preparing the budget for my unit requires my attention to a great number of details (.63); Item 17, I investigate favorable as well as unfavorable budget variances for my unit (.61); Item 5, I work with my subordinates in preparing the budget for my unit (.50); Item 30, I personally investigate budget variances in my unit (.46); and Item 2, I spend time outside of normal working hours preparing the budget for my unit (.43). Many of these items describe a manager's *own* budget-oriented behavior. For example, in preparing his unit's operating budget, he must pay attention to a great number of details. Moreover, he works with his subordinates and spends considerable time outside of normal working hours in preparing this budget. Similarly, in using this budget he personally investigates budget variances. Thus, this factor reflects budget-oriented behavior that is essentially self- and subordinate-oriented. This factor accounts for 6.6 percent of the combined variance on all items.

Descriptive Budget Factor X:
Involvement in Budgeting

This factor tends to reflect the extent of a manager's involvement in a company's budgeting system. The items with the highest loadings on this factor are Item 15, I am shown comparisons of actual and budgeted performance for other units (.79); Item 26, I ask for assistance from staff departments concerned with budgeting (.47); and Item 39, The budgeting system is changed in accordance with my suggestions (.43). Managers who more often are shown comparisons of actual and budgeted performance for other units, ask for assistance from budgeting personnel, and have the budgeting changed in accordance with their suggestions have higher scores on this factor. This factor accounts for 7 percent of the combined variance on all items.

Descriptive Budget Factor XI:
Expressive about Budgeting

Managers with higher scores on this factor more often exhibit oral expressive behavior. The items with the highest loadings on this factor are Item 37, I express my opinions on budget matters (.82); Item 36, Budget matters are mentioned in informal discussions (.80); and Item 40, I discuss budget items when problems occur (.59). These items reflect budget-oriented behavior that is essentially oral in nature. Managers with higher scores on this factor more often express their opinions on budget matters and discuss these matters informally. This factor accounts for about 8 percent of the combined variance for all items.

Descriptive Budget Factor XII:
Interactions with Peers and Financial Staff

This factor reflects budget-oriented interactive behavior with individuals other than manager's immediate superior or subordinate. The items with the highest loadings on this factor are Item 6, I work with other unit heads in preparing the budget for my unit (.69); and Item 7, I work with financial staff people in preparing the budget for my unit (.53). Managers with higher scores on this factor work with other unit heads and financial staff people in preparing their unit's operating budget. This factor accounts for about 6 percent of the combined variance on all items.

Descriptive Budget Factor XIII:
Time Demands of Budgeting

This factor reflects the time demands that a budgeting system places on managers; it also reflects managers' responses to these time demands. The items with the highest loadings on this factor are Item 3, I am not able to spend as much time as I would like preparing the budget for my unit (.63); Item 2, I spend time outside of normal working hours preparing the budget for my unit (.49); and Item 38, I offer suggestions for the improvement of budget systems (.41). Managers with higher scores on this factor are not able to spend as much time as they would like preparing the budget for their units, even though they spend time outside of

Table 4-6
MEANS AND STANDARD DEVIATIONS OF OCCURRENCE FOR NORMATIVE MEASURES OF FORTY-FOUR BUDGET-ORIENTED BEHAVIOR ITEMS
(N = 137)

Item No.	Means	Standard Deviations
1	3.50	1.42
2	1.90	1.07
3	1.69	1.15
4	3.07	1.46
5	3.94	1.29
6	3.03	1.46
7	3.63	1.35
8	4.04	1.24
9	3.69	1.09
10	3.81	1.38
11	3.40	1.33
12	3.35	1.33
13	3.58	1.23
14	1.99	1.13
15	3.26	1.59
16	3.31	1.33
17	4.11	1.04
18	2.54	1.29
19	2.85	1.55
20	3.21	1.24
21	3.05	1.24
22	2.97	1.23
23	4.13	1.07
24	3.04	1.46
25	3.02	1.26
26	3.28	1.38
27	2.93	1.48
28	3.90	1.16
29	2.95	1.39
30	3.98	1.15
31	2.70	1.31
32	2.49	1.26
33	2.26	1.29
34	1.45	0.88
35	1.31	0.77
36	2.86	1.30
37	3.80	1.06
38	3.29	1.27
39	2.68	1.13
40	3.73	1.16
41	2.73	1.35
42	2.77	1.35
43	3.22	1.23
44	3.70	1.20

normal working hours preparing these budgets. Moreover, these managers also offer suggestions for the improvement of budget systems. This factor accounts for 5.6 percent of the combined variance for all items.

Analysis of Normative Measures of Managers' Budget-Oriented Behavior

Marginal Distributions of the Measures

Table 4-6 presents the means and standard deviations of occurrence for the normative measures of managers' budget-oriented behavior (How often should it take place?) based on data obtained from our total sample. From inspection of this table we can obtain a general idea about what the managers in our sample think about their budget-oriented behavior. The items managers indicate they think should occur most frequently suggest that our sample of managers think that they should experience a relatively high degree of personal involvement in budgeting. For example, these items include the following: My superior accepts my explanations of budget variances in my unit (Item 23), I investigate favorable as well as unfavorable budget variances for my unit (Item 17), I am consulted about special factors I would like to have included in the budget being prepared (Item 8), I personally investigate budget variances in my unit (Item 30), and I work with my subordinates in preparing the budget for my unit (Item 5). Recall that Table 4-2 revealed that our sample of managers indicated that four of the five items presented above actually occur most frequently.

The items managers indicate they think should occur least frequently include the following: I have to shift figures relating to operations to reduce budget variances (Item 35), I find it necessary to charge some activities to other accounts when budgeted funds have been used up (Item 34), I am not able to spend as much time as I would like preparing the budget for my unit (Item 3), I spend time outside of normal working hours preparing the budget for my unit (Item 2), and I have difficulty meeting the budget for my unit (Item 14).

Table 4-7 presents the means, standard deviation, and t-values for differences between the descriptive (what is) and normative measurements (what should be) for each of the 44 budget-oriented behavior items. The differences reported in Table 4-7 were calculated by subtracting the descriptive measure from the normative measure for each item for each manager. Thus, a positive mean difference for an item indicates that on average, the descriptive measures for that item exceed the normative measures for that item. A negative mean difference for an item indicates that, on average, the normative measures for that item exceed the descriptive measures for that item.

67

Table 4-7
MEANS AND STANDARD DEVIATIONS FOR DIFFERENCES
BETWEEN DESCRIPTIVE AND NORMATIVE MEASURES OF
FORTY-FOUR BUDGET-ORIENTED BEHAVIOR ITEMS — (N = 137)

Item No.	Means	Standard Deviations	t-Values*
1	—0.56	1.21	3.165
2	0.71	1.26	4.574
3	0.44	1.34	2.776
4	—0.47	1.14	2.621
5	—0.20	0.72	
6	—0.48	0.98	2.744
7	—0.28	0.79	
8	—0.84	1.19	5.031
9	—0.32	0.87	2.250
10	—0.60	1.17	3.115
11	0.05	0.93	
12	—0.45	1.26	2.477
13	—0.64	1.12	4.101
14	0.35	1.35	2.413
15	—0.58	1.11	2.818
16	—0.88	1.21	5.105
17	—0.56	0.93	3.746
18	—0.39	0.94	2.402
19	—0.71	1.09	3.767
20	0.01	0.93	
21	0.25	1.03	
22	—0.66	1.10	4.203
23	0.03	0.81	
24	—0.69	1.09	3.892
25	—0.94	1.15	5.654
26	—0.19	0.63	
27	—0.86	1.17	4.682
28	—0.44	0.72	2.695
29	—0.63	1.11	3.596
30	0.20	0.68	
31	—0.35	0.76	2.157
32	—0.52	0.97	3.434
33	—0.18	0.89	
34	0.36	0.86	2.937
35	0.13	0.73	
36	0.08	0.74	
37	—0.10	0.60	
38	—0.39	0.89	2.619
39	—0.54	0.90	3.820
40	—0.31	0.64	2.027
41	—0.45	0.90	2.697
42	—0.47	0.98	2.780
43	—0.37	0.92	2.182
44	—0.51	0.85	3.097

* Only t-values over 2.00 are reported and are significant at the 5% level. Those t-values over 2.58 are significant at the 1% level, and those over 3.29 are significant at the .1% level.

Table 4-7 reveals that there are 11 descriptive items which managers indicate occur more frequently than they think they should. Item 2, for example, has the most significant positive mean difference. This item suggests that managers spend more time outside of normal working hours preparing the budgets for their units than they think they should. The other 33 items have negative mean differences. Item 25 has the most significant negative mean difference. This item suggests that managers think their superiors should mention budgets more often than they do when talking about their efficiency as managers.

Correlations Among the Measures

The simple correlation coefficients for pairs of the normative measures of the 44 budget-oriented behavior items are presented in Table 4-8. The coefficients reported in this table follow the same general pattern as those reported in Table 4-3 for the descriptive measures of these items. First, these coefficients suggest that these items are not highly intercorrelated; only 11 of the coefficients reported in Table 4-8 are above .50, and the highest coefficient is .69. Second, patterns of relations exist. Note the intercorrelations between the following sets of items: I am required to submit an explanation in writing about causes of large budget variances (Item 27), I am required to trace the cause of budget variances to groups or individuals within my unit (Item 29), I evaluate my subordinates by means of the budget (Item 31), and I am required to report actions I take to correct causes of budget variances (Item 32); My superior mentions budgets when talking to me about my efficiency as a manager (Item 25), The budget enables me to keep track of my success as a manager (Item 43), and The budget enables me to be a better manager (Item 44); I am shown comparisons of actual and budgeted performance for other units (Item 15), My explanation of budget variances is included in performance reports (Item 16), and I investigate favorable as well as unfavorable budget variances for my unit (Item 17).

Factor Analysis of Intercorrelations

To take advantage of these intercorrelations, a factor analysis was used to identify principal normative dimensions of managers' budget-oriented behavior. A principal components analysis resulted in identifying 14 characteristic roots that were greater than one and which accounted for 69 percent of the total variance. These roots are presented in Table 4-9. These 14 factors were then rotated using Kaiser's normal orthogonal varimax criterion.

Table 4-10 presents the rotated factor loading coefficients for the 14 normative budget-oriented behavior factors. These loading coeffi-

Table 4-8

CORRELATIONS AMONG NORMATIVE MEASURES OF FORTY-FOUR BUDGET-ORIENTED BEHAVIOR ITEMS

(N = 137)

	1	2	3	4	5	6	7	8	9	10	11	12	13	14	15	16	17	18	19	20	21	22
1		.25	.19	.18	.30	.25	.18	.21	.16	.18	.15	.07	.28	-.02	.24	.24	.23	.11	.34	.04	-.09	.26
2			.26	.23	.29	.20	.11	.09	-.09	.10	.03	.10	.12	.21	.28	.27	.11	.22	.41	-.10	-.17	.13
3				.24	.08	.15	.02	.07	-.02	.03	.11	-.01	.06	.09	.09	.08	-.03	.31	.22	-.02	-.13	.04
4					.21	.38	.29	.22	-.07	.06	.12	-.01	.07	-.04	.09	.05	-.04	.30	.15	-.17	-.14	.20
5						.25	.34	.46	.30	.38	.12	.15	.34	-.00	.27	.33	.39	-.03	.21	-.16	-.02	.19
6							.40	.17	.05	.10	.04	.26	.23	-.00	.22	.10	.01	.16	.19	-.06	-.05	.17
7								.39	.29	.16	.01	.14	.11	-.03	.27	.13	.25	.10	.21	-.02	.04	.15
8									.50	.34	.17	.18	.19	-.15	.14	.27	.30	.12	.12	.09	.06	.27
9										.41	.30	.22	.26	-.09	.12	.12	.27	-.05	.09	.16	.14	.18
10											.16	.17	.38	-.05	.11	.25	.28	.05	.01	.11	-.01	.11
11												.13	.15	-.01	.04	.07	.12	.08	.15	-.02	.05	.16
12													.37	-.00	.23	.20	.27	.04	.21	-.11	.01	.35
13														.00	.05	.29	.34	.06	.16	-.19	.05	.12
14															-.06	-.01	-.05	.12	.07	-.05	-.15	-.02
15																.38	.40	.17	.28	.07	-.04	-.32
16																	.57	.13	.45	.19	-.01	.35
17																			.24	-.09	-.20	.33
18																			.18	-.10	-.02	.36
19																					-.20	.32
20																					.50	-.08
21																						.02
22																						
23																						
24																						
25																						
26																						
27																						
28																						
29																						
30																						
31 through 43																						
44																						

	23	24	25	26	27	28	29	30	31	32	33	34	35	36	37	38	39	40	41	42	43	44
1																						
2	.02		.17		.36	.16	.22	.07	.32						.20				.09			
3	-.10		.22	.28	.10	.08	.15	-.06	.21	.25	.09				.03	.32		.07	.15			
4	-.11	.21	.05	.21	.13	-.06	.14	-.07	.08	.16	.30			.13	.03	.10		.13	-.16			.16
5	-.14	.19	.07	.11	.11	-.05	.17	.01	.02	.12	.21		-.05	.04	-.01	.11	.20	-.11	.07		.21	.13
6	-.04	.17	.18	.19	.14	.19	.26	.25	.29	.18	.16		.03	-.04	.27	.07	.12	-.13	.10		.09	.06
7	-.02	.28	.17	.28	.21	.17	.33	.01	.24	.11	.11	-.08	.29	.08	.09	.24	.23	.23	.12		-.08	-.05
8	.16	.27	.05	.30	.12	.20	.22	.07	.02	.19	.21	.16	.14	.13	.22	.24	.14	.17	.05		-.11	.25
9	.21	.10	.14	.50	.16	.19	.26	.08	.06	-.04	.10	.12	-.10	.03	.35	.23	.21	.14	.13		.22	.05
10	.24	.09	.07	.20	-.00	.25	.06	.21	.11	.12	.06	-.08	.08	.18	.27	.33	.29	.20	.07	.14	.05	.14
11	.09	.06	.23	.14	.18	.21	.11	.12	.20	.04	-.00	-.10	.02	.21	.16	.25	.25	.29	.13	.14	.03	.20
12	.12	.21	.09	.23	.10	.13	.09	.15	.02	.10	-.03	.03	-.03	.15	.19	.12	.33	.18	-.01	.18	.23	.19
13	-.12	.36	.26	.05	.23	.19	.22	.14	.16	.17	-.05	-.08	-.01	.16	.14	.17	.19	.20	-.02	.07	.17	.08
14	-.20	.29	.44	.25	.26	.35	.18	.22	.42	.15	.13	-.11	-.06	.06	.16	.13	.12	-.21	.25	.21	.01	.03
15	-.06	.05	.10	.24	-.05	-.09	.09	.01	.08	.24	.19	-.06	-.07	.16	-.08	-.05	-.01	.27	-.02	.19	.08	.41
16	.25	.18	.08	-.05	.26	.14	.17	.05	.09	.10	.12	-.21	-.01	.24	.17	.29	-.03	.06	.11	.07	.40	.03
17	.33	-.22	.38	.24	.40	.44	.26	.24	.37	.20	.16	-.15	-.02	-.20	.28	.22	-.00	-.15	.16	.18	-.00	.02
18	.27	.24	.32	.22	.18	.42	.11	.35	.26	.26	.12	-.08	-.05	.18	.25	.14	.33	-.13	.07	.15	-.00	.19
19	-.04	.28	.25	.40	.14	.18	.33	.19	.20	.08	.07	-.04	-.13	.17	.13	.22	.35	.25	.11	.18	.21	.24
20	-.00	.21	.20	.16	.41	.19	.36	.12	.17	.25	.22	.06	.33	.22	.22	.29	.21	.22	.16	.23	.20	.03
21	.35	.00	.08	.25	-.02	-.16	-.07	.22	.12	.24	.22	.01	.10	.12	.16	.05	.20	.19	.13	-.03	-.06	.15
22	.27	-.05	.21	.07	-.11	.26	-.02	.18	-.05	.00	-.05	-.18	.07	.11	.16	.02	.09	-.02	.15	.11	.06	.07
23	.11	.41	.36	.06	.37	.27	.32	.28	.22	.31	.04	-.19	.02	.12	.30	.34	-.07	-.31	.03	.13	.12	.20
24		.23	.26	.24	.15	.41	.01	.26	.12	.02	.21	-.03	.03	.30	.24	.14	.33	.19	.12	.15	.14	.15
25			.58	.24	.36	.26	.46	.16	.38	.37	-.03	-.08	.14	.16	.10	.26	.08	.31	.09	-.03	.12	.26
26				.32	.39	.49	.36	.24	.43	.50	.25	.02	.11	.11	.23	.24	.15	.26	.25	.00	.31	.25
27					.25	.26	.16	.14	.25	.04	.23	.05	.02	.19	.25	.25	.15	.21	.17	-.13	.50	.46
28						.35	.38	.20	.40	.51	.09	.04	-.17	.29	.18	.37	.28	.10	.22	.11	.14	.25
29							.32	.36	.34	.31	.09	-.06	.09	.09	.25	.09	.07	.28	.28	.06	.25	.31
30								.20	.33	.45	.16	-.16	.14	.18	.27	.34	.41	.29	.06	.24	.24	.25
31									.28	.22	.01	-.09	.01	.22	.41	.14	.06	.30	.05	.16	.19	.22
32										.44	.16	.06	.15	.01	.06	.24	.12	.23	.25	.25	.20	.33
33											.26	.00	.15	.07	.17	.25	.20	.20	.23	.25	.42	.24
34												.46	.40	.09	.04	.08	.17	.22	.22	.22	.31	.24
35													.36	-.01	-.05	.05	-.06	-.04	.02	.04	.10	.02
36														-.01	-.09	.02	.05	-.03	-.01	.05	-.04	.11
37															.56	.18	.14	.33	-.05	.04	.19	.27
38																.43	.34	.41	.22	.15	.26	.34
39																	.61	.30	.24	.37	.19	.22
40																		.26	.16	.23	.11	.15
41																			.16	.24	.15	.23
42																				.69	.25	.29
43																					.30	.32
44																						.67

Table 4-9

CHARACTERISTIC ROOTS FOR PRINCIPAL COMPONENTS ANALYSIS FOR NORMATIVE MEASURES OF BUDGET-ORIENTED BEHAVIOR ITEMS

Root Number	Characteristic Root	Cumulative Proportion of Total Variance
1	8.699	.198
2	3.300	.273
3	2.688	.334
4	1.986	.379
5	1.893	.422
6	1.715	.461
7	1.566	.497
8	1.478	.530
9	1.366	.561
10	1.293	.591
11	1.227	.618
12	1.120	.644
13	1.031	.667
14	1.001	.690
Total	30.363	

cients were used to develop the substantive descriptions of each factor provided in the following paragraphs.

Normative Budget Factor I:
Required Explanations of Budget Variances

This factor reflects managers' attitudes about the extent to which they should be required to perform various activities brought about by budget variances and the extent to which they should use the budget to evaluate their subordinates. The following items have the highest loadings on this factor: Item 32, I should be required to report actions I take to correct causes of budget variances (.71); Item 27, I should be required to submit an explanation in writing about causes of large budget variances (.65); Item 29, I should be required to trace the cause of budget variances to groups or individuals within my unit (.55); and Item 31, I should evaluate my subordinates by means of the budget (.45).

The combination of these items on this factor suggests that managers' attitudes about various activities brought about by budget variances may be interrelated. For example, this factor suggests that managers' attitudes about being required to report actions taken to correct the causes of budget variances, having to submit explanations in writing about the causes of these variances, and being required to trace the causes of these variances to groups or individuals within their units may be inter-related. Moreover, the combination of these items on this factor suggests that their attitudes about these activities may be related to their attitudes about using the budget to evaluate their subordinates.

Managers with higher scores on this factor think that they should be required to perform these activities more often and that they should use the budget to evaluate their subordinates more often. This is a relatively important factor, accounting for 9.5 percent of the combined variance for all items.

Normative Budget Factor II:
Acceptability of Methods

This factor reflects managers' attitudes about the acceptability of their methods of reaching budgeted performance and the acceptability of their explanations of budget variances. The following items have the highest loadings on this factor: Item 20, My methods of reaching budgeted performance should be accepted without question by my superior (.80); Item 21, My methods of reaching budgeted performance should be accepted without question by my subordinates (.64); and Item 23, My superior should accept my explanation of budget variances in my unit (.61). Managers with higher scores on this factor think that their methods of reaching budgeted performance more often should be accepted without question by their superiors and subordinates and that their superiors more often should accept their explanations of budget variances for their units. This factor accounts for 7.9 percent of the combined variance for all items.

Normative Budget Factor III:
Interactions with Peers and Financial Staff

This factor reflects managers' attitudes about the extent to which they think they should work with other individuals in preparing the budgets for their units. The following items have the highest loadings on this factor: Item 7, I should work with financial staff people in preparing the budget for my unit (.80); Item 6, I should work with other unit heads in preparing the budget for my unit (.68); Item 26, I should ask for assistance from staff departments concerned with budgeting (.53); and Item 4, I should work with my superior in preparing the budget for my unit (.50). Managers with higher scores on this factor think that they should work with these individuals more often in preparing the budgets for their units. This factor accounts for 7.5 percent of the combined variance for all items.

Table 4-10
ROTATED FACTOR LOADINGS FOR NORMATIVE MEASURES OF FORTY-FOUR BUDGET-ORIENTED BEHAVIOR ITEMS
(N = 137)

Item No.	I	II	III	IV	V	VI	VII	VIII	IX	X	XI	XII	XIII	XIV	Communality
1	.30	-.05	.18	-.04	.10	.10	.21	.09	.09	.01	-.03	-.14	.65	.04	.64
2	-.06	-.24	.12	.22	.08	-.04	.43	.03	-.11	.15	.04	.30	.36	.26	.64
3	-.01	-.10	-.08	.23	-.08	.14	.05	-.05	.12	.17	-.01	.02	.30	.62	.61
4	.12	-.21	.50	-.09	-.10	-.09	-.05	.06	.03	.04	.00	-.07	.12	.57	.69
5	-.07	.16	.37	-.12	.23	.16	.25	.06	.29	.00	.12	.25	.41	.04	.65
6	.26	-.06	.68	.09	-.11	.14	-.07	-.04	-.02	.15	.24	.03	.18	.05	.70
7	-.05	.00	.80	.01	.07	.15	.20	.08	.19	-.04	-.07	-.02	-.06	.00	.77
8	-.05	.05	.32	.11	.23	.34	.16	.09	.56	-.00	-.01	-.10	-.01	.15	.67
9	-.04	.18	.11	.03	.14	.16	.06	.10	.79	-.01	.10	.01	-.01	-.12	.75
10	-.15	.14	.06	-.25	.28	.11	.11	-.06	.44	.04	.36	.05	.25	.10	.61
11	.29	-.05	-.11	-.08	-.21	-.23	.01	.22	.64	.15	-.01	-.02	.11	.08	.70
12	.19	-.08	.14	.09	-.12	.00	.20	.12	.22	-.01	.68	-.05	-.05	-.21	.69
13	.16	.06	.13	.02	.41	-.27	.10	.10	.27	.19	.40	.01	.30	-.05	.67
14	.04	-.22	-.06	.09	.05	-.02	.02	-.08	-.03	-.02	.01	.77	-.03	.02	.66
15	.04	-.06	.17	.11	-.16	.25	.60	.10	-.17	.08	.18	-.08	.11	-.08	.57
16	.24	.13	-.01	-.13	.19	.12	.76	.01	.07	.04	.05	.03	.07	.10	.74
17	-.01	.31	.12	-.14	.15	-.04	.69	.17	.18	-.01	.20	.06	.01	-.03	.73
18	.25	.01	.09	.08	-.08	.08	.12	.22	-.11	.04	.09	.09	-.15	.67	.66
19	.36	-.23	.09	.12	-.05	.17	.56	.12	.09	.06	-.09	.05	.19	.08	.63
20	-.03	.80	-.05	.10	.02	.04	-.03	.02	.06	.01	-.07	-.09	.22	-.05	.73
21	.01	.64	.10	.12	.06	-.12	-.04	.11	.06	.18	-.10	-.09	-.29	-.11	.62
22	.35	-.09	.06	.04	.02	.20	.34	.42	.09	-.10	.30	-.08	-.08	.14	.61
23	-.03	.61	-.10	-.14	.09	.08	.21	.08	.08	.04	.28	-.18	.07	.03	.59
24	.29	.05	.08	.04	.27	.17	.08	.04	-.10	-.00	.66	.07	.06	.26	.73

Item No.	I	II	III	IV	V	VI	VII	VIII	IX	X	XI	XII	XIII	XIV	Communality
25	.38	.16	.03	.05	.49	-.03	.24	.12	-.08	.13	.40	.06	-.05	.13	.70
26	-.05	.12	.53	.10	.14	-.03	.31	.23	-.04	.09	.22	-.12	.19	.05	.58
27	.65	-.02	.04	.03	.17	.19	.28	-.04	-.01	.10	.14	-.24	.19	.02	.69
28	.39	.38	.20	-.16	.23	-.18	.36	.09	.12	.20	.13	-.00	-.21	.09	.71
29	.55	-.05	.26	-.05	.17	.35	.05	.14	.01	-.03	.14	.19	-.07	.19	.64
30	.34	.45	.02	-.03	.03	-.08	.09	.47	.10	-.10	.02	.31	.05	-.04	.67
31	.45	.21	.06	.04	.34	.03	.10	-.08	-.07	.16	.25	.23	.35	.04	.65
32	.71	-.01	-.04	.06	.20	.08	.06	.05	.03	.13	.13	.08	.08	.14	.63
33	.09	-.10	.13	.72	.14	.01	.17	.03	.02	.23	.15	.07	-.07	.17	.72
34	-.08	.09	-.03	.83	-.01	-.01	-.12	.04	-.14	-.04	.00	.08	.08	-.02	.76
35	.23	.17	-.01	.68	.12	.03	-.08	-.21	.08	-.13	-.08	-.11	-.13	.47	.76
36	-.09	.03	.10	.05	.25	.02	.11	.74	.02	-.07	.09	-.29	.04	.06	.74
37	.09	.16	.07	-.05	.17	.30	.12	.74	.16	.09	-.09	-.02	.06	-.03	.78
38	.21	.03	.09	.02	.04	.70	.05	.24	.11	.23	.14	-.06	.19	.01	.74
39	.15	-.04	.13	.03	-.01	.79	.25	.11	.08	.10	.01	.02	-.01	.10	.77
40	.05	.06	.06	.00	.02	.14	.02	.55	.20	.21	.34	.29	-.02	.16	.64
41	.06	.12	.04	.02	.18	.07	.09	.04	-.04	.86	-.05	-.02	.04	.06	.82
42	.13	.02	.06	.06	.16	.16	.03	.00	.12	.84	.10	.01	.01	.07	.81
43	.22	.06	-.03	.02	.79	.06	-.01	.10	.06	.14	.05	.01	.10	-.17	.77
44	.14	.02	.05	.12	.78	.03	.08	.23	.12	.20	-.02	.02	.01	-.02	.76
Contribution of Factor	2.899	2.387	2.265	1.958	2.601	2.052	2.881	2.326	2.115	2.015	2.086	1.327	1.583	1.868	30.36
Percent of Communality	9.5	7.9	7.5	6.4	8.6	6.8	9.5	7.7	6.9	6.6	6.9	4.4	5.2	6.1	

Normative Budget Factor IV:
Actions Brought About by Expected Budget Overruns

This factor reflects managers' attitudes about the extent to which they think they should undertake various activities in coping with budget variances. The items having the highest loadings on this factor include the following: Item 34, I should find it necessary to charge some activities to other accounts when budgeted funds for these activities have been used up (.83); Item 33, I should find it necessary to stop some activities in my unit when budgeted funds are used up (.72); and Item 35, I should have to shift figures relating to operations to reduce budget variances (.58). Managers with higher scores on this factor think that they should engage in these activities more often. This factor accounts for 6.4 percent of the combined variance for all items.

Normative Budget Factor V:
Usefulness of Budgeting

This factor reflects managers' attitudes about the usefulness of budgeting. The items with the highest loadings on this factor include the following: Item 44, The budget should enable me to be a better manager (.78); Item 43, The budget should enable me to keep track of my success as a manager (.79); and Item 25, My superior should mention budgets when talking to me about my efficiency as a manager (.49). Managers with higher scores on this factor have more positive attitudes about the usefulness of budgeting. They think that the budget should enable them to keep track of their success as managers. Moreover, they think that their superiors should mention budgets more often when talking to them about their efficiency as managers. This is a relatively important factor, accounting for 8.6 percent of the total variance for all items.

Normative Budget Factor VI:
Suggestions about Budgeting

This factor reflects managers' attitudes about the extent to which they think they should have an influential role in improving budgeting systems. The following two items have highest loadings on this factor: Item 38, I should offer suggestions for the improvement of budget systems (.70); and Item 39, The budgeting system should be changed in accordance with my suggestions (.79). Note that this factor encompasses managers' attitudes about whether they should offer suggestions for the improvement of budgeting systems and also their attitudes about whether these systems should be changed in accordance with their suggestions. Managers who think that they should offer these suggestions more often and that these systems should more often be changed in accordance with these suggestions have higher scores on this factor. This factor is a relatively important one, accounting for 6.8 percent of the combined variance for all items.

Normative Budget Factor VII:
Involvement in Budgeting

This factor reflects managers' attitudes about their involvement in the budgeting process. The following items have the highest loadings on this factor: Item 16, My explanation of budget variances should be included in performance reports (.76); Item 17, I should investigate favorable as well as unfavorable budget variances for my unit (.69); Item 15, I should be shown comparisons of actual and budgeted performance for other units (.60); and Item 2, I should spend time outside of normal working hours preparing the budget for my unit (.43). This factor suggests that the extent to which managers think that explanations of budget variances should be included in performance reports, that they should investigate favorable as well as unfavorable budget variances for their units, and that they should be shown comparisons of actual and budgeted performance for other units may be interrelated. Moreover, this factor suggests that their attitudes about these items may be related to their attitudes about whether they should spend time outside of normal working hours preparing the budget for their units. Managers with higher scores on this factor think that these events should occur more frequently. This is an important factor, accounting for 9.5 percent of the total variance for all items.

Normative Budget Factor VIII:
Expressive about Budgeting

Managers with higher scores on this factor think that they should take a more active, expressive role in the budgeting process. The following items have the highest loadings on this factor: Item 37, I should express my opinions on budget matters (.74); Item 36, Budget matters should be mentioned in informal conversations (.74); Item 30, I personally should investigate budget variances in my unit (.47); and Item 40, I should discuss budget items when problems occur (.55). This factor suggests that managers' attitudes about their expressing their opinions on budget matters, their mentioning budget matters in informal conversations, and their discussing budget items when problems occur may be interrelated. Moreover, it suggests that their attitudes about these events may be related to their attitudes about personally investigating budget variances in their units. This factor accounts for 7.7 percent of the combined variance for all items.

Normative Budget Factor IX:
Influence in Budget Setting

This factor is similar to normative budget factor VI in that it combines items which reflect managers' attitudes about assuming an influential role in the budgeting process. The following items have the highest loadings on this factor: Item 9, New budgets should include changes I have suggested (.79); Item 11, Preparing the budget for my unit should require my attention to a great number of details (.64); Item 8, I should be consulted about special factors I would like to have included in the budget being prepared (.56); and Item 10, The budget should not be finalized until I am satisfied with it (.44). Managers who think that their budgets should include changes they have suggested, that they should be consulted about special factors they would like to have included in the budget being prepared, and that the budget should not be finalized until they are satisfied with it have higher scores on this factor. This accounts for 6.9 percent of the combined variance for all items.

Normative Budget Factor X:
Influence on Flexibility and Innovation

This factor is essentially a two-item factor. The following two items have the highest loadings on this factor: Item 41, The budget should enable me to be more flexible (.86); and Item 42, The budget should enable me to be more innovative (.84). Note that both of these items are attitudinal items. Managers who think that the budget should enable them to be more flexible and innovative have higher scores' on this factor. This factor accounts for 6.6 percent of the combined variance for all items.

Normative Budget Factor XI:
Evaluation by Superiors

This factor also is essentially a two-item factor. The two items with the highest loadings on this factor are: Item 12, I should be reminded of the importance of meeting the budget for my unit (.68); and Item 24, My superior should express dissatisfaction to me about results in my unit when the budget has not been met (.66). Note that this factor suggests that managers' attitudes about being reminded of the importance of meeting their budgets and their attitudes about their superiors expressing dissatisfaction to them when their budgets have not been met may be interrelated. Managers with higher scores on this factor think that these events should occur more often. This factor accounts for 6.9 percent of the total variance for all items.

Normative Budget Factor XII:
Difficulty Meeting Budget

This factor is a one-item factor. The following item has the highest loading on this factor: Item 14, I should have difficulty meeting the budget for my unit (.77). Managers who think that they should experience more difficulty meeting their operating budgets have higher scores on this factor. This factor accounts for 4.4 percent of the combined variance for all items.

Normative Budget Factor XIII:
Anticipating Budget Preparation

This factor also is a one-item factor. The following item has the highest loading on this factor: Item 1, I should start preparing the budget for my unit before I am asked to (.65). Managers who think that they should start preparing the budgets for their units before they are asked to have higher scores on this factor. This factor accounts for 5.2 percent of the combined variance for all items.

Normative Budget Factor XIV:
Interactions with Superiors

This factor reflects managers' attitudes about the extent to which they should interact with their superiors. The following items have the highest loadings on this factor: Item 18, I should go to my superior for advice on how to achieve my budget (.67); and Item 3, I should not be able to spend as much time as I would like preparing the budget for my unit (.57). This factor suggests that managers' attitudes about whether they should go to their superiors for advice on how to achieve their budgets and whether they should work with their superiors in preparing the budgets for their units may be related to their attitudes about whether they are able to spend as much time as they would like in preparing their budgets. Managers who think that they should go to and work with their superiors more often and who think that they more often should not be able to spend as much time as they would like preparing their budgets have higher scores on this factor. This factor accounts for 6.1 percent of the combined variance for all items.

Comparison of Descriptive and Normative Factor Structures

Our analysis of the data obtained from our total sample of managers for the descriptive and normative measures of managers' budget-oriented behavior has led us to posit the existence of 13 descriptive and 14 separable summary factors or dimensions of this behavior. In this section we consider the structures of these summary descriptive and normative factors in more detail.

First, an examination of the loadings of items on the descriptive and normative budget factors reveals several striking similarities and differences in these factor structures. Note, for example, that items 33, 34 and 35 have the highest loadings on both descriptive budget factor II and normative budget factor IV. Similarly, note that items 36, 37 and 40 have the highest loadings on both descriptive budget factor XI and normative budget factor VIII; that items 6 and 7 have the highest loadings on both descriptive budget factor XII and normative budget factor III; and that items 20, 21 and 23 have the highest loadings on both descriptive budget factor VII and normative budget factor II. The relatively high loadings of these items on similar descriptive and normative budget factors suggest that some general patterns of relations may be similar for the two factor structures.

Even though these items are heavily loaded on similar descriptive and normative budget factors, the relative loadings of these items on these factors differ. For example, where items 6 and 7 have loadings of .69 and .53 respectively on descriptive budget factor XII, these items have loadings of .68 and .80 respectively on normative budget factor III. Moreover, some items are heavily loaded on different descriptive and normative budget factors. For example, where items 41, 42, 43 and 44 are heavily loaded on descriptive budget factor VI, items 41 and 42 are heavily loaded on normative budget factor X and items 43 and 44 are heavily loaded on normative budget factor V. Similarly, where items 7, 8, 9, 10 and 26 are heavily loaded on descriptive budget factor VIII, items 7 and 26 are heavily loaded on normative budget factor III, and items 8, 9 and 10 are heavily loaded on normative budget factor IX. The relatively high loadings of these items on different descriptive and normative budget factors suggest that these two factor structures also have some general patterns of relations which may be different.

Second, an examination of the relative contributions of individual factors to the total variance accounted for by each factor structure also reveals several striking similarities and differences in these factor structures. Our analysis of the descriptive measures of managers' budget-oriented behavior resulted in the identification of 13 summary behavioral factors which are capable of providing both an economical and reasonably complete description of how managers use budgeting in carrying out their management functions. The relative contribution of each of these factors to the total variance provides considerable insight into the relative importance of each factor for describing differences in managers' budget-oriented behavior.

Descriptive budget factors I and IV each account for about 10 percent of the total variance. These two factors reflect managers' budget-oriented behavior that is essentially evaluative in nature. Descriptive budget factor I reflects the extent to which a manager's superior mentions budgets when talking to him about his efficiency as a manager and expresses dissatisfaction to him when his budget has not been met. Descriptive budget factor IV reflects a manager's performance of various required activities which are brought about or related to the existence of budget variances.

Descriptive budget factors VI and VIII each account for about 9 percent of the total variance. These two factors reflect the extent to which managers tend to have positive attitudes about budgeting and tend to be influential in budget setting. Descriptive budget factor VI reflects a manager's attitudes about the extent to which he thinks that the budget enables him to be more flexible, more innovative, and a better manager, and to keep track of his success as a manager. Descriptive budget factor VIII reflects the extent to which a manager is consulted about special factors he would like to have included in the budgets being prepared and the extent to which his budgets include changes he has suggested and are not finalized until he is satisfied with them.

The relatively high contributions of these four factors suggest that they also may be important dimensions for describing differences in how managers use budgeting.

Descriptive budget factors II, VII and XI each account for about 8 percent of the total variance. These factors reflect different aspects of a manager's budget-oriented behavior, including his coping with large budget variances, the acceptability of his methods for achieving budgeted performance, and his oral expressive behavior.

The remaining six descriptive budget factors account for between 5 and 7 percent of the total variance. These factors also reflect various dimensions of a manager's budget-oriented behavior, including his general evaluative behavior, his interactions with his superiors, subordinates and others, his general level of involvement in budgeting, and the time demands he experiences because of budgeting. Even though these factors may be generally less important in terms of their contributions to the total variance explained, they represent separable behavioral dimensions which can be used to describe differences in mangers' budget-oriented behavior.

Similarly, our analysis of the normative measures of managers' budget-oriented behavior resulted in the identification of 14 summary attitudinal factors. These factors also differ in their relative importance for describing differences in what managers think about their use of budgeting.

Normative budget factors I, VI and VII each account for 9.5 percent of the total variance. These factors reflect managers' attitudes about their performing various activities brought about by budget variances, their using the budget to evaluate their subordinates, their taking an influential role in improving budgeting systems, and their being involved in the budgeting process. The relatively high contributions of these factors suggest that they may be the most important dimensions for describing differences in what managers think about their use of budgeting.

Normative budget factors II, III, V and VIII each account for between 7 and 9 percent of the total variance. These factors reflect a manager's attitudes about having his methods of achieving his budgets accepted by others, working with others in preparing his operating budgets, having the budget enable him to be a better manager and to keep track of his success as a manager, and taking an active and expressive role in the budgeting process.

Also, normative budget factors IV, IX, X, XI and XIV, which each account for between 6 and 7 percent of the total variance, reflect a manager's attitudes about his undertaking various activities in coping with large budget variances, assuming an active role in the budgeting process, being reminded of the importance of meeting his budgets, having his superior express dissatisfaction to him when his budget has not been met, and interacting with his superior.

Finally, normative budget factors XII and XIII, which each account for between 4 and 6 percent of the total variance, reflect a manager's attitudes about having difficulty meeting his operating budgets and starting to prepare his budgets before he is asked to. These factors represent separable attitudinal dimensions which can be used to describe differences in what managers think about their use of budgeting. However, the relatively low contributions of these factors to the total variance explained suggests that they may be less important for describing these differences.

Some of the factors which are most important for explaining differences in how managers use budgeting and in what they think about their use of budgeting suggest that there may be some important similarities in the two factor structures. For example, where the two most important descriptive budget factors reflect the evaluative budget-oriented behavior of managers and of their superiors, the most important normative budget factor reflects managers' attitudes about their evaluative budget-oriented behavior. Similarly, where an important descriptive budget factor reflects the extent to which managers are influential in budgeting, an important normative budget factor reflects managers' attitudes about the extent to which they should be influential in budgeting.

However, some of these factors suggest that important differences may also exist in these two factor structures. For example, where the normative budget factor that reflects managers' attitudes about being involved in budgeting is a relatively important factor in the normative factor structure, the corresponding descriptive budget factor which

Table 4-11

CORRELATIONS AMONG THIRTEEN DESCRIPTIVE AND FOURTEEN NORMATIVE BUDGET FACTORS

(N = 137)

Descriptive Budget Factors	Normative Budget Factors													
	I	II	III	IV	V	VI	VII	VIII	IX	X	XI	XII	XIII	XIV
I	.38	.22	−.03	−.03	.42	.08	−.06	−.06	−.14	−.04	.26	.22	.22	.09
II	.13	.06	−.05	.60	.04	−.18	.10	.08	.00	.00	.06	−.02	−.24	.25
III	−.19	−.04	−.02	−.00	.07	−.17	.14	−.07	.05	.14	.43	−.05	.19	−.06
IV	.40	.10	.06	−.04	−.06	.31	.29	−.02	−.02	.01	−.21	−.03	−.03	−.04
V	.08	−.10	.25	−.16	−.26	.02	−.06	.16	.09	.09	.13	−.07	−.20	.40
VI	.08	−.01	−.01	.10	.26	.00	.09	−.11	.13	.71	−.05	−.15	.01	−.05
VII	−.05	.71	.02	−.07	−.02	−.04	.08	.06	−.05	.04	.15	−.14	−.12	−.08
VIII	−.13	.14	.36	−.09	.12	.07	.05	−.04	.49	−.13	−.05	−.06	.09	−.04
IX	.09	.18	.00	−.03	−.06	−.16	.32	.21	.29	−.00	−.19	.32	.30	−.01
X	−.23	−.05	.28	.12	.03	.27	.51	.04	−.33	−.03	.08	−.16	.17	.01
XI	.01	−.01	.01	.03	.29	.21	−.00	.74	.11	−.01	.07	−.04	−.16	−.08
XII	.00	−.08	.60	.23	.08	−.00	−.01	−.06	−.05	.02	.07	.18	−.02	−.05
XIII	−.05	−.07	−.03	.19	−.28	.40	−.12	−.01	.16	.21	.20	.24	.24	.24

reflects the extent to which managers tend to be involved in budgeting is a relatively unimportant factor in the descriptive factor structure.

Finally, our examination of the loadings of items on the descriptive and normative budget factors and of the relative contributions of individual factors to the variance explained by each factor structure suggests that some of the descriptive and normative budget factors may be intercorrelated. Table 4-11 presents the simple correlation coefficients for pairs of the descriptive and normative budget factors. Note that only a few of these factors are highly intercorrelated. For example, the highest correlation coefficient is .74, and only six coefficients are above .50. However, note that those descriptive and normative budget factors which are intercorrelated tend to be closely related in terms of their substantive identification. For example, descriptive budget factor XI which reflects managers' oral expressive behavior is highly correlated with normative budget factor VIII which reflects managers' attitudes about taking an active, expressive role in budgeting.

Chapter 5

The Predictor Variables

A major part of our research was aimed at measuring managers' budget-oriented behavior and at developing sets of measures of this behavior. As reported in Chapter 4, our intensive analysis of this behavior resulted in the identification and description of 13 descriptive and 14 normative dimensions of this behavior. Another major part of our research was aimed at identifying some of the variables which may affect managers' budget-oriented behavior. The theoretical model presented in Chapter 2 hypothesized that this behavior may be a complex outcome of many variables. Some of these variables may include the structural properties of a company's use of participative budgeting; others may include several organizational, personality, and interpersonal variables which may mediate the relationship between a company's use of participative budgeting and managers' budget-oriented behavior.

In this chapter, we describe in detail the 17 predictor variables that were measured as part of the study and the overall approach we used to analyze the relationships between variables and the descriptive and normative measures of managers' budget-oriented behavior.

The first section describes the two categorical predictor variables which reflect the fact that our total sample was drawn from four different production companies and from different management levels within each company. The three subsequent sections describe the four demographic, three attitudinal, and eight personality variables also measured as part of the study. The chapter concludes with a brief description of the overall approach we used to analyze the relationships between the predictor variables and the descriptive and normative measures of managers' budget-oriented behavior.

Because we were unable to specify a priori how these predictor variables might be related to these measures, we used an analysis strategy which allowed us to observe which variables and combinations within them produced the greatest discrimination in explaining differences in these measures. The results of our analysis of the relationships between these variables and the measures of managers' budget-oriented behavior are reported in Chapters 6 and 7.

Categorical Predictor Variables

Four Production Companies

Our total sample of 137 managers was drawn from four production companies. The companies differed somewhat in their uses of participative budgeting. To isolate the effects of these differences as well as differences that may exist in each company's organizational context, we assigned the managers drawn from each company to one of four categories. Each category refers to the use of a different amount and form of participative budgeting within the context of a particular organization. The following paragraphs describe briefly each company's use of participative budgeting.

The 43 managers drawn from Company A were assigned to the first category. Company A uses both project budgets and departmental operating budgets. Project budgets are used to monitor spending on developmental and performance projects funded by various governmental agencies. The creator or developer of a project initially describes the technical performance characteristics of the project. These characteristics are then translated into estimates of the man-hours, material costs, and work orders necessary to complete the project. A technical review is made of the feasibility of successfully completing the proposed project and, if approved, a centralized pricing group completes a financial budget for the proposed project. This financial budget is then reviewed by top management and, if approved, the proposed project is processed through various negotiations with the appropriate governmental agencies. After governmental funding has been obtained for the proposed project, the project is undertaken, and a financial budget for the project is established. The project engineer responsible for completion of the project is given a weekly report which compares actual expenditures with those provided for in the project budget.

Company A also uses departmental operating budgets. Each year, estimates of man-hours, material costs and work orders are obtained from department managers. These estimates are compiled centrally and a company-wide operating budget is prepared. The company's top management then reviews this budget in the process of setting company-wide operating targets. Based on the targets set by top management, a revised company-wide financial operating budget is prepared and distributed to department managers. This budget, however, is not used generally to monitor and evaluate the company's actual performance during the year. Rather, the major use of this budget is to facilitate Government Accounting Office audits because almost all of the company's projects are funded by means of various types of contracts with governmental agencies. Monthly budget reports which compare actual operating results with this budget are prepared and reviewed by the company's top management. However, these reports are not distributed to department managers.

Observe that the top management of Company A uses its operating budgets to obtain information from department managers, compiles this information centrally in preparing a company-wide financial operating budget, and then reviews this budget in the process of setting company-wide operating targets. Observe further, however, that department managers do not participate directly in the process of setting these operating targets, do not use the revised company-wide operating budget to monitor and evaluate the actual operating performance of their departments, and are not evaluated on the basis of a comparison of actual and budgeted performance. Rather, evaluation of departmental managerial performnace is based almost entirely on the technical performance of projects.

The 28 managers drawn from Company B were assigned to the second category. Company B uses financial budgets to prepare an annual profit plan which is used initially to inform the company's operating managers and also the top management of its parent company about its targets for the coming year and later to inform them about how the company's operating performance compares with this plan. Because the company's profit plan is also used by its parent company in preparing its annual profit plan, the parent company's planning schedule is used to develop the company's annual profit plan schedule. This schedule reflects the due dates of the various informational items required to prepare the preliminary operating budgets and profit and loss summaries which are reviewed and considered by the company's top management in setting operating targets for the coming year. It usually takes about 30 days to obtain the information required to prepare these budgets and summaries and another 30 days for top management to set operating targets and for the annual profit plan to be prepared and distributed to operating managers.

In late August, expected revenue forecasts are prepared by a marketing services manager and a marketing research manager. In preparing these forecasts, these managers rely on data about current sales orders as well as on sales estimates they obtain from marketing field personnel. These forecasts are reviewed by the marketing vice-president and then are broken down by customers — for example, by telephone industry sales, other industrial sales, governmental sales, etc.; by products — for example, by standard products, repair and replacement products, etc.; and also by gross sales prices within product and customer classifications.

The forecasts then are used to obtain expected cost forecasts from operating managers. First, gross sales prices and historical variable cost ratios for labor and material costs are used to generate the labor and work requirements forecasts which, in turn, are used to obtain expected variable cost estimates from the managers of operating departments.

These estimates then are used to prepare a standard variable cost of sales schedule. Next, a capacity costing system is used to obtain estimates of expected fixed costs, including expected repairs and maintenance costs and expected occupancy costs, from managers of non-operating departments. A set of preliminary operating budgets and profit and loss summaries is prepared on a direct or variable costing basis and then converted to an absorption costing basis so that they are consistent with financial reporting and Internal Revenue Service requirements.

The company's president meets with members of the budgeting staff to review these preliminary budgets and summaries. Next, the company's president holds a group meeting with the company's function managers. The purpose of this meeting is to have these managers reach agreement and consensus about the company's operating targets for the coming year. Considerable bargaining occurs in this meeting. The operating targets that are set in this meeting are used to prepare a revised set of budgets and summaries. These revised budgets and summaries are used to prepare the annual profit plan which is sent to the parent company to facilitate its planning activities. The parent company subsequently receives quarterly budget reports which include comparisons of actual and budgeted performance. The revised budgets and summaries also are used to prepare revised budgets for all operating and non-operating departments in the company. These budgets are revised quarterly to reflect current sales and spending levels.

Budget reports which include comparisons of actual and budgeted performance are prepared monthly and distributed to department managers. These reports are used as a basis for performance evaluation only to the extent that they provide the basis for letters written each month to the company's president and to function managers by members of the budgeting staff. The purpose of these letters is to highlight potential problem areas that are indicated by comparisons of actual and budgeted performance for each operating unit.

Company B's use of budgeting is similar to that of Company A in that department managers do not participate directly in the target-setting process; rather, the role of these managers in this process is effectively limited to that of providing information which is used to prepare the set of preliminary budgets and summaries. Observe further, however, that Company B's use of budgeting differs from that of Company A in that the targets set by top management are used to develop revised operating budgets for all departments. Moreover, these budgets are distributed to department managers and are used to monitor actual performance. However, these budgets are not used as a basis for performance evaluation, at least not in the sense of being used to judge managers based on comparisons of actual and budgeted performance. Rather, they are used only to inform top mangement of potential problem areas.

The 17 managers drawn from Company C were assigned to the third category. Company C uses company-wide financial operating budgets; however, the procedures used to prepare operating budgets differ somewhat in its two operating groups. The company's instrument group is a cohesive operating group. Its operating divisions have product lines which use similar technologies and which share similar markets. The products manufactured by the group's operating divisions are presented together in a single sales catalogue and are sold by a centralized group marketing staff.

Preparation of the instrument group's annual profit plan begins with the formulation of a sales forecast by the group's marketing staff. This forecast is then used to obtain expected cost estimates from the group's operating divisions. Each division uses the marketing staff's sales forecasts to develop its own preliminary operating budgets. These budgets are then compiled by the group's controller into a preliminary group operating plan which is reviewed by the group vice-president. The group vice-president presents the preliminary group operating plan to the company's chief executive officer for approval.

A bargaining process then ensues between the group vice-president and the chief executive officer. The group's operating targets for the coming year are set in this bargaining process and are used to prepare revised operating budgets for the group for each operating division and for each department within each division. These operating budgets are revised quarterly, and monthly reports which compare actual with budgeted performance are prepared and distributed to operating managers.

The company's transducer group is less cohesive as an operating group. The operating divisions which are included in this group have product lines which use different technologies and sell in different markets. Because of this, each operating division is essentially a separate and distinct operating unit.

In preparing the transducer group's annual profit plan, each operating division prepares its own preliminary operating budgets. Each division develops its own expected revenue and cost estimates and prepares a complete operating budget. Each division manager then submits his division's preliminary operating budget to the group vice-president for approval.

A bargaining process ensues between each division manager and the group vice-president. Preliminary divisional operating targets are set in this bargaining process and revised divisional operating budgets are prepared. These revised divisional operating budgets are then compiled by the group controller into a preliminary group operating plan which the group vice-president presents to the company's chief executive for approval.

Another bargaining process ensues between the group vice-president and the chief executive officer. The group's operating targets are set in this bargaining process and are used to prepare revised operating budgets for the group, for each operating division, and for each department within each division. These operating budgets also are revised quarterly, and monthly reports which compare actual with budgeted performance are prepared and distributed to operating managers.

Observe that the instrument group's use of budgeting is similar to that of Company B. The role of department managers is again effectively limited to providing information which can be used to prepare the preliminary operating budgets submitted to top management. Similarly, the transducer group's use of budgeting effectively limits the participation of department managers to the role of providing information used to prepare preliminary divisional operating budgets. Observe further that Company C's use of budgeting is similar to that of Company B in that the operating targets set in bargaining processes at higher management levels are used to prepare revised operating budgets for operating groups, division, and departments. However, Company C's use of budgeting differs from that of Company B in that operating budgets are used as a basis for performance evaluation of managers at various levels in the company. Because of this, it is important that managers at various levels reach agreement and consensus on the targets set, and this is reflected in the extensive use of bargaining in this company.

Finally, the 49 managers drawn from Company D were assigned to the fourth category. Company D uses financial targets that are based on three overlapping accounting systems. One system is the company's "legal" accounting system which collects and processes the financial data necessary to prepare the company's financial statements. The second system is a "facility" management accounting system in which the basic units of accountability are the company's manufacturing facilities. The third system is a "product line" accounting system in which the basic units of accountability are the company's worldwide product types.

The annual financial targeting process begins with the development, review, and acceptance of worldwide product type sales forecasts and estimated corporate consolidated earnings targets for the year by the company's operations council. These forecasts and targets are reviewed and accepted by the office of the president and used to develop product type guidelines which are distributed to the company's product line managers, regional sales managers, and the finance managers of facilities and sales regions.

These managers negotiate and refine these product type guidelines, resulting in the development of annual sales order estimates by product line, reconciled between regional sales managers, facility product line managers, and product type group marketing managers. The product group marketing managers then forward their reconciled annual sales order estimates, staffing targets, and estimated cost per order dollar projections, by product type, to the company's marketing staff. These estimates, targets, and projections are sent to the office of the president for review.

The approved sales order estimates are sent to the product type groups, facilities, and sales regions, and the approved staffing targets are sent to product type groups and sales regions. At the same time, company overhead guidelines are established by the company's executive vice-president and are reviewed by the office of the president. Based on these guidelines, overhead cost allocation estimates are sent to the appropriate facilities.

The product type group managers, sales region managers and facility managers send their management and legal accounting targets to the company's corporate accounting staff. This staff reconciles these two sets of targets and sends them to the office of the president for review. Operating managers then are notified about whether their targets have been accepted. Reports comparing actual with targeted performance are prepared monthly for facilities and quarterly for product type groups.

Observe that Company D's use of budgeting differs dramatically from that of the other three companies. Company D's budgeting has a general top-down orientation. Targets and guidelines are set at top management levels, without operating manager participation, and then are distributed to operating managers to facilitate preparation of their operating budgets. Moreover, there is considerable top management direction and review as these overall targets and guidelines are operationalized at lower management levels. Finally, there is top management review and acceptance of the operating budgets that have been prepared and compiled. Observe further that even though there is no operating manager participation in the target-setting process, there is considerable participation by these managers in the process of operationalizing these targets and in preparing their operating budgets. In fact, operating managers essentially prepare their own budgets, even though they are given considerable guidance and direction in preparing these budgets. However, these operating budgets are not used formally to evaluate managerial performance.

As reflected in the descriptions presented above, the four companies differ somewhat in their uses of participative budgeting. For example, where the operating managers in Company A tend to be the least involved in budgeting, operating managers in Company D tend to be the most involved, and operating managers in Companies B and C tend to be somewhat intermediate. Where operating managers in Companies A, B and C participate at least in a limited way in budget or target setting, operating managers in Company D do not participate in target setting. Where operating budgets are used to monitor operating unit performance in Companies B, C and D, operating budgets are used only to monitor overall company performance in Company A.

The four categories reflect the fact that our total sample of managers was drawn from four production companies which differ in their uses of participative budgeting. These differences reflect, at least in part, the fact that these companies operate in different contexts or environments, and because of this, it is impossible to isolate each company's use of participative budgeting from its broader context. Consequently, these four categories are used to represent not only each company's use of participative budgeting, but also the broader organizational context within which participative budgeting is used.

Focal and Other Managers

As discussed in Chapter 3, our total sample was drawn in two stages, and because of this, our sample essentially included two sub-samples. One sub-sample included the 46 Focal Managers drawn from the same management level in each company. These managers generally were department managers who reported to divisional general managers. The second sub-sample included the 91 Other Managers drawn from lists of names obtained from the Focal Managers. Each Focal Manager was asked to list the names of the individuals with whom he spent the most time in drafting and using budgets. Each Focal Manager typically listed seven or eight names of other individuals, and these lists were then used to obtain our sample of Other Managers. Because the individuals listed by the Focal Managers occupied positions in various levels of management, the sample of Other Managers included managers in different levels of management.

To reflect the existence of these two sub-samples, and to reflect the fact that the managers included in these two sub-samples differed in terms of the level of their positions in their companies, we assigned the 46 Focal Managers to one category and the 91 Other Managers to a second category. Also, because 68 percent of the Other Managers turned out to be subordinates of the Focal Managers, these two categories essentially reflect higher versus lower management levels. That is, the Focal Manager category tends to reflect managers who occupy higher management positions, and the Other Manager category tends more heavily to reflect managers who occupy lower management positions.

Demographic Predictor Variables

Our earlier research (Swieringa and Moncur, 1972) suggested that several demographic variables may be important for understanding managers' budget-oriented behavior. This research suggested that a manager's generalized work experience, his tenure in his company and position, and the amount of time he spends on budgeting may influence his budget-oriented behavior. To obtain measures of these variables, each manager was asked to indicate how long he had worked since leaving school and how long he had worked for this company and in his present position. Also, each manager was asked to consider the last month and to indicate what percent of his time was spent on budget-related activities. Managers' responses to these questions were used as measures of their time out of school, time in company, time in position, and time spent budgeting.

Table 5-1 presents the means and standard deviations for these four demographic variables. The means and standard deviations for the time out of school, time in company, and time in position variables are expressed in terms of years; the time spent budgeting variable is expressed in terms of a percentage. Note that the managers included in our total sample have been out of school an average of 17.66 years, have been with their present companies an average of 9.61 years, but have occupied their present positions an average of 3.66 years. Note further that these managers spent an average of 16.07 percent of their time on budgeting during the previous month.

Table 5-1

MEANS AND STANDARD DEVIATIONS FOR
FOUR DEMOGRAPHIC PREDICTOR VARIABLES
$(N = 137)$

Predictor Variable	Mean	Standard Deviation
Time Out of School	17.66	9.17
Time In Company	9.61	6.15
Time In Position	3.66	3.02
Time Spent Budgeting	16.07	20.40

Attitudinal Predictor Variables

Earlier research by Argyris (1952), Fertakis (1967), and Hofstede (1967) suggested that attitudinal variables may be important in understanding how managers used budgeting. For example, Argyris (1952) concluded that how supervisors used budgeting was a way of expressing their own patterns of leadership; Fertakis (1967) concluded that supervisors who felt greater budget-induced pressure tended to exhibit both more task-oriented and more considerate leadership behavior toward their subordinates; and Hofstede (1967) concluded that the way in which budget problems were handled by superiors was one of the most powerful determinants of the effects of budgeting on managerial motivation.

Because we were interested in the extent to which managers' attitudes might be important for understanding managers' budget-oriented behavior, we obtained measures on three variables.

The first attitudinal variable was the "Least-Preferred Co-worker" (LPC) index developed by Fiedler (1967). This index is based on Fiedler's Contingency Model theory of leadership which rests on the findings that effective group performance depends upon the proper match between the leader's style of interacting with his subordinates and the degree to which the situation gives control and influence to the leader. The Contingency Model classifies leadership style on an index called the LPC score. An individual is asked to think of all the persons he has ever worked with, then to describe the one person in his life with whom he worked least well. The individual rates this co-worker on a 16-item scale modeled after Osgood's Semantic Differential (Osgood, *et. al.*, 1957), which reveals the individual's reactions to the person he rates. The individual who describes his least-preferred co-worker in relatively favorable terms primarily is interested in good personal relations with his fellow workers. He tends to be relationship-motivated. The individual who describes his least-preferred co-worker in relatively unfavorable terms, who rejects someone he cannot work with, is interested primarily in performing well. He tends to be task-motivated.

The second attitudinal variable was the "Machiavellianism" (Mach) test which is based on the work of Christie (1970) and others (Geis, 1964; Geis and Christie, 1965; and Christie and Geis, 1970). The test is based on the hypothesis that individuals who think like Machiavelli, or who at least agree with his speculations about how to be a successful manipulator, may themselves be skilled controllers and manipulators of others. The test consists of 10 descriptive statements which either reflect or support a Machiavellian viewpoint. Individuals are asked to indicate the extent to which they agree or disagree with each statement. Individuals who have a more pro-Machiavellian viewpoint tend to obtain higher scores on this test. A higher test score tends to reflect a greater tendency to be good manipulators, to be more resistant to social influence, to appraise situations more logically and cognitively, and to take a more initiating and controlling role in their activities. Individuals who tend to have a less pro-Machiavellian viewpoint tend to obtain lower scores on this test. A lower test score tends to reflect a greater tendency to be more susceptible to social influence, to appraise situations more emotionally, and to take a more accepting and following role.

The third attitudinal variable was the "Internal versus External Feelings of Locus of Control" test developed by Rotter (1961, 1966) and others (Battle and Rotter, 1963; Gore and Rotter, 1963; and Rotter, Seeman and Liverant, 1962). This test is based on the premise that the behavior of individuals is affected by whether they believe that they tend

Table 5-2
MEANS AND STANDARD DEVIATIONS FOR
THREE ATTITUDINAL PREDICTOR VARIABLES
(N = 137)

Predictor Variable	Mean	Standard Deviation
LPC	57.75	17.74
Mach	19.51	5.29
Internal-External Control	6.20	3.11

to be masters of their own destinies or whether they believe that they tend to be victims of chance, luck or fate. Whether something tends to reward or reinforce an action of an individual depends, to some extent, on whether the individual views the reward as being the result of his action or as being merely fortuitous. In situations where the causes of rewards or reinforcements are ambiguous, some individuals may be more likely to consistently attribute these rewards or reinforcements to their own actions. These individuals tend to have internal feelings of control. Other individuals may be more likely to consistently attribute these rewards and reinforcements to chance or fate. These individuals tend to have external feelings of control. The test designed to measure internal versus external feelings of control consists of 29 forced-choice items, including six fill-in items to make the purpose of the test somewhat more ambiguous. Individuals who tend to have generalized expectancies that rewards and reinforcements following their actions are not entirely contingent upon their own actions but tend to result because of luck, chance, fate, the control of others, or the unpredictability of other forces tend to have higher external feelings of control and tend to have higher scores on this test. Individuals who tend to believe that the rewards and reinforcements they receive depend on their own actions tend to have higher internal feelings of control and tend to have lower scores on this test.

The means and standard deviations for these three attitudinal predictor variables are presented in Table 5-2. The LPC index, with 16 items scored on an eight-point scale, has a possible maximum score of 128 and a possible minimum score of 16. Table 5-2 reveals that the average LPC score for the managers included in our total sample was 57.75. The Mach test, with 10 items scored on a five-point scale, has a possible maximum score of 50 and a possible minimum score of 10. Table 5-2 reveals that the average Mach score for the managers included in our total sample was 19.51. Finally, the internal-external control test has a possible maximum score of 23 and possible minimum score of zero. Table 5-2 reveals that the average score on this test for the managers included in our total sample was 6.20.

Personality Predictor Variables

The Gordon Personality Profile and Personality Inventory (Gordon, 1963) were used to obtain measures on eight personality dimensions. These two instruments have been widely used, are relatively easy to administer, do not tend to irritate respondents, and yield scores on personality dimensions which appear to be meaningful for managers in industrial settings. The Personality Profile consists of 18 sets of four descriptive phrases called tetrads. Each of the four dimensions measured by the Profile is represented by one of the phrases in each tetrad. Each tetrad contains two items which are likely to be highly preferred and two which are not likely to be highly preferred. For each tetrad, an individual is asked to select which phrase is most like himself and which phrase is least like himself. Similarly, the Personality Inventory consists of 20 sets of tetrads, and an individual is asked to select which phrase included in each tetrad is most like himself and which phrase is least like himself. Scoring of the Profile and Inventory is accomplished with a template that fits over the set of responses for each tetrad. Scores are obtained for the following eight personality dimensions:

Cautiousness

Individuals who tend to be more cautious, to consider matters more carefully before making decisions, and to dislike taking more risks tend to have higher scores on this dimension. Individuals who tend to be more impulsive, to act on the spur of the moment, to make more hurried or snap decisions, to enjoy taking chances, tend to have lower scores on this dimension.

Original Thinking

Individuals who tend to like to work on difficult problems, to be more intellectually curious, to enjoy thought-provoking questions and discussions, and to like to think about new ideas tend to have higher scores on this dimension. Individuals who tend to dislike working on more difficult or complicated problems, to care less about acquiring knowledge, and to be less interested in thought-provoking questions or discussions tend to have lower scores on this dimension.

Personal Relations

Individuals who tend to have more faith and trust in people, to be more tolerant, patient, and understanding tend to have higher scores on this dimension. Individuals who tend to have less trust or confidence in people, who tend to be more critical of others, and to more often become annoyed or irritated by what others do tend to have lower scores on this dimension.

Vigor

Individuals who tend to be more vigorous and energetic, to like to work and move more rapidly, and to accomplish more than the average person tend to have higher scores on this dimension. Individuals who tend to have lower vitality or energy levels, to prefer to set a slower pace, to have a tendency to tire more easily, and to be below average in terms of sheer output or productivity tend to have lower scores on this dimension.

Ascendency

Individuals who tend to be more verbally ascendent, to adopt a more active role in the group, to be more self-assured and assertive in relationships with others, and to make more decisions independently tend to have higher scores on this dimension. Individuals who tend to adopt a more passive role in the group, to listen rather than talk, to lack self-confidence, to let others take the lead, and to be more dependent on others for advice tend to have lower scores on this dimension.

Responsibility

Individuals who tend to be more able to stick to any job assigned to them, to be more persevering and determined, and to be more reliable tend to have higher scores on this dimension. Individuals who tend to be less able to stick to the tasks that do not interest them, and to be more flighty and irresponsible tend to have lower scores on this factor.

Emotional Stability

Individuals who tend to be more well-balanced, more stable emotionally, and relatively free from anxieties and nervous ten-

Table 5-3
MEANS AND STANDARD DEVIATIONS FOR
EIGHT PERSONALITY PREDICTOR VARIABLES
(N = 137)

Predictor Variable	Mean	Standard Deviation
Cautiousness	19.57	4.41
Original Thinking	20.46	4.47
Personal Relations	19.50	4.25
Vigor	20.42	4.47
Ascendency	20.01	3.60
Responsibility	20.69	3.95
Emotional Stability	20.33	4.03
Sociability	18.94	3.65

sion tend to have higher scores on this dimension. Individuals who tend to be more anxious, more nervous, and to have a lower tolerance for frustration tend to have lower scores on this dimension.

Sociability

Individuals who tend to like to be with and work with people and to be more gregarious and sociable tend to have higher scores on this dimension. Individuals who tend to be less gregarious, to be more restrictive in their social contacts and to actually avoid social relationships tend to have lower scores on this dimension.

The means and standard deviations for these eight personality variables are presented in Table 5-3.

Method

Automatic Interaction Detector (AID)

There was little in the way of either theory or empirical evidence that could help us specify how the predictor variables might be related to a particular descriptive or normative measure of managers' budget-oriented behavior. Given these deficiencies, we had no choice but to be thrust back upon our own data and to use an analysis strategy that would allow us to observe which predictor variables and combinations of predictor variables produced the greatest discrimination in explaining differences in the measures of managers' budget-oriented behavior.

To facilitate our analysis of these relationships, we utilized a search algorithm entitled the Automatic Interaction Detector (AID) developed by Sonquist and Morgan (1964) and revised by Sonquist, Baker and Morgan (1971). AID is a multivariate technique for determining what independent (predictor) variables and categories within them combine to produce the greatest discrimination in the group means of a dependent variable. It can be used to consider up to 35 predictor variables simultaneously, to define the most significant combinations of these variables, and to demonstrate the joint effects of these variables. The independent or predictor variables must be catgorical, with a maximum of 63 categories per variable. The dependent variable may take any form.

The AID program divides the total sample through a series of binary splits into the set of mutually exclusive subgroups for which the group means account for more of the total sum of squares of the dependent variable than the means of any combination of predictor variables. First, the program splits the total sample into the two subgroups that provide the largest reduction in the unexplained sum of squares of the dependent variable. To do this, the program determines the group means for each classification of all the predictor variables and examines all dichotomous groupings of each variable. Using companies as an example, the group mean for managers in Companies A, B, C and D is examined first. Next, the group means for all dichotomous groupings are examined — for example, the group mean for managers in Company A is compared with the group mean for managers in Companies B, C and D; the group mean for managers in Companies A and B is compared with the group mean for managers in Companies C and D, etc. Each predictor then is split into the two non-overlapping subgroups which provide the largest reduction in the unexplained variance. Thus, managers might be divided by company into one subgroup consisting of managers who are in Company B, C or D, by sample selected into one subgroup consisting of Focal Managers and another subgroup consisting of Other Managers, etc.

After binary splits have been formed for each predictor variable so that the between sum of squares is maximized, the ratio of the between to total sum of squares for the group to be split is computed for each independent variable. The program then selects that independent variable with the highest ratio and divides the total sample into two subgroups on the basis of that variable. Once the total sample has been divided into two subgroups, the program treats each subgroup as a separate sample, and the same process is repeated. Within each subgroup, the program again dichotomizes the remaining independent variables at the optimal point, computes a between to total sum of squares ratio for each variable, and selects the variable with the highest ratio for the next split. After the second series of splits, additional subgroups are formed. The program again treats each subgroup as a separate sample, and another iteration determines which predictor variable, when split, will best reduce the unexplained sum of squares for that subgroup. The program continues to iterate, subject to stopping rules for (1) the minimum subgroup sample size, (2) the minimum percentage of the original sum of squares required in order for a subgroup to be considered eligible for splitting, and (3) a split reducibility criterion which requires that the size of the between sum of squares for the group to be split has to be a minimum percentage of the original sum of squares.

The program requires a relatively large number of observations or cases and assumes that the dependent variable is well-behaved, without extreme cases or bimodalities, and that the independent variables are categorical. Also, several limitations or restrictions are inherent in the program itself. For example, the program relies on dichotomous splits only. This represents a limitation because in some cases three- or four-way splits may reduce the unexplained variance more than a two-way split. Moreover, the program selects the variable with the highest between to total sum of squares ratio to split the sample, and all subsequent splits are contingent on the subgroups formed by the first split. This limitation, however, can be partially overcome by running the program again, eliminating the variable which defines the first two subgroups, to give an alternative variable a chance to split. Subsequent subgroups can then be examined to determine if they differ markedly from the original run.

The AID technique was selected because we were unable to quantify a priori the functional form of the relationships between the predictor variables and the measures of managers' budget-oriented behavior. The AID program helps us to do this. In principle, it uses a prestated strategy to search for the predictors that increase the power to account for the variance of a dependent variable. It follows the basic principle of least squares and focuses on power in reducing error. Moreover, it starts with the most stable and dependable findings and works down to less and less dependable and powerful findings on smaller and smaller subgroups.

Categorical Predictor Variables

Because the AID program requires that the independent or predictor variables be categorical, some of the 17 predictor variables described in Chapter 5 were recoded into classes or categories. Table 5-4

Table 5-4
SEVENTEEN CATEGORICAL PREDICTORS OF MANAGERS' BUDGET-ORIENTED BEHAVIOR

Description	Classes	Constraint Type	Rank
Company	4	Free	1
Sample Selected	2	Monotonic	1
Time Out of School	2	Monotonic	1
Time in Company	2	Monotonic	1
Time in Position	2	Monotonic	1
Time Budgeting	2	Monotonic	1
LPC	2	Monotonic	1
Mach	2	Monotonic	1
I/E Control	2	Monotonic	1
Cautiousness	2	Monotonic	1
Original Thinking	2	Monotonic	1
Personal Relations	2	Monotonic	1
Vigor	2	Monotonic	1
Ascendency	2	Monotonic	1
Responsibility	2	Monotonic	1
Emotional Stability	2	Monotonic	1
Sociability	2	Monotonic	1

Table 5-5
CORRELATIONS AMONG SEVENTEEN CATEGORICAL PREDICTOR VARIABLES
(N = 137)

Predictor Variables	1	2	3	4	5	6	7	8	9	10	11	12	13	14	15	16	17
1 Company		.03	.04	.40	.07	-.00	.02	-.03	-.10	-.16	-.08	-.05	-.05	-.10	-.08	-.05	-.11
2 Sample Selected			-.10	-.16	-.04	-.00	.05	.10	.07	-.30	.38	-.39	.22	.23	.20	-.34	-.24
3 Time out of School				.38	.21	.05	-.04	-.02	-.06	.10	-.07	.15	-.06	.08	.01	.10	.06
4 Time in Company					.30	.11	.20	.02	-.15	-.07	-.17	-.01	-.06	-.18	-.13	.01	-.05
5 Time in Position						.10	.10	-.02	-.09	-.10	-.01	.07	.02	-.03	-.10	-.06	-.06
6 Time Budgeting							.00	.13	.06	-.04	.00	-.02	-.09	.09	-.01	-.05	.03
7 LPC								.05	.08	.01	.02	-.01	.07	-.11	-.13	-.02	-.08
8 Mach									.18	.10	.06	.03	.12	.10	-.09	.02	.05
9 I/E Control										.16	-.04	.04	.08	.01	.01	-.06	.06
10 Cautiousness											.05	.39	.23	.03	.03	.16	.19
11 Original Thinking												-.05	.35	.24	.08	-.03	.00
12 Personal Relations													.06	-.13	.02	.26	.21
13 Vigor														.30	.20	.02	.14
14 Ascendency															.26	.11	.20
15 Responsibility																.16	.15
16 Emotional Stability																	.19
17 Sociability																	

shows the number of classes or categories used for each predictor variable, the type of constraints placed on these categories, and the rank assigned to each predictor variable. The company- and sample-selected predictor variables were originally classification or categorical variables and were not recoded. The other 15 predictor variables were recoded into dichotomous high and low classes or categories. An overall sample median was calculated for each of these 15 predictor variables. Managers with scores above the overall sample median for a predictor variable were assigned to the "high" class or category for that variable; managers with scores below the overall sample median for a predictor variable were assigned to the "low" class or category for that variable.

Each predictor variable also was designated as either a "free" or "monotonic" variable. A "free" variable can have its classes or categories rearranged during the partitioning process. Only the company predictor variable was designated as a "free" variable. A "monotonic" variable has the order of its classes maintained in the partitioning process; its classes cannot be rearranged in this process. The remaining 16 predictor variables were designated as "monotonic" variables.

Since the AID program chooses from among alternative predictor variables and from alternative combinations of these variables, it is important that these variables not be highly intercorrelated. Table 5-5 presents simple correlation coefficients for pairs of the 17 categorized predictor variables. Inspection of this table reveals that the predictor variables are not highly intercorrelated. Only 10 correlation coefficients in Table 5-5 are above .30 and the highest correlation coefficient is .40.

Chapter 6

Analysis of Relationships Between Predictor Variables and the Descriptive Measures of Managers' Budget-Oriented Behavior

Our efforts at variable definition, reported in the last two chapters, yielded a list of 13 descriptive and 14 normative measures, as well as a list of some 17 predictor variables. In this chapter we will report the results of our analysis of the relationships between these predictor variables and the descriptive measures of managers' budget-oriented behavior.

The first section reports the results of our analysis of these relationships. Our analysis reveals that different variables may be important for predicting different aspects of how managers use budgeting. For example, these results show that a company's budgeting system and the organizational context within which it operates may be the most important predictors of the extent to which managers tend to engage in various budget-related coping behaviors, to be personally involved in budgeting, to be shown comparisons of actual and budget performance for other units, and to experience intensive time demands from budgeting.

These results also reveal that the personality variables of emotional stability and ascendency and the interpersonal variable of internal-external control may be the most important predictors of the extent to which managers' methods of achieving their budgets tend to be accepted by others and the extent to which managers are relatively influential in the budgeting process, are expressive about budgeting, and have positive attitudes about budgeting.

Next, they reveal that the demographic variables of managers' time in position and time spent on budgeting may be the most important predictors of the extent to which managers use budgets as evaluative devices, perform various budget variance related activities, and are involved in the budgeting process.

Finally, these results show that managers' levels in their companies may be the most important predictor of the extent to which managers work with their superiors and others in preparing operating budgets.

The chapter concludes with a brief discussion of the implications of our findings. A more speculative discussion of the implications of these findings is presented in Chapter 11.

Analysis

In this section, we will report the results of our analysis of the relationships between these predictor variables and the descriptive measures of managers' budget-oriented behavior presented in Chapter 4. The results of our analysis of each measure will be presented in the form of a "tree diagram" showing the various splits made among the predictor variables and the resulting subgroups of the sample developed by combinations of these variables. In addition, the size of each subgroup, N, and the average factor score for each subgroup, $\overline{Y}$, are reported for each subgroup in the tree diagram. Finally, the r^2 and t-value that occasion each split are entered at the vertex of the split.

Descriptive Budget Factor I:
Evaluation by Superiors and of Subordinates

Descriptive budget factor I reflects the use of a budget as an evaluative device. Managers who have higher scores on this factor more often use the budget to evaluate their subordinates, and their superiors more often use it to evaluate them. Figure 6-1 presents the results of our analysis of the relationship between this factor and the predictor variables.

The most important variable explaining differences in the extent to which managers use budgets as evaluative devices is managers' time in company.

Managers who have been in their companies for a shorter time (Group 2) generally use the budget as an evaluative device less often. This is particularly true for Other Managers who are relatively less energetic (Group 8).

These results suggest that the longer a manager has been with his company the more likely he may be to use the budget as an evaluative device. Presumably, a manager becomes sensitized to this use of a budget as his experience with his company and its use of budgeting increases. At the outset a manager may not have much familiarity with or confidence in a company's use of budgeting and may rely on other criteria to evaluate his subordinates. Moreover, he may even believe that he is being evaluated on the basis of other criteria. As time passes, however, he may become more comfortable with the company's use of budgeting and may begin to use operating budgets to evaluate his subordinates' performances.

Of the managers who have been with their companies for a shorter period of time, those who are Focal Managers use the budget as an

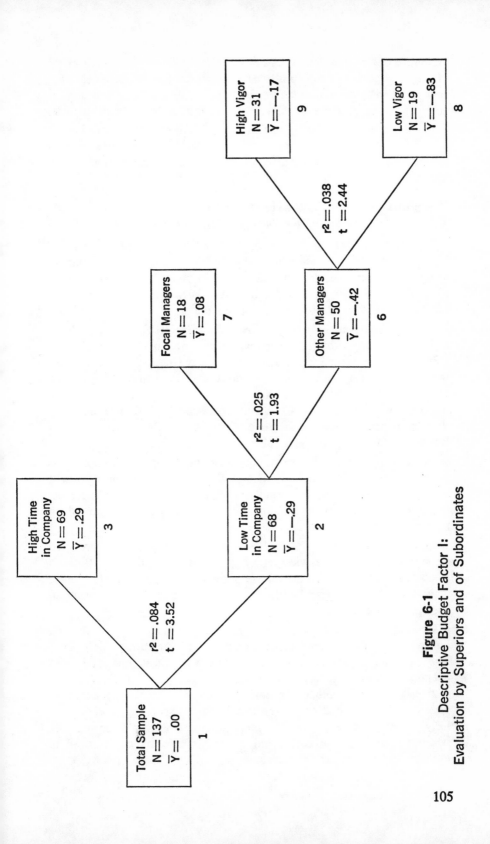

Figure 6-1
Descriptive Budget Factor I:
Evaluation by Superiors and of Subordinates

evaluative device more often than those who are Other Managers. Focal Managers generally occupy positions at higher levels of management and, as a result, may be more likely to be involved in the budgeting process and to be more sensitive to the use of a budget as an evaluative device.

Finally, these results suggest that the managers who use the budget as an evaluative device the least often may be those who have been in their companies for a shorter time, are Other Managers, and are relatively less energetic.

Descriptive Budget Factor II:
Actions Brought About by Expected Budget Overruns

This factor reflects budget-oriented coping behavior. Managers with higher scores on this factor generally find it necessary more often to charge some activities to other accounts, to shift figures, and to stop some activities when budgeted funds have been used up. Figure 6-2 presents the results of our analysis of this factor.

Managers who are in Company B or D (Group 2) engage in these activities less often than those managers who are in Company A or C (Group 3). Of the managers who are in either Company A or C, those who are relatively intellectually curious and less emotionally stable (Group 9) engage in these activities the most often. Of the remaining managers who are in these Companies (Group 4), those who are relatively more self-assured and assertive (Group 6) engage in these activities less often than those who lack self-confidence (Group 7).

In general, the incidence of budget-oriented coping behavior was relatively low for our sample of managers. However, differences do exist among managers in the frequency of this type of behavior. The most important variable for explaining differences in the extent to which managers engage in these activities is the company they work in.

Companies B and D are similar in that operating budgets are used essentially as planning devices and not as evaluative devices. Because these budgets are not used to evaluate or reward managerial performance, managers who use these budgets may experience less felt pressure to engage in these activities.

Companies A and C are similar in that operating budgets are used either to evaluate and reward performance or to inform managers about how their actual spending levels compare with those budgeted. For example, managers in Company A are more likely to shift figures or to charge activities to other accounts in order to successfully complete governmentally funded projects within budgeted spending levels. Similarly, managers in Company C are more likely to engage in these activities because comparison of actual and budgeted performance are used to evaluate and reward their performance.

106

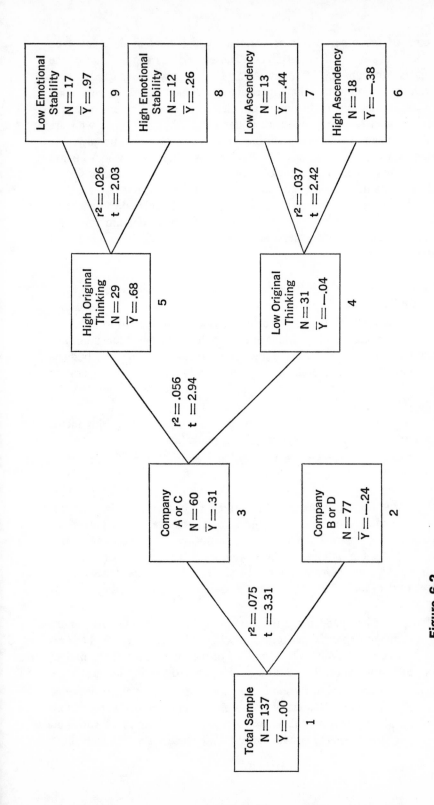

Figure 6-2
Descriptive Budget Factor II:
Actions Brought About by Expected Budget Overruns

Some of the other predictor variables which explain differences on this factor are personality variables. These variables suggest that of the managers who are in Company A or C, those who engage in these activities more often may have personality profiles that differ somewhat from those who engage in these activities less often. For example, the managers who engage in these activities most often are those who are relatively more intellectually curious but less stable emotionally; the managers who engage in these activities less often are those who are relatively less intellectually curious but more self-assured and assertive in their relationships with others. These results suggest that the extent to which managers engage in these activities may be related to the extent to which they are intellectually challenged by their job, are relatively free from anxieties and nervous tension, and are self-assured and assertive.

Descriptive Budget Factor III:
Responsibility for Meeting Budget

This factor reflects evaluative behavior that is not limited to superior-subordinate relationships. Managers who have higher scores on this factor more often are reminded of the importance of meeting their budgets and more often are evaluated on their ability to meet the operating budgets for their units. Figure 6-3 presents the results of our analysis of this factor.

The most important variable for explaining differences on this factor is the amount of time managers spend on budgeting.

Managers who spend more time on budgeting (Group 3) are more often reminded of the importance of the budget and are more often evaluated on their ability to meet their operating budgets. This is particularly true for those managers who tend to believe that they are not the masters of their own destinies and who are relatively more gregarious and sociable (Group 9). Conversely, those managers who spend less time on budgeting, who are relatively new to their positions, and who are more cautious (Group 6) are reminded of the importance of the budget and evaluated on their ability to meet their operating budgets least often.

Managers who spend more time on budgeting are likely to be more involved in a company's budgeting process. Consequently, these managers may be more likely to be reminded of the importance of the budget and to be evaluated on their ability to meet their operating budgets.

Figure 6-3 reveals that those managers who experience the occurrence of these events most frequently spend more time on budgeting, think they have less control over their own destinies, and like to be with and work with others. These results suggest that those managers who think

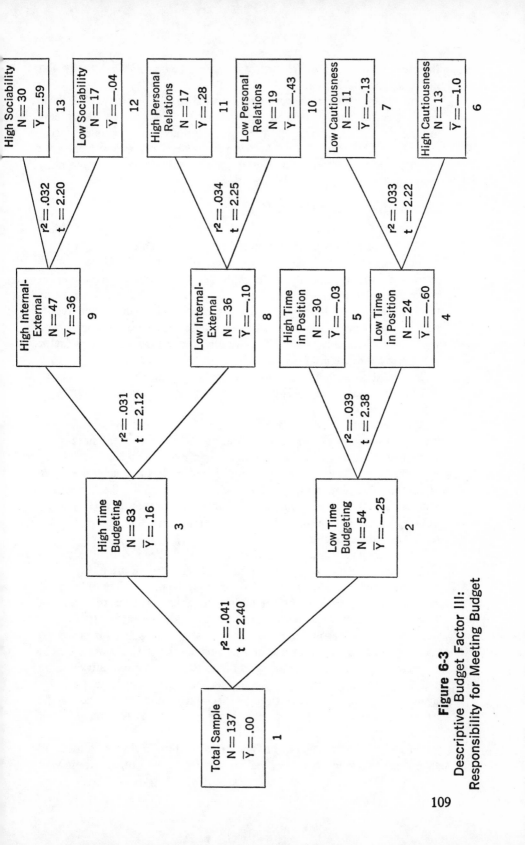

Figure 6-3
Descriptive Budget Factor III:
Responsibility for Meeting Budget

109

these events occur most frequently may tend to be more externally and interpersonally oriented.

Conversely, those managers who experience the occurrence of these events less frequently spend less time on budgeting, are relatively new to their positions, and are relatively more cautious. These results suggest that those managers who think that these events occur less frequently may be less involved in the budgeting process and may be more internally oriented.

Descriptive Budget Factor IV:
Required Explanations of Budget Variances

This factor reflects a set of required activities which are brought about by budget variances. Managers who more often are required to prepare reports comparing actual results with budget, submit explanations in writing about the causes of large budget variances, trace the causes of these variances to groups and individuals within their units, and report actions they have taken to correct the causes of these variances have higher scores on this factor. The results of our analysis of this factor are presented in Figure 6-4.

The most important variable in explaining differences in the extent to which managers are required to engage in these activities is managers' time in position.

Managers who have been in their positions longer (Group 3) are required to engage in these activities more often. Moreover, those managers who have been in their positions longer and who lack confidence in themselves (Group 5) are required to engage in these activities more often. Of the remaining managers who have been in their positions longer (Group 4), those who are relatively more responsible (Group 7) are required to engage in these activities more often than those who are less responsible (Group 6).

These results suggest that managers who have been in their positions longer may be required to perform these activities more often. Managers who have longer tenure in their positions may be more likely to have the responsibility for accounting for budget variances assigned to them and thus may be required to perform these activities more often.

Moreover, of the managers who have longer tenure in their positions, those who lack self-confidence and let others take the lead are required to perform these activities more often than those who are relatively more self-assured and assertive. This suggests that the extent to which managers are required to perform these activities may be related to the extent to which they tend to take an active or passive role in their relationships with others.

Finally, of the managers who have longer tenure in their positions and take a relatively active role in their relationships with others, those who

110

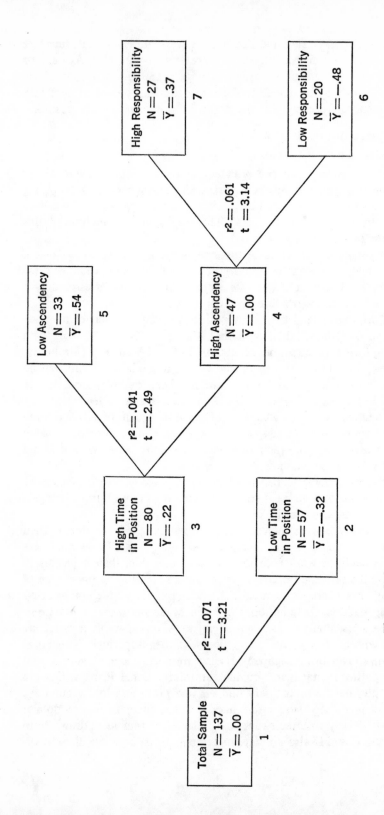

Figure 6-4
Descriptive Budget Factor IV:
Required Explanations of Budget Variances

are relatively persevering and determined are required to perform these activities more often than those who are less responsible. Again, this suggests that the extent to which managers are required to perform these activities may be related to the extent to which they think that they should responsibly carry out the activities assigned to their positions.

Descriptive Budget Factor V: Interactions with Superiors

This factor reflects superior-oriented behavior. Managers with higher scores on this factor more often work with their superiors in preparing the budgets for their units and more often go to their superiors for advice on how to achieve their budgets. The results of our analysis of this factor are presented in Figure 6-5.

The most important variable for explaining differences in the extent to which managers work with and go to their superiors is whether these managers are Focal or Other Managers. This variable is essentially a surrogate for a manager's level in a company.

Focal Managers tend to occupy positions at higher levels of management than do Other Managers. Other Managers (Group 3) work with and go to their superiors more often than do Focal Managers (Group 2). Moreover, those Other Managers who believe that reinforcements depend on their own behavior and who have not been out of school longer (Group 11) go to and work with their superiors more often.

Of the Other Managers who do not believe that reinforcements depend on their own behavior (Group 6), those who are more assertive (Group 9) go to and work with their superiors more often than those who are more susceptible to social influence (Group 8).

Finally, those Focal Managers who are in Company A or B (Group 4) go to and work with their superiors less often than those Focal Managers who are in Company C or D.

The Focal Managers included in our total sample were drawn from relatively high management levels in each company. These managers are more likely to work with their subordinates than their superiors in preparing the operating budgets for their units, depending upon type of company. For example, Company A places relatively little emphasis on operating budgets. In addition, the Focal Managers drawn from Company A are essentially department managers who prepare their operating budgets with relatively little interaction with their superiors. The Focal Managers drawn from Company B also are department managers, and these department managers provide the informational items which are used to prepare the preliminary budgets and profit and loss summaries. Again, in providing these informational items, these managers do not work very closely with their superiors. The Focal Managers drawn from Companies C and D also are department managers; however, these man-

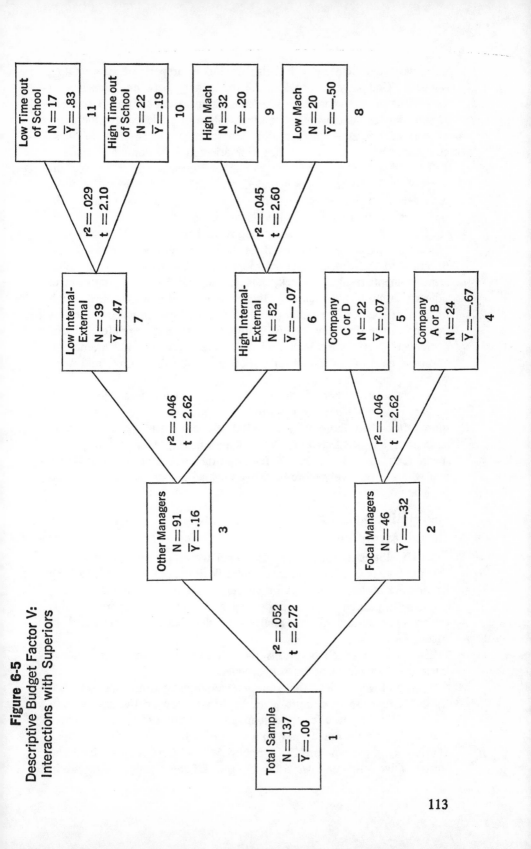

Figure 6-5
Descriptive Budget Factor V:
Interactions with Superiors

113

agers work more closely with their superiors in preparing their operating budgets. Company C provides for bargaining between managers at various levels of management in preparing operating budgets. Company D provides for the downward communication of guidelines for the preparation of operating budgets for departments. Thus, both of these companies bring about more superior-oriented behavior.

The Other Managers included in our total sample tend to be subordinates of the Focal Managers included. Thus it is not surprising that these managers go to and work with their superiors, as opposed to their subordinates, more often than do the Focal Managers.

However, it is somewhat surprising to find that Other Managers who think that reinforcements depend on their own behavior (Group 7) go to and work with their superiors more often than those who think that reinforcements result from luck, chance, fate, and the control of powerful others (Group 6). Presumably, those Other Managers who have a high internal orientation think that going to and working with their superiors does not mean that they are giving up control over their reinforcements. Moreover, those Other Managers who have a low external orientation and have been out of school for a shorter period of time go to and work with their superiors the most often.

Finally, those Other Managers who have a high external orientation and are relatively better manipulators go to and work with their superiors more often than those who are relatively more susceptible to social influence. This suggests that Other Managers who think that reinforcements result from luck, chance, fate, and the control of powerful others and who are relatively more assertive engage in more superior-oriented behavior.

Descriptive Budget Factor VI:
Usefulness of Budgeting

This factor is essentially an attitudinal factor. Managers who think that the budget enables them to be more flexible and innovative, to keep better track of their success as a manager, and to be better managers have a relatively positive view of budgeting and have higher scores on this factor. The results of our analysis of this factor are presented in Figure 6-6.

The variable which occasions the initial split on this factor is the internal-external locus of control variable.

Managers who believe that reinforcements result from their own behavior (Group 3) have more positive attitudes toward the budget, and this is particularly true for those managers who are also Focal Managers (Group 9). Of the managers who tend to have high external orientations (Group 2), those who are in Company A, B or C (Group 4) have the least positive attitudes toward the budget. Of the managers who are in

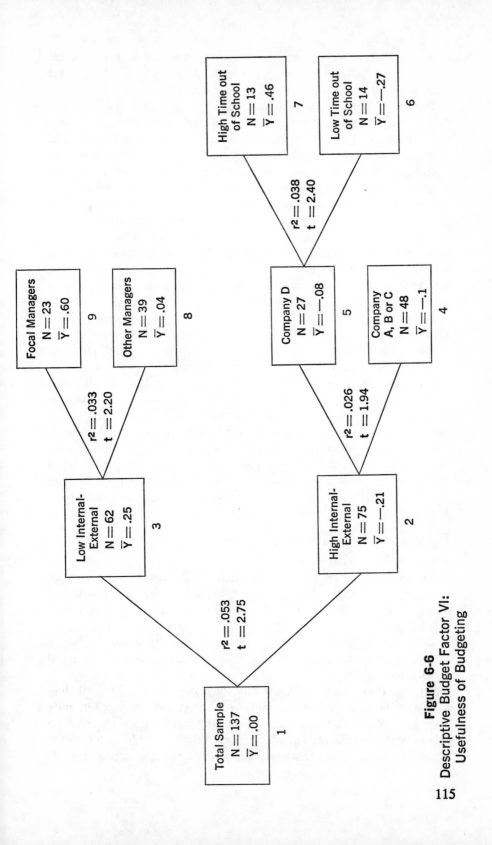

Figure 6-6
Descriptive Budget Factor VI:
Usefulness of Budgeting

Company D (Group 5), those who have been out of school a shorter period of time (Group 6) have less positive attitudes toward the budget than those who have been out of school longer (Group 7).

Our analysis of this factor suggests that managers who tend to believe that they are masters of their own destinies may have more positive attitudes toward budgeting. Presumably these managers view budgeting as a tool that can assist them in carrying out their management functions.

However, of the managers who have relatively high internal orientations, those who occupy higher management positions have more positive attitudes toward budgeting than those who occupy lower management positions. This suggests that managers' attitudes toward the budget may also be related to their positions in the company. Those managers who have relatively high external orientations are less positively disposed towards budgeting. Presumably they view their success more as being the result of fate, chance, and the control of powerful others and view budgeting as being of relatively less assistance to them.

Moveover, of those managers who have high external orientations, those who are in Company A, B or C are somewhat less positively disposed toward budgeting than those who are in Company D. This suggests that differences between companies may affect the extent to which managers who have high external orientations have positive attitudes toward budgeting. For example, the managers who are in Company D essentially prepare their own operating budgets, even though they receive guidelines from top management before preparing these budgets. The managers who are in Company A, B or C initially prepare their own operating budgets; however, these budgets are subsequently either revised by top management or are subject to negotiations with outside funding agencies. Thus, the use of budgeting in Company A, B or C may reinforce the high external orientations of some managers.

Descriptive Budget Factor VII:
Acceptability of Methods

Managers who think that their methods of achieving their budgets are accepted more often by their superiors and subordinates have higher scores on this factor. Figure 6-7 presents the results of our analysis of this factor.

The most important variable for explaining the extent to which managers think that their methods of achieving their budgets are accepted is emotional stability.

Managers who tend to be emotionally stable (Group 3) think that their methods of achieving their budgets are more often accepted by their superiors and subordinates. This is especially true for managers who are relatively emotionally stable and intellectually curious (Group 9). Managers who are relatively less emotionally stable and in Company B or C

116

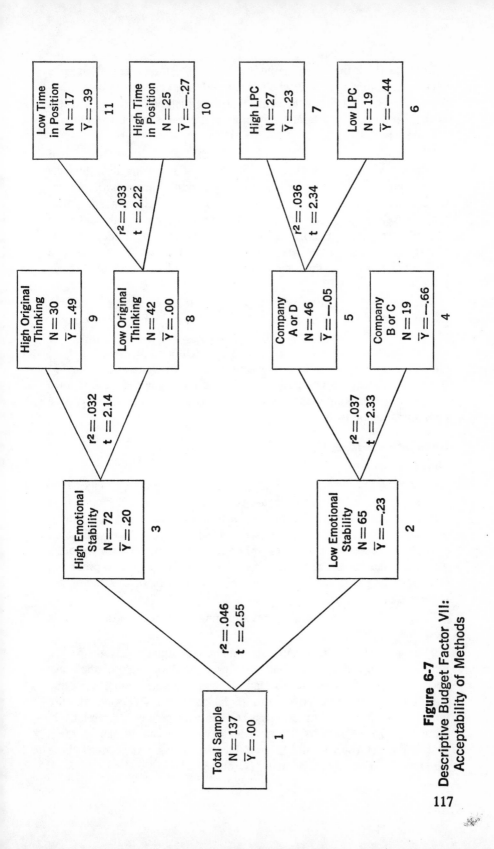

Figure 6-7
Descriptive Budget Factor VII:
Acceptability of Methods

(Group 4) think that their methods are accepted least often. Managers who are in Company A or D who are relatively less concerned about interpersonal relations (Group 6) think that their methods are accepted less often than those who are relatively more concerned about these relations (Group 7).

This factor is essentially an attitudinal factor which reflects the extent to which managers think that their methods of achieving their budgets are accepted by others. Some personality variables are most important for explaining differences on this factor. For example, managers who are relatively free from anxieties and nervous tension think that their methods are accepted more often by their superiors and subordinates. Managers who are emotionally stable and intellectually curious and challenged think that their methods are accepted by these individuals most often.

The finding that the company variable may be important for explaining differences on this attitudinal factor is somewhat surprising. For example, of the managers who are relatively more anxious and nervous, those who are in Company A or D think that their methods are accepted more often than those who are in Company B or C. Yet, Companies A and D place less reliance on comparisons of actual and budgeted performance and provide operating managers with more latitude in how they achieve their operating budgets.

Descriptive Budget Factor VIII:
Influence in Budget Setting

Managers whose operating budgets more often include changes they have suggested, who more often are consulted about special factors they would like to have included in the budgets being prepared, and whose budgets more often are not finalized until they are satisfied with them have higher scores on this factor. Moreover, these managers more often work with and ask for assistance from financial staff people in preparing their operating budgets. The results of our analysis of this factor are presented in Figure 6-8.

The most important variable for explaining differences on this factor is emotional stability.

Managers who are relatively more stable emotionally (Group 3) are more often influential in the budgeting process. Moreover, of the managers who are more emotionally stable, those who take a more accepting and following role and have high internal orientations (Group 11) are influential in this process most often. Of the managers who are relatively more assertive (Group 6), those who have been out of school for a shorter time (Group 9) are more influential in this process than those who have been out of school longer (Group 8).

118

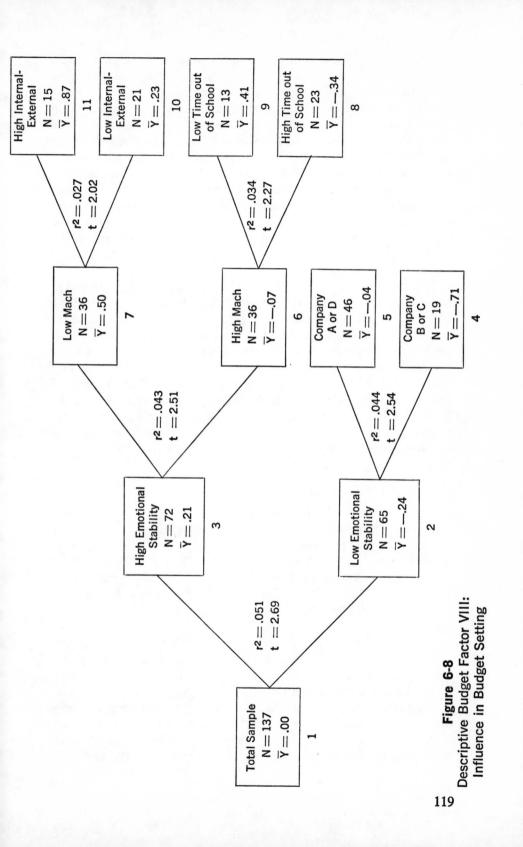

Figure 6-8
Descriptive Budget Factor VIII:
Influence in Budget Setting

119

Managers who are relatively less stable emotionally (Group 2) are less influential in this process, and this is particularly true for those managers who are in Company B or C (Group 4).

This factor also is essentially an attitudinal factor; it reflects the extent to which managers are influential in the budgeting process. The results of our analysis of this factor are similar to those described above for descriptive budget factor VII in that personality variables are the most important for explaining differences on this factor. For example, managers who are relatively more stable emotionally, less assertive, and more externally oriented are most influential in budgeting. This suggests that the extent to which managers are more influential in budgeting may be related to the extent to which they are anxious and nervous, susceptible to influence, and believe that reinforcements depend on luck, fate, and the control of powerful others.

The results of our analysis of this factor are similar to those found in our analysis of descriptive budget factor VII in that the company variable also is important in explaining differences on this factor. Of the managers who are less stable emotionally, those who are in Company B or C are less influential in budgeting than those who are in Company A or D. Managers who are in Company A or D generally prepare their own operating budgets; managers who are in Company C or D generally prepare initial operating budgets which are subsequently revised on the basis of targets set by top management. Thus, those managers who are more anxious and nervous and who are allowed to prepare their own operating budgets may think that they are more influential in the budgeting process than those who are not.

Descriptive Budget Factor IX:
Personal Attention to Budgeting

This factor reflects the extent to which managers are personally involved in budgeting. Managers who have higher scores on this factor pay more attention to a great number of details, personally investigate more budget variances, work more with their subordinates, and spend more time outside of normal working hours preparing their operating budgets. The results of our analysis of this factor are presented in Figure 6-9.

These results are not particularly strong. However, they do reveal that managers who are in Company B (Group 3) are somewhat more personally involved in budgeting. This is particularly true for those managers who are relatively more assertive (Group 5).

The results suggest that the extent to which managers are personally involved in budgeting may be related to the company they are in. Managers who are in Company B apparently find it to be a relatively more demanding one personally; it requires that they more often undertake

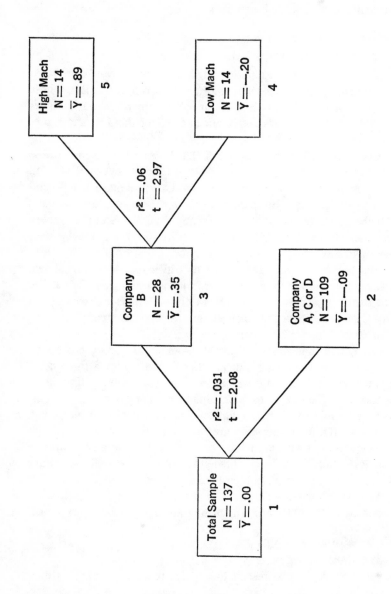

Figure 6-9
Descriptive Budget Factor IX:
Personal Attention to Budgeting

various budget-oriented activities and engage in various budget-oriented interactions. Moreover, the results suggest that the extent to which the managers who are in Company B find it to be demanding personally may be related to the extent to which they take an initiating and controlling role in performing their activities.

Descriptive Budget Factor X:
Involvement in Budgeting

This factor reflects the extent to which managers are shown comparisons of actual and budgeted performance for other units. Those managers who are shown these comparisons more often have higher scores on this factor. The results of our analysis of this factor are presented in Figure 6-10.

Managers who are in Company C or D (Group 3) are shown these comparisons more often than those who are in Company A or B (Group 2). Of the managers who are in Company C or D, those who spend more time on budgeting (Group 11) are shown these comparisons most often. Of the managers who are in Company A or B (Group 2), those who are relatively less sociable and older (Group 6) are shown these comparisons least often.

These results suggest that the extent to which managers are shown comparisons of actual and budgeted performance for other units may be related to the company they are in. For example, managers who are in Company C or D indicate that they are shown these comparisons more often than those who are in Company A or B.

However, of the managers who are in Company C or D, those who spend more time on budgeting indicate that they are shown these comparisons more often than those who spend less time on budgeting. This also suggests that the extent to which managers are shown these comparisons may be related to the amount of time they spend on budgeting.

Moreover, of the managers who are in Company A or B, those who dislike being with and working with others are shown these comparisons somewhat less often than those who tend to like to be with and work with others. This finding is not particularly strong. However, it does suggest that the extent to which managers are shown these comparisons may be related to the extent to which they are interpersonally oriented.

Descriptive Budget Factor XI:
Expressive about Budgeting

Managers with higher scores on this factor more often express their opinions on budget matters, mention budget matters in informal conversations, and discuss budget items when problems occur. The results of our analysis of this factor are presented in Figure 6-11.

Managers who are relatively more self-assured and assertive in their

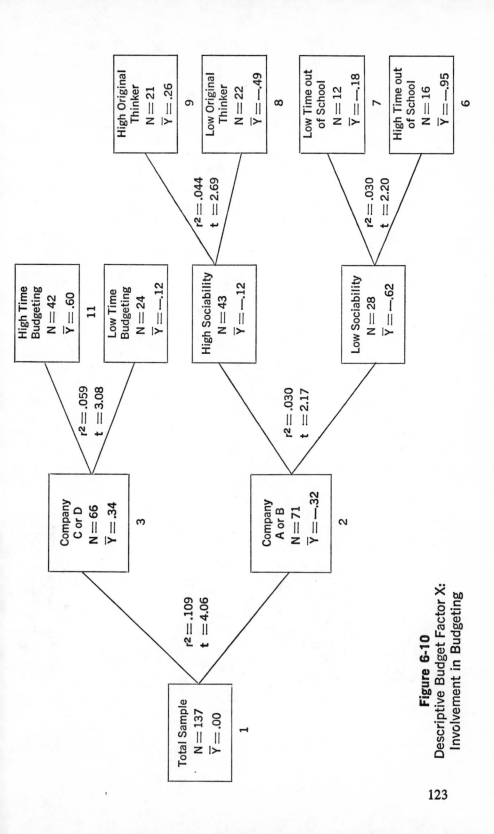

Figure 6-10
Descriptive Budget Factor X:
Involvement in Budgeting

123

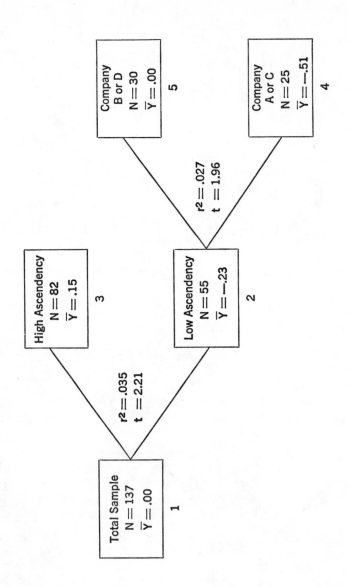

Figure 6-11
Descriptive Budget Factor XI:
Expressive About Budgeting

relationships with others (Group 3) are more expressive about budgeting. Of the managers who are relatively more passive and less self-confident (Group 2), those who are in Company A or C (Group 4) are less expressive about budgeting.

The results of our analysis of this factor are not relatively strong. However, these results suggest that managers who are relatively more verbally ascendent may be more expressive about budgeting. That is, those managers who are relatively self-assured, more assertive, and take a more active role are likely to be more expressive on budgeting.

These results also suggest that the extent to which managers are relatively more passive and less assertive and expressive on budgeting may be related to the company they are in. For example, the managers who are less verbally ascendent who are in Company A or C are less expressive than those who are in Company B or D.

Descriptive Budget Factor XII:
Interactions with Peers and Financial Staff

Managers who think they more often work with other unit heads and financial staff people have higher scores on this factor. The results of our analysis of this factor are presented in Figure 6-12.

Managers who occupy higher management positions (Group 3) think they more often work with these other individuals. Of the managers who occupy lower management positions (Group 2), those who are less stable emotionally (Group 5) think they work with these individuals more often than those who are more stable emotionally (Group 4). Finally, of the managers who occupy lower management positions and are relatively less stable emotionally (Group 5), those who are relatively more assertive (Group 7) think they work with these individuals more often than those who are more susceptible to social influence (Group 6).

The most important variable for explaining differences on this factor is the level of a manager's position in a company.

Focal Managers are generally department managers and, as a result, they are more likely to work with other department managers and financial staff people in preparing their operating budgets. Other Managers are generally subordinates of department managers and thus are less likely to interact with these individuals.

However, the results of our analysis also suggest that the extent to which Other Managers interact with these other individuals may be related to their emotional stability and assertiveness. For example, those Other Managers who are relatively more anxious and more assertive interact with these other individuals more often.

125

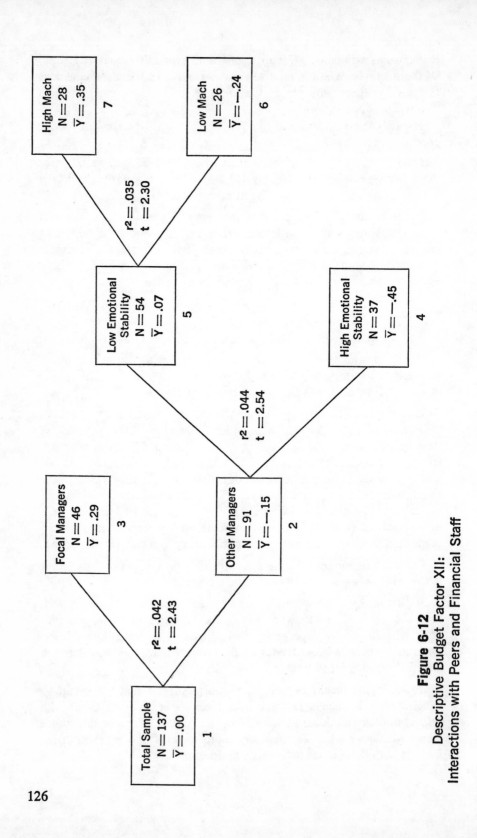

Figure 6-12
Descriptive Budget Factor XII:
Interactions with Peers and Financial Staff

126

Descriptive Budget Factor XIII:
Time Demands of Budgeting

Managers who have higher scores on this factor are more often not able to spend as much time as they would like preparing their operating budgets, even though they more often tend to spend time outside of normal working hours preparing these budgets. The results of our analysis of this factor are presented in Figure 6-13.

Managers who are in Company C or D (Group 3) experience more intensive time demands than those who are in Company A or B (Group 2). Of the managers who are in Company C or D, those who are relatively less stable emotionally and more trusting of others (Group 11) think that they experience the intensive budgeting time demands most often. Of the managers who are in Company A or B, those who are relatively more gregarious and sociable (Group 4) think that they experience intensive budgeting time demands least often.

This factor reflects the extent to which managers think that they experience intensive time demands because of a company's budgeting system.

The results of our analysis of this factor suggest that the company variable may explain most of the variance. Managers who are in Company C or D more often think that they are not able to spend as much time as they would like in preparing their operating budgets and think that they more often spend time outside of normal working hours preparing these budgets.

Discussion

Our analysis of the relationships between the 17 predictor variables and the 13 descriptive measures of managers' budget-oriented behavior suggests that different variables may be most important for explaining differences on measures of how managers actually use budgeting. The literature on the behavioral effects of budgeting suggests that personality and attitudinal variables may be important predictors of how managers use budgeting. In part, our results confirm this suggestion. For example, the personality variables of emotional stability and ascendency and the attitudinal variable of internal-external control are the most important predictors of the extent to which managers' methods of achieving their budgets tend to be accepted by others and the extent to which managers tend to be influential in the budgeting process, to be expressive about budgeting, and to have positive attitudes about budgeting.

Our results also suggest that other variables may be important predictors of various aspects of managers' budget-oriented behavior. For example, the company variable is the most important predictor of the extent to which managers tend to engage in various budget-related coping

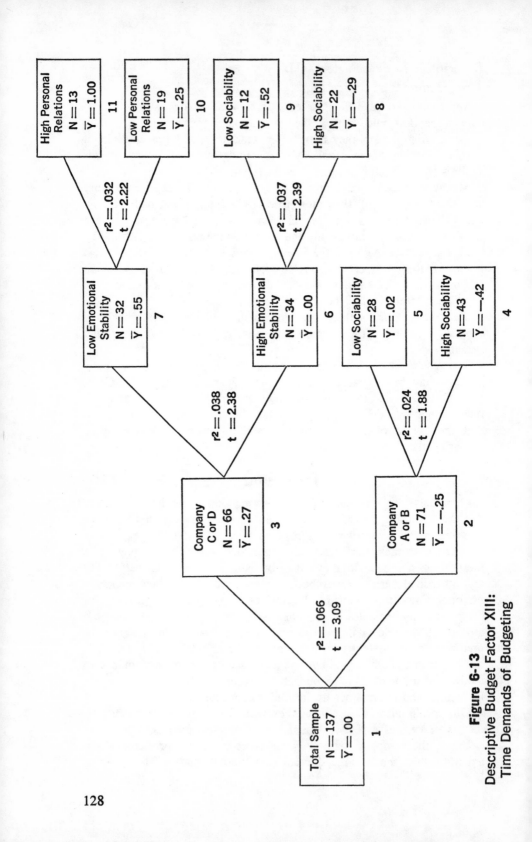

Figure 6-13
Descriptive Budget Factor XIII:
Time Demands of Budgeting

behaviors, to be personally involved in budgeting, to be shown comparisons of actual and budgeted performance for other units, and to experience intensive time demands from budgeting. Moreover, the demographic variables of managers' time in company, time in position, and time spent on budgeting are the most important predictors of the extent to which managers use budgets as evaluative devices, to perform various activities brought about by budget variances, and to be involved in the budgeting process. Finally, the level of managers' positions in their companies is the most important predictor of the extent to which managers work with their superiors and others in preparing their operating budgets.

These results are somewhat satisfying, especially those that suggest that a company's use of budgeting and the organizational context within which it is used may be important determinants of some aspects of managers' budget-oriented behavior.[1] These variables have received little, if any, consideration in the literature about the behavioral effects of budgeting. Moreover, various demographic and organizational variables have received relatively little attention in this literature. However, the results of our analysis suggest that these variables also may be important determinants of some aspects of how managers use budgeting in carrying out their management functions.

Our analysis of the relationships between the predictor variables and the descriptive measures of managers' budget-oriented behavior also reveals what combinations of these variables are most important for explaining differences in these measures. The most important predictor of each descriptive budget factor accounts for between 3.1 and 10.9 percent of the total variance on each factor. On average, this predictor accounts for 5.8 percent of the variance on each factor. Additional predictors account for between 2.7 and 16.9 percent of the total variance on each factor. On average, these additional predictors account for 11.3 percent of the variance on each factor. These results suggest that the combination of budget systems and organizational, demographic, and personality variables allows us to explain a higher percentage of the variance on each factor. Moreover, a careful examination of the results of our analysis of each factor reveals that different combinations of these variables exist for each factor. This suggests that different managerial profiles may be important for explaining differences in how managers use budgeting.

---

[1] As discussed in Chapter 5, the company variable also is essentially a surrogate variable for both a company's budgeting system and the organizational context within which it operates.

Chapter 7

Analysis of Relationships Between Predictor Variables and the Normative Measures of Managers' Budget-Oriented Behavior

We reported the results of our analysis of the relationships between the 17 predictor variables and the 13 descriptive measures of managers' budget-oriented behavior in Chapter 6. In this chapter, we focus on the relationships between these predictor variables and the normative measures of this behavior. The results of our analysis of these relationships are presented in the next section.

This analysis reveals that different variables may be important for predicting different dimensions of what managers think about their use of budgeting. For example, these results reveal that a company's use of participative budgeting and the organizational context within which it is used may be the most important predictors of managers' attitudes about the extent to which they think they should perform certain budget-variance-related activities, work with their superiors and others, suggest changes or improvements in the budgeting system, be expressive about budgeting, and have positive attitudes about the usefulness of budgeting.

These results also reveal that a manager's level in his company may be the most important predictor of his attitudes about budget-oriented interaction with his superiors and that the demographic variables of a manager's time in company, time in position and time spent budgeting may be the most important predictors of his attitudes about the extent to which he thinks he should offer suggestions for the improvement of budgeting systems, interact with his superiors, have difficulty meeting his budgets and be involved in the budgeting process.

Further, they show that the personality variables of emotional stability and cautiousness may be the most important predictors of managers' attitudes about the extent to which they think they should work with others in preparing their budgets, perform various budget-oriented activities, have positive attitudes about the usefulness of budgeting, and be influential in budgeting.

The chapter concludes with a brief discussion of the implications of the findings. A more speculative discussion of the findings is presented in Chapter 11.

Analysis

To determine which predictors and combinations of predictors produce the greatest discrimination in the group means of the normative measures of managers' budget-oriented behavior, we again used the Automatic Interaction Detector (AID) technique described in Chapter 5. The results of our analysis of each measure is again presented in the form of a "tree diagram" showing the various splits made among the predictor variables and the resulting subgroups of the sample developed by combinations of these variables. We report the size, N, and the average factor score, $\overline{Y}$, for each subgroup in the tree diagram and show the r^2 and t-value that occasion each split at the vertex of the split.

Normative Budget Factor I:
Required Explanations of Budget Variances

Managers with higher scores on this factor think that they more often should be required to report the actions they take to correct large budget variances, to submit more often explanations in writing about large budget variances, and to trace more often the causes of these variances to groups and individuals within their units. The results of the analysis of this factor are presented in Figure 7-1.

Managers who are in Company B or C (Group 3) think they should engage in these activities more often than those who are in Company A or D (Group 2). Moreover, those managers who are in Company A or D and who are relatively less persevering and determined (Group 4) think they should engage in these activities least often.

Our analysis of this factor suggests that the company in which the managers work may be an important variable in explaining differences in the extent to which they think they should perform these activities.

Managers who are in Company B or C think they should perform these activities more often than those who are in Company A or D. Companies B and C may place relatively more reliance on comparisons of actual and budgeted performance. This suggests that the extent to which managers think they should perform these activities may be related to the extent to which a company emphasizes these comparisons.

The results of our analysis of this factor also suggest that the extent to which managers in specific companies think they should perform these activities may be related to the extent to which they are relatively persevering and responsible. For example, of those managers who are in Company A or D, those who are relatively more persevering think

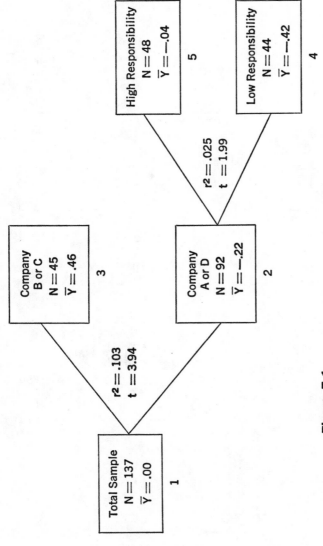

Figure 7-1
Normative Budget Factor I:
Required Explanations of Budget Variances

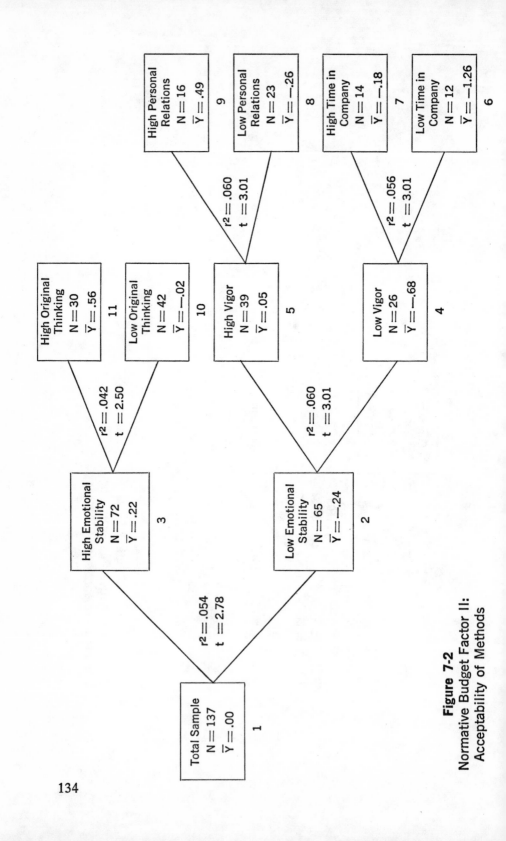

Figure 7-2
Normative Budget Factor II:
Acceptability of Methods

they should perform these activities more often than those who are relatively less persevering.

Normative Budget Factor II:
Acceptability of Methods

Managers who have higher scores on this factor think that their methods of reaching budgeted performance more often should be accepted without question by their superiors and subordinates and that their superiors more often should accept their explanations of budget variances for their units. Figure 7-2 presents the results of our analysis of this factor.

Managers who are relatively more stable emotionally (Group 3) think that their methods and explanations should be accepted more often. This is particularly true for those managers who also are relatively more intellectually curious (Group 11). Managers who are relatively less stable emotionally, are less vigorous and energetic, and have been in their companies for a shorter time (Group 6) think that their methods should be accepted by these individuals least often.

Of the managers who are relatively less stable emotionally but more energetic (Group 5), those who have relatively more trust in people (Group 9) think that their methods should be accepted more often by these individuals than those who have relatively less confidence or trust in people (Group 8).

Our analysis of this factor suggests that the most important variables for explaining differences on this factor are personality variables.

Managers who have relatively strong personalities think that their methods should be accepted more often. For example, managers who are relatively less anxious and nervous and more intellectually challenged think that their methods should be accepted most often. Managers who have relatively weaker personalities think that their methods should be accepted less often. Moreover, of the managers who are relatively more anxious, those who are relatively less energetic think that their methods should be accepted less often than those who are more energetic.

Normative Budget Factor III:
Interactions with Peers and Financial Staff

This factor reflects the extent to which managers think they should work with their superiors, other unit heads, and financial staff people in preparing the budgets for their units. Managers who think they should work with these individuals more often have higher scores on this factor. The results of our analysis of this factor are presented in Figure 7-3.

Managers who are in Company C or D (Group 3) think they should work with these individuals more often. This is particularly true for those managers who are in these companies and spend more time on

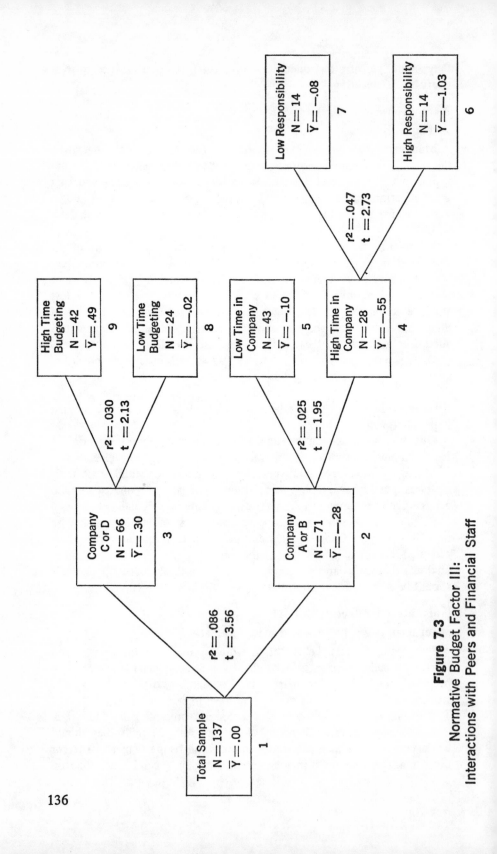

Figure 7-3
Normative Budget Factor III:
Interactions with Peers and Financial Staff

budgeting (Group 9). Of the managers who are in Company A or B (Group 2), those who have longer tenure in their companies and are relatively more persevering and determined (Group 6) think they should work with these people least often.

These results suggest that a company's use of budgeting may be an important determinant of managers' attitudes about their budget-oriented interactions with others, as most of the variance on this factor is explained by the company variable. Managers who are in Company C or D think that in preparing their operating budgets they should work with their superiors, other unit heads, and financial staff people more often than those who are in Company A or B.

However, these results also suggest that managers' attitudes about these interactions may be affected by the amount of time they spend on budgeting and by how long they have been with their companies. For example, of the managers who are in Company B or C, those who spend more time on budgeting think they should interact with these other individuals more often. Of the managers who are in Company A or B, those who have been with their company longer think that they should interact with these individuals somewhat less often.

Normative Budget Factor IV:
Actions Brought About by Expected Budget Overruns

Managers who have higher scores on this factor think that they should more often find it necessary to charge some activities to other accounts, stop some activities in their units, shift figures relating to operations when budgeted funds are used up, or reduce budget variances. Figure 7-4 presents the results of our analysis of this factor.

Managers who tend to be less stable emotionally (Group 3) think they should engage in these activities more often. Managers who tend to be less stable emotionally and who occupy relatively higher management positions (Group 7) think that they should engage in these activities most often. Managers who tend to be more stable emotionally and who have been in their positions longer (Group 4) think that they should engage in these activities least often.

This factor reflects managers' attitudes about various budget-oriented activities. Even though we noted in Chapter 4 that our sample of managers generally did not think they should engage in these activities very often, differences exist among managers to the extent to which they think they should engage in these activities, and these differences are reflected in this factor.

The results of our analysis of this factor suggest that the most important variable for explaining these differences is emotional stability. Managers who are relatively more anxious and nervous think that they should perform these activities more often.

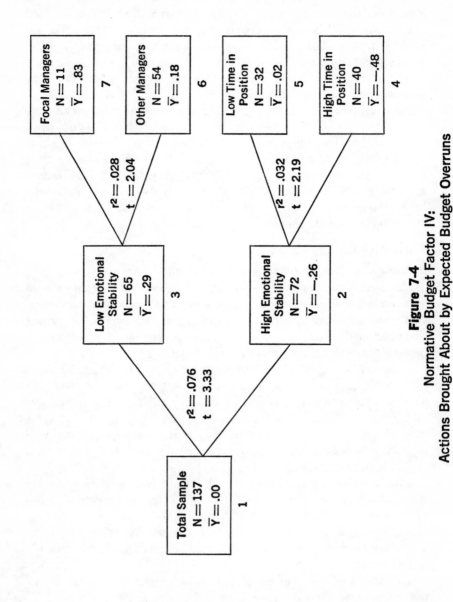

Figure 7-4
Normative Budget Factor IV:
Actions Brought About by Expected Budget Overruns

However, a manager's position also may be an important variable in explaining these differences. For example, of the managers who tend to be less stable emotionally, those who occupy relatively higher management positions think they should engage in these activities more often than those who occupy lower management positions. Of the managers who tend to be more stable emotionally, those who have occupied their positions longer think that they should engage in these activities less often than those who have occupied their positions a shorter time. These results suggest that the extent to which a manager thinks he should engage in these activities may not only be related to his emotional stability, but also to the level of his management position and how long he has occupied it.

Normative Budget Factor V:
Usefulness of Budgeting

Managers who have higher scores on this factor think that the budget more often should enable them to be better managers and to keep better track of their success as managers. Figure 7-5 presents the results of our analysis of this factor.

Managers who are in Company D (Group 3) think that the budget more often should enable them to be better managers and to keep track of their success as managers. Managers who are in Company A, B or C (Group 2) think that the budget should less often enable them to be better managers and to keep better track of their success, and this is particularly true for those managers who also are relatively more persevering (Group 4).

This factor reflects essentially the extent to which managers tend to have positive attitudes about the usefulness of budgeting. The results of our analysis of this factor reveal that managers who are in Company D have more positive attitudes about the usefulness of budgeting than those who are in Company A, B or C. This is an important finding since it suggests that a company's use of budgeting may be an important determinant of managers' attitudes about the usefulness of budgeting.

Moreover, the results of our analysis of this factor reveal that of the managers who are in Company A, B or C, those who are relatively more persevering and diligent have less positive attitudes about budgeting than those who are less persevering. This suggests that managers who are more determined may not think that the budget should be more useful to them.

Normative Budget Factor VI:
Suggestions About Budgeting

Managers who have higher scores on this factor think that they should more often offer suggestions for the improvement of budgeting systems

139

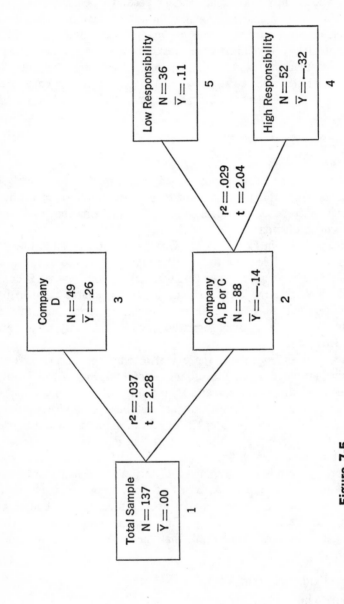

Figure 7-5
Normative Budget Factor V:
Usefulness of Budgeting

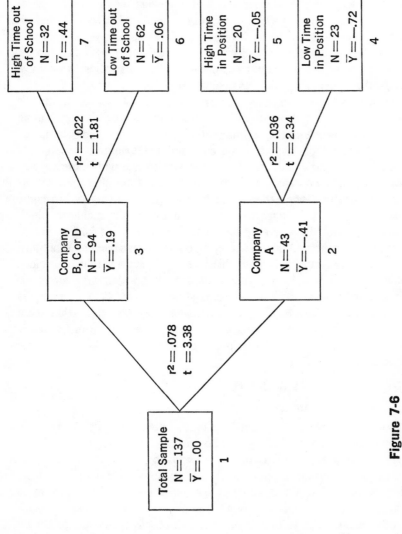

Figure 7-6
Normative Budget Factor VI:
Suggestions about Budgeting

and that these systems more often should be changed in accordance with these suggestions. Figure 7-6 presents the results of our analysis of this factor.

Managers who are in Company B, C or D (Group 3) think that they should more often make suggestions and that budgeting systems should more often be changed in accordance with these suggestions. This is particularly true for managers who are older (Group 7). Managers who are in Company A (Group 2) think that they should make suggestions and that budgeting systems should be changed in accordance with these suggestions less often. Moreover, of the managers who are in Company A, those who have been in their positions longer (Group 5) think that these events should occur more often than those who have been in their positions a shorter time (Group 4).

The results of our analysis of this factor suggest that a company's way of budgeting may be the most important variable for explaining the extent to which managers think they should offer suggestions for the improvement of budgeting systems and the extent to which they think these systems should be changed in accordance with these suggestions. Managers who are in Company B, C or D think that these events should occur more often than those who are in Company A. In some respects, these results suggest that the extent to which managers think these events should occur may be related to the relative importance of the budgeting system to them in carrying out their management functions.

The results of our analysis of this factor also suggest that how old a manager is and how long he has occupied his position may affect his attitudes about how often these events should occur. Of the managers who are in Company B, C or D, those who are older think that these events should occur more often. Of the managers who are in Company A, those who have been in their positions longer think that these events should occur more often.

Normative Budget Factor VII:
Involvement in Budgeting

This factor reflects managers' attitudes about their involvement in the budgeting process. Managers who have higher scores on this factor think that their explanations of budget variances more often should be included in performance reports, that they more often should investigate favorable as well as unfavorable budget variances, and that they more often should be shown comparisons of actual and budgeted performance for other units. The results of our analysis of this factor are presented in Figure 7-7.

Managers who spend more time on budgeting (Group 3) think that they should be involved in budgeting more often, and those managers who also are less verbally ascendent (Group 7) think that they should

142

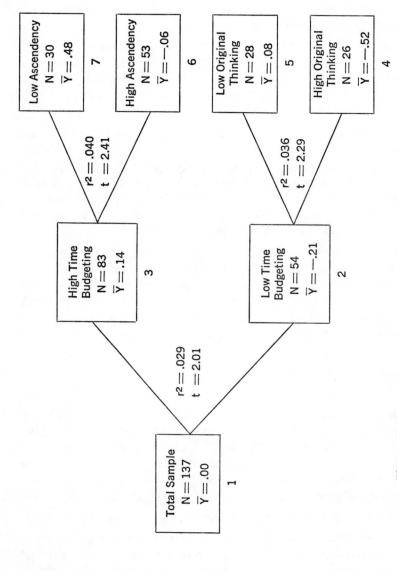

Figure 7-7
Normative Budget Factor VII:
Involvement in Budgeting

Low Ascendency
N = 30
$\bar{Y}$ = .48
7

High Ascendency
N = 53
$\bar{Y}$ = −.06
6

Low Original
Thinking
N = 28
$\bar{Y}$ = .08
5

High Original
Thinking
N = 26
$\bar{Y}$ = −.52
4

r^2 = .040
t = 2.41

r^2 = .036
t = 2.29

High Time
Budgeting
N = 83
$\bar{Y}$ = .14
3

Low Time
Budgeting
N = 54
$\bar{Y}$ = −.21
2

r^2 = .029
t = 2.01

Total Sample
N = 137
$\bar{Y}$ = .00
1

be involved in budgeting most often. Managers who spend less time on budgeting (Group 2) think that they should be involved in budgeting less often, and those managers who are relatively more curious intellectually (Group 4) think that they should be involved in budgeting least often.

The most important variable for explaining differences in managers' attitudes about this type of involvement in the budgeting process is the amount of time managers spend on budgeting.

Managers who spend more time on budgeting think that they should be involved in budgeting more often. Presumably managers who spend more time on budgeting are more involved in budgeting. Consequently, it is not too surprising to find that these managers also think that they should be more involved in budgeting.

Of the managers who spend more time on budgeting, those who are assertive and less self-confident think that they should be more involved in budgeting. This suggests that managers' attitudes about their involvement in budgeting may be related to the extent to which they are relatively ascendent in their relationships with others. Managers who are relatively more passive in their relationships with others may think that they should be more involved in budgeting.

Of the managers who spend less time on budgeting, those who are relatively more intellectually curious think that they should be less involved in budgeting. This suggests that managers' attitudes about their involvement in budgeting may also be related to the extent to which they are intellectually challenged. Those managers who are more intellectually challenged think that they should be less involved in budgeting.

Normative Budget Factor VIII: Expressive About Budgeting

This factor reflects managers' attitudes about the extent to which they think they should be expressive about budgeting. Managers with higher scores on this factor think that they should more often express their opinions on budget matters and should more often mention these matters in informal conversations. The results of our analysis of this factor are presented in Figure 7-8.

The company variable explains most of the variance of this factor.

This suggests that a company's use of budgeting may be an important determinant of managers' attitudes about the extent to which they should be more expressive about budgeting. Managers who are in Company A or B (Group 3) think that they should be more expressive about budgeting than those who are in Company C or D (Group 2).

144

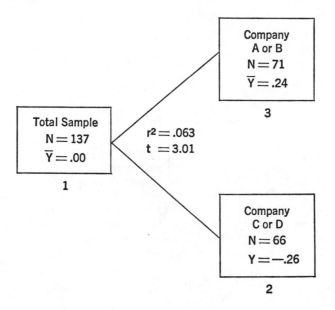

Figure 7-8
Normative Budget Factor VIII:
Expressive about Budgeting

Normative Budget Factor IX:
Influence in Budget Setting

This factor reflects managers' attitudes about the extent to which they think they should be more influential in budgeting. Managers with higher scores on this factor think that their budgets should more often include changes they have suggested, that they more often should be consulted about special factors they would like to have included in the budget being prepared, and that their budgets more often should not be finalized until they are satisfied with them. The results of our analysis of this factor are presented in Figure 7-9.

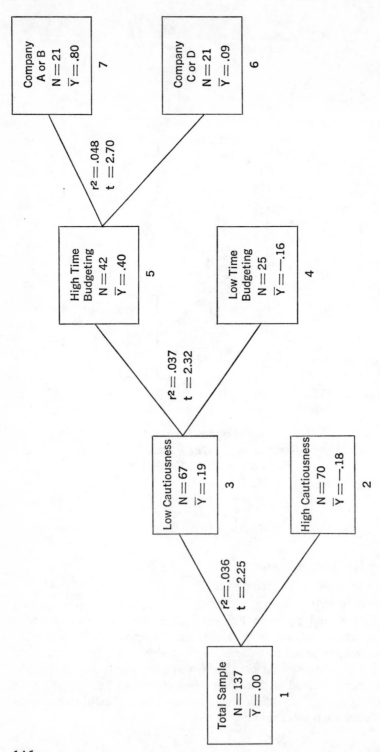

Figure 7-9
Normative Budget Factor IX:
Influence in Budget Setting

Managers who are relatively less cautious (Group 3) think that these events should occur more often. Those managers who are less cautious, spend more time on budgeting, and are in Company A or B (Group 7) think that these events should occur most often.

The most important variable for explaining differences in managers' attitudes about the extent to which they think they should be more influential in budgeting is the personality variable cautiousness.

Managers who are relatively more cautious think that they should be less influential in budgeting than those who are more aggressive. Presumably the tendency of managers either to be more calculative and careful or more impulsive in decision making may be reflected in their attitudes about the extent to which they think they should be more influential in budgeting.

The results of our analysis of this factor also suggest that the extent to which the personality variable cautiousness is related to managers' attitudes about their being more influential in budgeting may be affected by the amount of time they spend on budgeting and the budgeting system they use. For example, the managers who are relatively less cautious, spend more time on budgeting, and are in Company A or B think that they should be more influential in budgeting.

Normative Budget Factor X:
Influence on Flexibility and Innovation

This factor reflects the extent to which managers have positive attitudes about the usefulness of budgeting. Managers with higher scores on this factor think that the budget should more often enable them to be more flexible and innovative. The results of our analysis of this factor are presented in Figure 7-10.

The only important variable for explaining differences on this factor is emotional stability.

Managers who are relatively more stable emotionally (Group 3) think that the budget should more often enable them to be more flexible and innovative. Presumably managers who are relatively free from anxieties and nervous tension may be more likely to view budgeting as a useful tool and have positive attitudes about the usefulness of budgeting.

Normative Budget Factor XI:
Evaluation by Superiors

Managers who think that they should more often be reminded of the importance of meeting their budgets and that their superiors should more often express dissatisfaction to them when their budgets have not been met have higher scores on this factor. Figure 7-11 presents the results of our analysis of this factor.

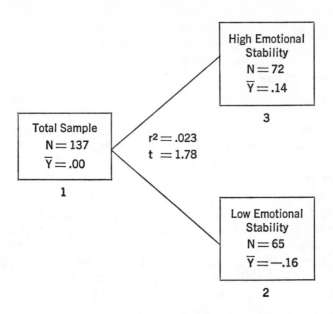

Figure 7-10
Normative Budget Factor X:
Influence on Flexibility and Innovation

The only variable which explains differences on this factor is managers' time in company.

Managers who have been with their companies longer (Group 3) think that these events should occur more often. This suggests that managers' attitudes about the importance of budgeting may be related to their tenure with their companies. Managers who have been with their companies longer may be more familiar and comfortable with how these companies use and rely on budgeting. Thus they may be more likely to think that these events should occur more often.

Normative Budget Factor XII:
Difficulty Meeting Budget

This factor reflects the extent to which managers think they should have difficulty meeting the budgets for their units. Managers who think that they should more often have difficulty meeting their budgets have higher scores on this factor. Figure 7-12 presents the results of our analysis of this factor.

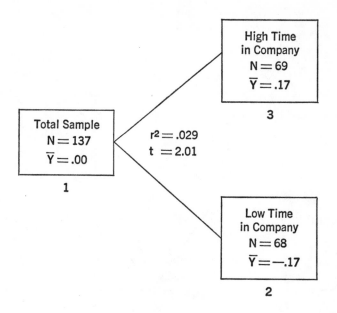

Figure 7-11
Normative Budget Factor XI:
Evaluation by Superiors

Managers who have occupied their present positions longer (Group 3) think that they should more often have difficulty meeting their operating budgets. Managers who have occupied their present positions a shorter time (Group 2) think they should less often have difficulty meeting their operating budgets, and those who also are relatively more gregarious and sociable (Group 4) think that they should least often have difficulty meeting these budgets.

The most important variable for explaining differences on this factor is managers' time in their positions. This finding is not too surprising.

Managers who have occupied their positions longer are more likely to be familiar with and to have been able to adjust to the various activities assigned to their positions. Consequently, these managers may be more likely to be challenged by operating budgets which are more difficult to achieve.

Managers who have occupied their positions for a shorter period of time are less likely to be as familiar with and to have been able to adjust to these activities. Because of this, these managers may be less likely to be comfortable with more difficult operating budgets.

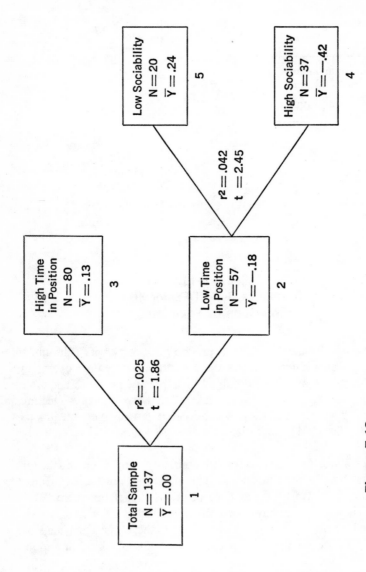

Figure 7-12
Normative Budget Factor XII:
Difficulty Meeting Budget

Also, of the managers who have been in their positions for a shorter time, those who are relatively more gregarious and sociable think they should less often have difficulty meeting their operating budgets. This suggests that managers who tend to like to be with and work with others may think that having difficulty meeting their operating budgets interferes with their social relationship with others.

Normative Budget Factor XIII:
Anticipatory Budget Preparation

This factor reflects the extent to which managers think they should start preparing the budgets for their unit before they are asked to. Managers with higher scores on this factor think that they should initiate the early preparation of their budgets more often. The results of our analysis of this factor are presented in Figure 7-13.

Managers who have been with their companies longer (Group 3) think that they should initiate the early preparation of their operating budgets more often. This is particularly true for those managers who also are relatively more anxious (Group 9). Of the managers who have been in their companies a shorter time (Group 2), those who occupy lower management positions and spend more time on budgeting (Group 6) think that they should initiate the preparation of the budgets least often.

The most important variable for explaining differences on this factor is managers' time in their companies.

Managers who have been with their companies longer think that they should more often initiate the preparation of their operating budgets. Presumably, managers who have been with their companies longer may be more likely to think that they should assume the responsibility for initiating the preparation of their operating budgets, and this may be particularly true for those managers who tend to be more anxious, tense, and to have a lower tolerance for frustration. Managers who have been with their companies a shorter time may be less likely to think that they should assume this responsibility, especially those managers who already spend more time on budgeting.

Normative Budget Factor XIV:
Interactions with Superiors

This factor reflects managers' attitudes about their budget-oriented interactions with their superiors. Managers who think that they should more often go to their superiors for advice on how to achieve their budgets and who think that they should more often work with their superiors in preparing the budgets for their units have higher scores on this factor. The results of our analysis of this factor are presented in Figure 7-14.

151

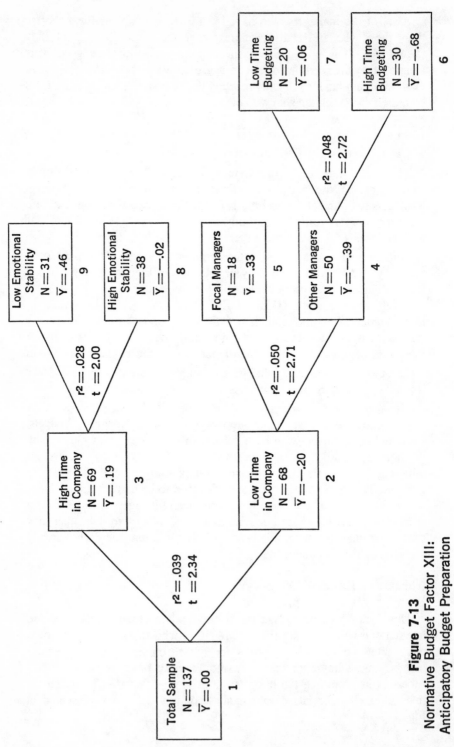

Figure 7-13
Normative Budget Factor XIII:
Anticipatory Budget Preparation

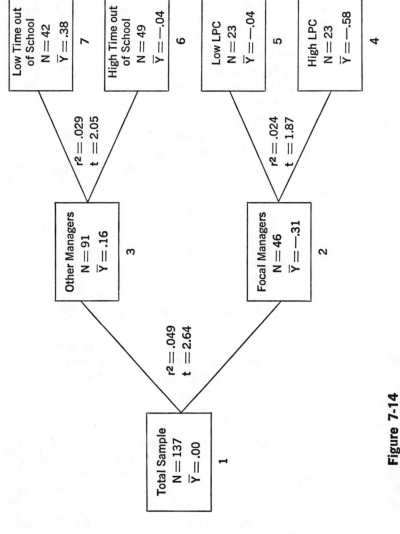

Figure 7-14
Normative Budget Factor XIV:
Interactions with Superior

The most important variable for explaining differences on this factor is the level of a manager's position in a company.

Managers who occupy lower management positions (Group 3) think that they should more often go to and work with their superiors. This is particularly true for younger managers who generally occupy lower management positions (Group 7). Of the managers who tend to occupy higher management positions (Group 2), those who are relatively less task-oriented (Group 4) think that they should go to and work with their superiors least often.

These results suggest that a manager's attitudes about his budget-oriented interactions with his superiors may be related to the level of his position in a company. For example, the Other Managers included in our sample are generally subordinates of the Focal Managers. Results suggest that these managers think they should more often go to and work with the Focal Managers. Moreover, those managers who are relatively younger think that they should interact with their superiors most often. Presumably, they think that they should receive more guidance and instruction from their superiors on how to achieve their operating budgets.

Discussion

Our analysis of the relationships between the 17 predictor variables and the 14 normative measures of managers' budget-oriented behavior reveals that different variables may be important for explaining differences on measures of what managers think about their budget-oriented behavior. For example, the company variable is the most important predictor of managers' attitudes about the extent to which they think they should perform certain activities brought about by budget variances, work with their superiors and others, suggest changes or improvements in the budgeting system, be expressive about budgeting, and have positive attitudes about the usefulness of budgeting. The level of managers' positions in their companies is the most important predictor of managers' attitudes about budget-oriented interaction with their superiors, and the demographic variables of managers' time in company, time in position, and time spent on budgeting are the most important predictors of managers' attitudes about the extent to which they should offer suggestions for the improvement of budgeting systems, interact with their superiors, have difficulty meeting their budgets, and be involved in the budgeting process. Finally, the personality variables of emotional stability and cautiousness are important predictors of managers' attitudes about the extent to which they think they should work with others in preparing their budgets, perform various budget-oriented activities, have positive attitudes about the usefulness of budgeting, and be influential in budgeting.

The results of our analysis of these relationships are also somewhat satisfying. The company variable explains the highest percentage of the variance on more normative budget factors than any other predictor variable, and it explains the highest percentage of the variance on three of the four most important normative budget factors. These results suggest that a company's use of budgeting and the organizational context within which it is used may be important determinants of what managers think about some aspects of their budget-oriented behavior. Also, these results suggest that even though certain organizational, demographic, and personality variables may be important predictors of some dimensions of managers' attitudes about their budget-oriented behavior, these variables generally are less important in terms of the percentage of the variance they explain on each dimension. Moreover, these variables generally are important predictors for those normative budget factors which are relatively less important.

Our analysis of the relationships between the predictor variables and the normative measures of managers' budget-oriented behavior reveals what combinations of these variables are most important for explaining differences on these measures. The most important predictor for each normative budget factor accounts for between 2.3 and 10.3 percent of the total variance on each factor. On average, this predictor accounts for 5.2 percent of the total variance on each factor. Additional predictors account for between 0.0 and 21.8 percent of the total variance on each factor. On average, these predictors account for 6.2 percent of the total variance on each factor.

These results suggest that the combination of various predictor variables allows us to explain a higher percentage of the variance on each factor. However, additional predictors generally are less powerful in explaining differences in managers' attitudes about their budget-oriented behavior than they were for explaining differences in managers' budget-oriented behavior. There are, of course, notable exceptions. Note, for example, that additional predictor variables account for 21.8 percent of the variance on normative budget factor II. For the most part, however, the combination of predictor variables is of relatively less significance in explaining differences in what managers think about how they use budgeting.

Chapter 8

Measures of Managers' Attitudes About Their Positions

Two major parts of our research were aimed at (1) measuring managers' budget-oriented behavior and identifying dimensions or aspects of that behavior and (2) identifying some of the variables which may affect these dimensions. Our analysis of managers' budget-oriented behavior, reported in Chapter 4, resulted in the identification and description of 13 descriptive and 14 normative measures of this behavior. In Chapter 5, we described 17 predictor variables we measured as part of the research, and in Chapters 6 and 7, we presented the results of our analysis of the relationships between these predictor variables and the measures of budget-oriented behavior.

A third major part of our research was aimed at identifying some effects of managers' budget-oriented behavior. The theoretical model presented in Chapter 2 suggested that both positive and negative effects might be associated with managers' budget-oriented behavior.

In this chapter, we will report the results of our analysis of managers' attitudes about their positions.

The first section describes the questionnaire used to measure these attitudes and the measures it was designed to obtain. Twenty attitudinal items were used to measure managers' attitudes about their positions. These items were drawn from questionnaires developed and used by Porter (1964), Haire, Ghiselli, and Porter (1966), and Porter and Lawler (1968) to measure managers' job attitudes and by Kahn et al. (1964) to measure job-related tension, satisfaction, and ambiguity. Descriptive, normative and evaluative measures of each of these items were obtained by asking managers to indicate how frequently each item described takes place, should take place and how important it is to him.

The second section reports the results of our analysis of the descriptive measures of these attitudes. This analysis results in the identification and description of five summary descriptive position factors which reflect job-related influence, ambiguity, tension, self-actualization, and satisfaction. The third section reports the results of our analysis of the normative measures of these attitudes. This analysis also results in the identification and description of five summary normative factors which reflect job-related influence, ambiguity, self-actualization, tension, and social interaction.

The chapter concludes with a comparison of the descriptive and normative factor structures.

Method

Questionnaire Construction

The 20 questionnaire items used to measure managers' attitudes about their positions are presented in Table 8-1. Nine of the 20 items presented in this table were drawn from questionnaires developed and used previously by Porter (1964), Haire, Ghiselli, and Porter (1966), and Porter and Lawler (1968) to measure managers' job attitudes. These items are based on Maslow's theory of personality and motivation (Maslow, 1954). Maslow categorized and ranked sets of human needs into a conceptual hierarchy. At the bottom of this hierarchy are physiological — or primary — needs which the individual must satisfy, at least to a minimal degree, before he can turn his attention to other, so-called "higher order" needs. Next in priority after the physiological needs are the needs concerned with safety and security, belongingness and love, esteem, and self-actualization.

Nine of the items included in Table 8-1 are based on and generally follow some of the higher order need categories included in Maslow's hierarchy of needs. Items 1 and 2 relate to Maslow's social needs category, items 5 and 6 relate to his need for esteem category, items 7, 9, 10 and 11 relate to a need for autonomy category, and item 13 relates to the need for self-realization or self-actualization category.

In our earlier studies (Swieringa and Moncur, 1972; Moncur and Swieringa, 1973), we used several items drawn from the job-related tension index, job-satisfaction index, and job-related ambiguity measures developed by Kahn et al. (1964). Eleven of the items included in Table 8-1 were selected from these indices and measures for use in the present study. Items 3, 4, 8, 12, 14, 15 and 16 were drawn from the Kahn et al. job-related tension index. These items are designed to cover a wide variety of job-relevant problems, and managers are asked to indicate the degree to which they are bothered by each of these problems. Items 17, 19 and 20 were drawn from the Kahn et al. job-related ambiguity measures. These items are designed to measure the clarity of a manager's expectations about his position. Finally, item 18 was drawn from the Kahn et al. job-satisfaction index; it was designed to measure the extent to which a manager thinks his position gives him a chance to do what he is best at.

Table 8-1
LIST OF TWENTY ATTITUDINAL ITEMS

1. My management position gives me the opportunity to give help to others.

2. My management position gives me the opportunity to develop close friendships.

3. My management position forces me to decide things that affect the lives of people that I know.

4. My management position forces me to resolve conflicting demands that people make on me.

5. My management position gives me prestige within the company.

6. My management position gives me prestige outside the company.

7. My management position gives me authority.

8. My management position forces me to do things that are against my better judgment.

9. My management position gives me opportunities for independent thought and action.

10. My management position gives me opportunities for participation in the setting of goals.

11. My management position gives me opportunities for participation in determining methods and procedures.

12. My management position gives me more to do than I can accomplish within a working day.

13. My management position gives me opportunities for personal growth and development.

14. My management position gives me opportunities for advancement and promotion.

15. My management position gives me more to do than I can do my best at.

16. My management position conflicts with my family life.

17. I am clear about the tasks I must perform in my management position.

18. My management position gives me opportunities to do the things I am best at.

19. I know when something is wanted or expected of me in my management position.

20. I know when I am doing well in my management position.

The Sets of Measures Obtained

Managers were asked to give three ratings for each item in Table 8-1:

a. How often does it take place?　　(Descriptive)
b. How often should it take place?　(Normative)
c. How important is it to me?　　　(Evaluative)

Each rating was made on a line which looked like this:

(min)＿＿＿＿＿＿＿＿＿＿＿＿＿＿＿(max)

Each rating was scored on a five-point scale by placing a clear plastic template divided into five equally spaced intervals over the line. A score of 1 on a given rating meant that the item "never" takes place, and a score of 5 meant that the item "always" takes place.

These ratings were designed to give us a view of what managers think they are getting from their jobs, what they think about what they are getting and how concerned they are with what they can get. The first question was designed to obtain information about a manager's job environment. This question asked each manager to indicate how frequently the item described *takes place*. Managers' responses to this question for each item were used as *descriptive* measures of their attitudes about their positions. The second question was designed to obtain information about both a manager's job environment and the manager himself. This question asked each manager to indicate how frequently the item described *should take place*. Managers' responses to this question for each item were used as *normative* measures of their attitudes about their positions. Finally, the third question was designed to obtain information about each manager as an individual. This question asked each manager to indicate *how important* the item described was to him. Managers' responses to this question for each item were used as *evaluative* measures of managers' attitudes about their positions. In the next two sections we will present the results of our analysis of the data obtained from our total sample of managers for the descriptive and normative measures of managers' attitudes about their positions. The results of our analysis of the data obtained for evaluative measures of managers' attitudes about their positions are presented elsewhere.[1]

Analysis of Descriptive Measures of Managers' Attitudes About Their Positions

Table 8-2 presents the means and standard deviations for descriptive measures of the 20 attitudinal items based on data obtained from our

---

[1] See Moncur (1975) for an analysis of the data obtained from our total sample of managers for the evaluative measures of their attitudes about their positions.

total sample of managers. An inspection of Table 8-2 provides a general idea of what managers think they get from their management positions. For example, managers think that their positions more often give them opportunities to help others (Item 1) and to participate in determining methods and procedures (Item 11). Moreover, managers think that they more often know when something is wanted or expected of them (Item 19), are clear about the tasks they must perform (Item 17), and know when they are doing well (Item 20). Managers also think that their positions less often force them to do things that are against their better judgment (Item 8), conflict with their family life (Item 16), and give them opportunities to develop close friendships (Item 2).

Table 8-2

MEANS AND STANDARD DEVIATIONS FOR DESCRIPTIVE MEASURES OF TWENTY ATTITUDINAL ITEMS

(N = 137)

Item No.	Means	Standard Deviations
1	4.10	1.11
2	2.66	1.32
3	3.38	1.30
4	3.74	1.20
5	3.20	1.31
6	3.03	1.29
7	3.54	1.18
8	1.54	0.95
9	3.74	1.21
10	3.64	1.40
11	3.80	1.22
12	3.45	1.43
13	3.66	1.28
14	3.31	1.48
15	2.74	1.50
16	2.50	1.32
17	3.80	1.18
18	3.64	1.22
19	3.92	1.11
20	3.72	1.23

Table 8-3

CORRELATIONS AMONG DESCRIPTIVE MEASURES OF
TWENTY ATTITUDINAL ITEMS

(N = 137)

Item No.	1	2	3	4	5	6	7	8	9	10	11	12	13	14	15	16	17	18	19	20
1		.43	.47	.55	.46	.38	.42	.15	.63	.52	.49	.14	.38	.18	.07	−.10	.15	.35	.10	.04
2			.15	.21	.23	.19	.19	.10	.35	.33	.26	−.06	.23	.12	.06	−.14	.05	.25	.08	−.07
3				.63	.45	.41	.37	.12	.34	.47	.39	.17	.27	.23	−.05	−.01	.05	.16	−.01	−.01
4					.43	.39	.36	.16	.43	.46	.45	.29	.25	.15	.17	−.10	−.06	.08	−.09	−.07
5						.49	.70	.03	.35	.50	.42	.15	.43	.33	.12	.04	.11	.25	.09	.17
6							.46	.18	.16	.24	.33	.11	.24	.13	−.00	.02	.09	.19	.06	.05
7								.02	.42	.48	.35	.05	.39	.28	.09	.02	.03	.13	.04	.17
8									−.08	−.08	.09	.04	−.25	−.30	.08	.12	−.12	−.17	−.25	−.26
9										.61	.35	.13	.46	.30	.10	−.12	.11	.36	.12	.14
10											.59	.21	.60	.53	.06	−.09	.16	.45	.15	.20
11												.26	.50	.41	.14	−.08	.20	.34	.17	.07
12													.29	.26	.55	.37	−.01	.14	.04	.06
13														.68	.19	.11	.18	.55	.28	.40
14															.21	.15	.18	.37	.22	.31
15																.49	−.03	.03	−.09	.02
16																	.07	−.00	−.10	.02
17																		.49	.55	.40
18																			.35	.35
19																				.52
20																				

The simple correlation coefficients for pairs of the descriptive measures of the 20 attitudinal items are presented in Table 8-3. Inspection of this table reveals that these measures are intercorrelated. For example, 41 of the coefficients presented in this table are above .40.[2] Moreover, a closer inspection of this table reveals that patterns of relations exist. Note, for example, the intercorrelations between items 1, 3 and 4; items 1, 9, 10 and 11; items 5, 6 and 7; and items 17, 19 and 20.

To take advantage of these intercorrelations, a factor analysis was used to identify principal descriptive dimensions of managers' attitudes about their positions. A principal components analysis resulted in the identification of five characteristic roots which were greater than one. These roots are presented in Table 8-4 and account for 65 percent of the total variance. These five factors were then rotated using Kaiser's normal orthogonal varimax criterion. Table 8-5 presents the rotated factor loading coefficients for the five descriptive position factors. These loading coefficients were used to develop substantive descriptions for each factor. These descriptions are presented in the following paragraphs.

Table 8-4

CHARACTERISTIC ROOTS FOR PRINCIPAL COMPONENTS
ANALYSIS FOR DESCRIPTIVE MEASURES OF
TWENTY ATTITUDINAL ITEMS

Root Number	Characteristic Root	Cumulative Proportion of Total Variance
1	5.840	.292
2	2.625	.424
3	2.051	.526
4	1.284	.590
5	1.222	.652
Total	13.022	

Descriptive Position Factor I:
Job-Related Influence

The following items have the highest loading on this factor: Item 5, My management position gives me prestige within the company (.79);

---

[2] It should be noted, however, that these measures of these items are not *highly* intercorrelated. For example, only six of the coefficients presented in Table 8-3 are above .60 and the highest coefficient is .70.

Table 8-5

ROTATED FACTOR LOADINGS FOR DESCRIPTIVE MEASURES OF TWENTY ATTITUDINAL ITEMS

(N = 137)

Item No.	I	II	III	IV	V	Communality
1	.43	.10	.02	—.07	.72	.72
2	.03	.06	—.08	—.11	.70	.52
3	.66	—.07	.01	—.00	.32	.54
4	.57	—.21	.13	—.05	.48	.62
5	.79	.10	.07	.18	.17	.70
6	.75	.16	.03	—.20	.07	.64
7	.78	.00	—.01	.24	.11	.67
8	.19	—.13	.18	—.74	.12	.65
9	.25	.03	—.01	.30	.69	.62
10	.42	.10	.05	.43	.60	.73
11	.40	.16	.17	.14	.53	.52
12	.10	—.01	.78	.10	.14	.65
13	.30	.28	.25	.62	.37	.76
14	.22	.18	.28	.70	.20	.68
15	—.02	—.07	.84	.04	.10	.72
16	.04	.07	.76	—.06	—.27	.66
17	.02	.85	.02	—.06	.10	.73
18	.05	.60	.09	.24	.45	.63
19	—.01	.79	—.09	.15	.05	.65
20	.13	.65	.02	.39	—.14	.61
Contribution of Factor	3.344	2.397	2.140	2.114	3.027	13.02
Percent of Communality	25.7	18.4	16.4	16.2	23.3	

Item 7, My management position gives me authority (.78); Item 6, My management position gives me prestige outside the company (.75); and Item 3, My management position forces me to decide things that affect the lives of people that I know (.66). Managers who have higher scores on this factor more often think that their management positions give them prestige, authority, and responsibility. Note that this factor is somewhat interpersonal in nature. Prestige derives from others respecting a manager and his position, authority derives from others having to comply with a manager's directives, and responsibility derives from having to make decisions that affect the lives of others. This is the most important descriptive position factor, accounting for 25.7 percent of the total variance explained.

Descriptive Position Factor II:
Job-Related Ambiguity

The following items have the highest loadings on this factor: Item 17, I am clear about the tasks I must perform in my management position (.85); Item 19, I know when something is wanted or expected of me in my management position (.79); Item 20, I know when I am doing well in my management position (.65); and Item 18, My management position gives me opportunities to do the things I am best at (.60). Managers who have higher scores on this factor tend to experience less job-related ambiguity; that is, they more often are clear about the tasks they must perform, know when something is expected of them, and know when they are doing well. Note that this factor suggests that lower job-related ambiguity may be related to higher job-satisfaction. Managers who tend to experience less job-related ambiguity also tend to think that their positions give them more opportunities to do the things they are best at. This factor accounts for 18.4 percent of the total explained variance.

Descriptive Position Factor III:
Job-Related Tension

The items with the highest loading on this factor are: Item 15, My position gives me more to do than I can do my best at (.84); Item 12, My management position gives me more to do than I can accomplish within a working day (.78); and Item 16, My management position conflicts with my family life (.76). Managers with higher scores on this factor more often experience job-related tension. They more often think that their positions give them more than they can do their best at, more than they can accomplish in a working day, and conflict with their family life. This factor accounts for 16.4 percent of the total explained variance.

Descriptive Position Factor IV:
Job-Related Self-Actualization

The following items have the highest loadings on this factor: Item 8, My management position forces me to do things that are against my better judgment (−.74); Item 14, My management position gives me opportunities for advancement and promotion (.70); and Item 13, My management position gives me opportunities for personal growth and development (.62). Managers with higher scores on this factor more often think that their management positions do not force them to do things that are against their better judgment, but rather that their positions more often give them opportunities for advancement and promotion and personal growth and development. This factor accounts for 16.2 percent of the total variance explained.

Descriptive Position Factor V:
Job-Related Satisfaction

The items with the highest loadings on this factor are as follows: Item 1, My management position gives me the opportunity to give help to others (.72); Item 2, My management position gives me the opportunity to develop close friendships (.70); Item 9, My management position gives me opportunities for independent thought and action (.69); Item 10, My management position gives me opportunities for participation in the setting of goals (.60); and Item 11, My management position gives me opportunities for participation in determining methods and procedures (.53). Managers with higher scores on this factor more often think that their management positions give them opportunities for meaningful social interaction, independent thought and action, and participation in decision making. This factor is the second most important descriptive position factor, accounting for 23.3 percent of the total variance explained.

Analysis of Normative Measures of
Managers' Attitudes About Their Positions

Table 8-6 presents the means and standard deviations for normative measures of the 20 attitudinal items based on data obtained from our total sample of managers. An inspection of Table 8-6 provides a general notion of what managers think about what they should get from their management positions. For example, managers think that they should more often know when something is wanted or expected of them (Item 19), should know more often when they are doing well (Item 20), and should more often be clear about the tasks they must perform (Item 17). Moreover, they think that their management positions more often should give them the opportunity to give help to others (Item 1), give them opportunities for personal growth and development (Item 13), and give them opportunities to do the things they are best at (Item 18). Conversely, managers think that their management positions should less often force them to do things that are against their better judgment (Item 8), conflict with their family life (Item 16), and give them more to do than they can do their best at (Item 15).

Table 8-6

MEANS AND STANDARD DEVIATIONS FOR NORMATIVE
MEASURES OF TWENTY ATTITUDINAL ITEMS

(N = 137)

Item No.	Means	Standard Deviations
1	4.35	1.06
2	2.80	1.29
3	3.18	1.35
4	3.49	1.32
5	3.33	1.28
6	3.01	1.18
7	3.55	1.19
8	1.21	0.59
9	4.20	1.02
10	4.22	1.10
11	4.11	1.08
12	2.55	1.22
13	4.23	1.04
14	3.95	1.15
15	2.05	1.22
16	1.55	0.86
17	4.35	1.19
18	4.23	1.04
19	4.49	0.92
20	4.45	0.94

Table 8-7 presents the simple correlation coefficients for pairs of the normative measures of the 20 attitudinal items. This table reveals that measures of these items are intercorrelated. For example, 46 of the coefficients presented in Table 8-7 are above .40. Table 8-7 also reveals that patterns of intercorrelations exist. For example, note the intercorrelations between items 5, 6 and 7; items 18, 19 and 20; and items 11, 13 and 14.

The correlation coefficients presented in Table 8-7 were factor analyzed to identify principal normative dimensions of managers' attitudes about their positions. A principal components analysis resulted in the identification of five characteristic roots which were greater than one. These roots, which account for 63.4 percent of the total variance, are

Table 8-7

CORRELATIONS AMONG NORMATIVE MEASURES OF
TWENTY ATTITUDINAL ITEMS

(N = 137)

Item No.	1	2	3	4	5	6	7	8	9	10	11	12	13	14	15	16	17	18	19	20
1		.43	.40	.52	.45	.39	.42	.12	.65	.58	.46	.15	.60	.43	.11	−.04	.23	.42	.31	.14
2			.25	.30	.21	.19	.12	.18	.26	.17	.12	.15	.30	.15	.21	−.02	.02	.12	.03	−.03
3				.62	.48	.39	.38	.20	.32	.40	.27	.30	.40	.35	.10	.06	.05	.14	.12	−.01
4					.42	.38	.37	.12	.32	.44	.27	.25	.34	.28	.18	.03	.06	.13	.13	−.03
5						.56	.59	.06	.40	.49	.34	.21	.43	.26	.06	.04	.07	.20	.31	.12
6							.58	.15	.29	.33	.20	.28	.32	.19	.13	.16	.11	.20	.15	.09
7								.05	.43	.51	.30	.02	.39	.24	.10	.05	.11	.02	.14	.02
8									−.01	.04	−.06	.19	−.02	−.05	.20	.23	−.02	−.08	−.11	−.09
9										.62	.45	.07	.53	.31	.04	−.07	.14	.29	.24	.25
10											.65	.26	.53	.38	.15	.03	.16	.21	.29	.22
11												.28	.64	.51	.17	.01	.28	.37	.44	.41
12													.26	.25	.35	.30	.06	.20	.20	.14
13														.68	.16	.06	.39	.56	.47	.41
14															.21	.11	.40	.47	.43	.36
15																.35	.22	.06	.01	−.03
16																	.04	−.01	−.08	−.17
17																		.49	.30	.41
18																			.44	.45
19																				.59
20																				

presented in Table 8-8. These five factors were then rotated using Kaiser's normal orthogonal varimax criterion. The rotated factor loading coefficients for these five factors are presented in Table 8-9 and were used to develop substantive descriptions for each normative position factor. These descriptions are presented in the following paragraphs.

Normative Position Factor I:
Job-Related Influence

This factor reflects the extent to which managers think their management positions should give them authority, prestige, and opportunities to participate in goal setting. The following items have the highest loadings on this factor: Item 7, My management position gives me authority (.85); Item 5, My management position gives me prestige within the company (.78); Item 6, My management position gives me prestige outside the company (.70); and Item 10, My management position gives me opportunities for participation in the setting of goals (.67). Managers who have higher scores on this factor think that their positions should be given these characteristics and opportunities more often. This factor is one of the two most important normative position factors, accounting for 30.1 percent of the total variance explained.

Table 8-8

CHARACTERISTIC ROOTS FOR PRINCIPAL COMPONENTS ANALYSIS FOR NORMATIVE MEASURES OF TWENTY ATTITUDINAL ITEMS

Root Number	Characteristic Root	Cumulative Proportion of Total Variance
1	6.275	.314
2	2.475	.437
3	1.745	.525
4	1.172	.583
5	1.012	.634
Total	12.679	

Normative Position Factor II:
Job-Related Ambiguity and Self-Actualization

This factor reflects the extent to which managers think they should experience job-related ambiguity and the extent to which they think

Table 8-9

ROTATED FACTOR LOADINGS FOR NORMATIVE MEASURES OF TWENTY ATTITUDINAL ITEMS

(N = 137)

Item No.	I	II	III	IV	V	Communality
1	.49	.34	—.00	.63	—.04	.76
2	.04	.01	.03	.79	.21	.66
3	.55	.06	—.02	.34	.43	.61
4	.52	.04	.00	.45	.33	.58
5	.78	.15	—.08	.06	.21	.68
6	.70	.08	.07	—.04	.35	.62
7	.85	.01	.09	.02	—.12	.75
8	.02	—.19	.30	.22	.47	.40
9	.54	.30	—.03	.46	—.30	.68
10	.67	.32	.13	.28	—.15	.67
11	.40	.61	.15	.17	—.14	.61
12	.12	.28	.26	.04	.66	.60
13	.41	.68	.11	.34	—.01	.76
14	.23	.67	.21	.21	.03	.59
15	—.00	.12	.76	.18	.16	.65
16	.10	—.05	.77	—.18	.15	.65
17	—.03	.64	.24	.02	—.09	.48
18	.01	.75	—.04	.17	.11	.61
19	.18	.73	—.22	—.10	.15	.65
20	.01	.78	—.22	—.14	.04	.68
Contribution of Factor	3.815	3.869	1.599	1.995	1.401	12.68
Percent of Communality	30.1	30.5	12.6	15.7	11.1	

they should experience self-realization or self-actualization. The items with the highest loadings on this factor are: Item 20, I know when I am doing well in my management position (.78); Item 18, My management position gives me opportunities to do the things I am best at (.75); Item 19, I know when something is wanted or expected of me in my management position (.73); Item 13, My management position gives me opportunities for personal growth and development (.68); and Item 14, My management position gives me opportunities for advancement and promotion (.67). This factor consists of two sets of items. The first set reflects managers' attitudes about job-related ambiguity; that is, it reflects the extent to which managers think they should know when they are doing well and should know when something is expected or wanted of them. The second set reflects managers' attitudes about their job-related self-actualization. This set reflects the extent to which managers think that their positions give them opportunities to do the things they are best at and opportunities for personal growth and development and for advancement and promotion. Managers with higher scores on this factor think that they should experience less job-related ambiguity and more opportunities for self-actualization in their management positions. This factor is the most important normative position factor, accounting for 30.5 percent of the total variance explained.

Normative Position Factor III:
Job-Related Tension

This factor reflects the extent to which managers think they should experience job-related tension in their management positions. The following two items have the highest loading on this factor: Item 16, My management position conflicts with my family life (.77); and Item 15, My management position gives me more to do than I can do my best at (.76). Managers who have higher scores on this factor think that they should more often experience job-related tension. This factor accounts for 12.6 percent of the total variance explained.

Normative Position Factor IV:
Job-Related Social Interaction

This factor reflects managers' attitudes about job-related social interaction. The two items which have the highest loadings on this factor are as follows: Item 2, My management position gives me the opportunity to develop close friendships (.79); and Item 1, My management position gives me the opportunity to give help to others (.63). Managers who have higher scores on this factor think that their management positions should more often give them the opportuntiy to develop close friendships and to give help to others. This factor accounts for 15.7 percent of the total variance explained.

Normative Position Factor V: Job-Related Tension

This factor also is a job-related tension factor. The following items have the highest loading on this factor: Item 12, My management position gives me more to do than I can accomplish within a working day (.66); Item 8, My management position forces me to do things that are against my better judgment (.47); and Item 3, My management position forces me to decide things that affect the lives of people I know (.43). Managers who think that they should experience more job-related tension because of their positions have higher scores on this factor. This factor accounts for 11.1 percent of the total variance explained.

Comparison of the Descriptive and Normative Position Factors

The preceding analyses have served to identify sets of descriptive and normative dimensions or factors of managers' attitudes about their positions. The factors included in each set are independent of one another, and all have natural and useful interpretations. The results of our analysis of the relationships between measures of managers' budget-oriented behavior and these descriptive and normative position factors are reported in Chapter 9. However, at this point it may be useful to consider the structures of these two sets of position factors in more detail.

An examination of the loadings of the 20 attitudinal items on each of the descriptive and normative position factors reveals that, in general, the two factor structures are relatively similar. For example, note that items 5, 6 and 7 have high loadings on both descriptive position factor I and normative position factor I. Similarly, note that items 18, 19 and 20 have high loadings on descriptive position factor III and normative position factor III. Finally, note that items 1 and 2 have high loadings on descriptive position factor V and normative position factor IV. These results suggest that these two factor structures may have some similar general patterns of relations.

However, even though these items have high loadings on particular descriptive and normative position factors, the relative loadings of these items of these factors differ. For example, where items 15 and 16 have loadings of .84 and .76, respectively, on descriptive position factor III, these items have loadings of .76 and .77, respectively, on normative position factor III. Moreover, some items have high loadings on different descriptive and normative position factors. For example, where items 13 and 14 have high loadings on descriptive position factor IV, these items have high loadings on normative position factor II. Similarly, where item 12 has a high loading on descriptive position factor III, it has a high loading on normative position factor V, and where items 9, 10 and 11 have high loadings on descriptive position factor V, they do not have high loadings on any one normative position factor. These results suggest that the two factor structures also may have some different patterns of relations.

An examination of the relative contributions of individual factors to the total variance explained by each factor structure also reveals some similarities between the two factor structures. First, consider the relative contribution of each descriptive position factor. Descriptive position factors I and V, which account for 25.7 and 23.3 percent, respectively, of the total variance explained, reflect the extent to which managers think they experience job-related ambiguity and job-related tension. Finally, descriptive position factor IV, which accounts for 16.2 percent of the total variance explained, reflects the extent to which managers experience job-related self-actualization.

Next, consider the relative contributions of each of the normative position factors. Normative position factors I and II account for 30.1 and 30.5 percent, respectively, of the total variance explained. These factors reflect managers' attitudes about the extent to which managers think their management positions should give them more influence and have them experience less job-related ambiguity and more job-related self-actualization. Normative position factor IV, which accounts for 15.7 percent of the total variance explained, reflects managers' attitudes about the extent to which they think their positions should give them more opportunities for meaningful social interaction. Finally, normative position factors III and V account for 12.6 and 11.1 percent, respectively, of the total variance explained. These factors reflect managers' attitudes about the extent to which they think they should experience job-related tension.

The position factors which are most important for explaining differences in what managers think they get from their management positions and what they think about what they should get from their management positions suggest that there may be some important similarities in the two factor structures. For example, where the three most important descriptive position factors reflect how much influence, job satisfaction and job-related ambiguity managers get from their positions, the three most important normative position factors reflect managers' attitudes about how much influence, job-related ambiguity, job-related self-actualization, and meaningful social interaction they should get from their management positions. Moreover, where the least important descriptive position factors reflect how much job-related tension and self-actualization managers get from their positions, the least important normative position factors reflect managers' attitudes about how much job-related tension they should get from their positions. Note that the only attitudinal aspect that differs between the two factor structures is self-actualization. Combined with managers' attitudes about job-related ambiguity, self-actualization is relatively more important for explaining differences in managers' attitudes about their positions than it is in explaining differences for what managers think they get from their management positions.

Chapter 9

Analysis of Relationships Between Descriptive Measures of Managers' Budget-Oriented Behavior and Measures of Managers' Attitudes About Their Positions

In this chapter, we report the results of our analysis of the relationships between the descriptive measures of managers' budget-oriented behavior described in Chapter 4 and the descriptive and normative measures of managers' attitudes about their positions described in Chapter 8. The next section reports the results of our analysis of these relationships.

These results suggest that how often managers experience job-related tension may be related to how often they experience time pressure from budgeting, that how often they experience job-related self-actualization may be related to how often they are influential in budgeting, and that how often they tend to experience job-related ambiguity may be related to how often they tend to have positive attitudes about the usefulness of budgeting.

In addition, the results suggest that managers' attitudes about how often they think they should experience job-related tension may be related to how much time pressure they experience from budgeting and how involved they are in budgeting.

Further, results suggest that managers' attitudes about how much job-related tension they think they should experience may be related to how much time pressure they experience from budgeting, how expressive they are about budgeting, and how involved they are in the budgeting process.

The chapter will conclude with a brief discussion of the implications of our findings.

Analysis

Because we derived both the descriptive budget factors and the normative and descriptive position factors from our empirical data, we had little in the way of either theory or empirical evidence that could help us specify a priori what the nature of the relationships between these two sets of measures might be. Accordingly, we had no choice but to again be thrust back upon our empirical data to analyze these relationships. To facilitate this analysis, we again used the Automatic Interaction Detector (AID) to determine which budget factors and combinations of them would produce the greatest discrimination in the group means of the position factor scores. Because the AID program requires that the independent or predictor variables be categorical, we recoded the descriptive budget factors into dichotomous high and low categories. To do this, we calculated an overall sample median for each budget factor and then assigned managers with factor scores above this median to the "high" category and managers with factor scores below this median to the "low" category.

The results of our analysis of each factor will be presented in the form of a "tree diagram" showing the various splits made by the budget factors and the resulting subgroups which are brought about by combinations of these factors. The size, N, and the average factor score, $\overline{Y}$, are reported for each subgroup. Also, the r^2 and t-value that occasion each split are entered at the vertex of the split. Appendix A, which presents an abbreviated dictionary of variables, provides the reader with a quick reference for the variables presented in the tables that follow.

Descriptive Position Factor I:
Job-Related Influence

Managers who have higher scores on this factor think that their management positions give them more prestige, authority, and responsibility. The results of our analysis of this factor are presented in Figure 9-1.

Managers who more often tend to use the budget to evaluate their subordinates and whose superiors more often tend to use it to evaluate them (Group 3) think that their positions give them more job-related influence. Managers who less often tend to evaluate their subordinates and who less often are evaluated by means of the budget (Group 2) think that their positions give them less job-related influence, and this is particularly true for those managers who more often are not able to spend as much time as they would like preparing the budgets for their units and who are not shown comparisons of actual and budgeted results for other units (Group 6).

These results suggest that the extent to which managers think their positions give them job-related influence may be related to the extent to which they use the budget as an evaluative device, experience greater time pressure from budgeting, and are involved in budgeting.

176

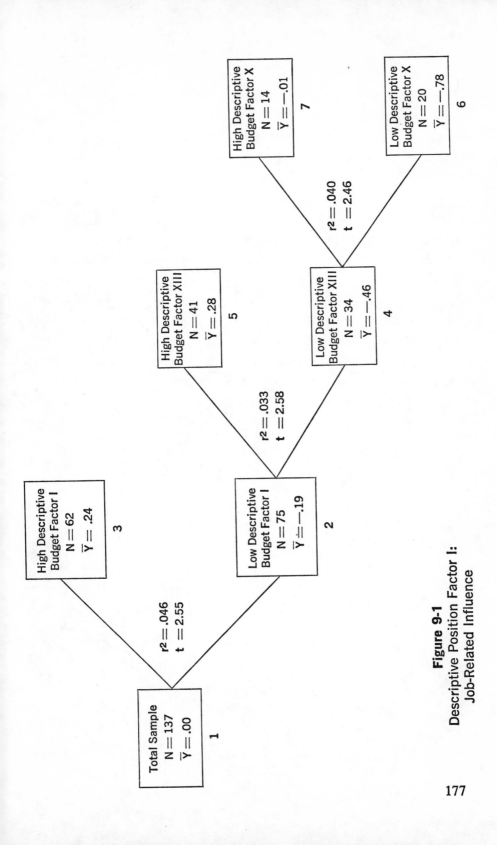

Figure 9-1
Descriptive Position Factor I:
Job-Related Influence

177

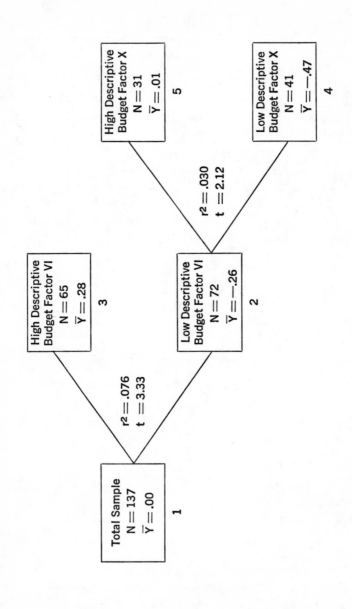

Figure 9-2
Descriptive Position Factor II:
Job-Related Ambiguity

Descriptive Position Factor II:
Job-Related Ambiguity

Managers who have higher scores on this factor have lower job-related ambiguity; that is, they are more clear about the tasks they must perform, more often know when something is wanted or expected of them, and more often know when they are doing well in their positions. The results of our analysis of this factor are presented in Figure 9-2.

Managers who view budgeting as a more worthwhile and useful process (Group 3) experience less job-related ambiguity. Managers who view budgeting as a less worthwhile and useful process (Group 2) experience more job-related ambiguity, and those managers who also are not shown comparisons of actual and budgeted results for other units (Group 4) experience the most job-related ambiguity.

These results suggest that the extent to which managers think they experience job-related ambiguity may be related to their attitudes about the usefulness of budgeting and the extent to which they are involved in the budgeting process.

Descriptive Position Factor III:
Job-Related Tension

Managers who have higher scores on this factor think that their management positions give them more to do than they can do their best at, more to do than they can accomplish in a working day, and conflict more with their family life. The results of our analysis of this factor are presented in Figure 9-3.

Managers who more often are not able to spend as much time as they would like preparing the budgets for their units and who more often spend time outside of normal working hours preparing the budgets for their units (Group 3) experience relatively higher job-related tension. Managers who experience the time demands of the budgeting system less often (Group 2) experience lower job-related tension, and those managers who, in addition, are less involved in the budgeting process experience even less job-related tension.

These results suggest that the extent to which managers think that they experience job-related tension may be somewhat related to how much time pressure they experience from budgeting and how involved they are in the budgeting process.

Descriptive Position Factor IV:
Job-Related Self-Actualization

Managers with higher scores on this factor think that their management positions less often force them to do things that are against their better judgment and that they give them more opportunities for advance-

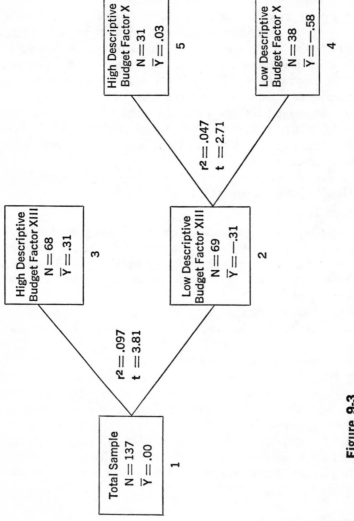

Figure 9-3
Descriptive Position Factor III:
Job-Related Tension

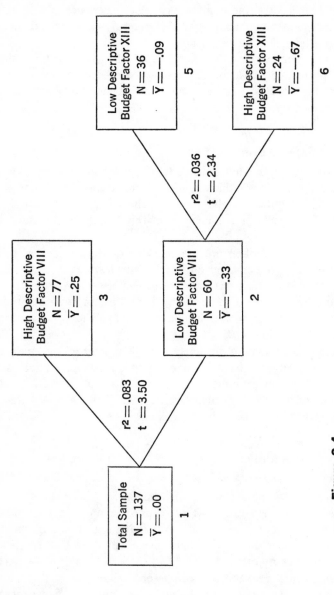

Figure 9-4
Descriptive Position Factor IV:
Job-Related Self-Actualization

ment and promotion and personal growth and development. The results of our analysis of this factor are presented in Figure 9-4.

Managers who are more influential in budget setting (Group 3) experience higher job-related self-actualization. Those who are relatively less influential in budget-setting (Group 2) experience less job-related self-actualization. Also, those managers who experience higher time demands because of a budgeting system (Group 6) experience the least amount of job-related self-actualization.

These results suggest that the extent to which managers think they experience job-related self-actualization may be related to how influential they are in budget setting and what time demands they experience because of budgeting.

Descriptive Position Factor V:
Job-Related Satisfaction

This factor is a job-related social interaction factor: managers with higher scores on this factor think that their management positions give them more opportunities to give help to others and to develop close friendships. The results of our analysis of this factor are presented in Figure 9-5.

Managers who more often are reminded of the importance of their operating budgets and evaluated on their ability to meet these budgets (Group 2) think that their positions give them fewer opportunities to give help to others and to develop close friendships, and this is particularly true of those managers who also have a relatively less positive view of budgeting (Group 4).

Even though the results of our analysis of this factor are not particularly strong, they suggest that the extent to which managers think their positions give them opportunities for meaningful social interaction with others may be related to how often they are reminded of the importance of their budgets and whether they are evaluated on their ability to meet their budgets.

Normative Position Factor I:
Job-Related Influence

This factor reflects the extent to which managers think their management positions should give them authority, prestige, and opportunities to participate in goal setting. Managers who have higher scores on this factor think that their positions should give them these characteristics and opportunities more often.

As presented in Figure 9-6, the results of our analysis of this factor suggest that managers who tend to be more influential in budget setting (Group 3) think their management positions should give them these characteristics and opportunities more often than those who are rela-

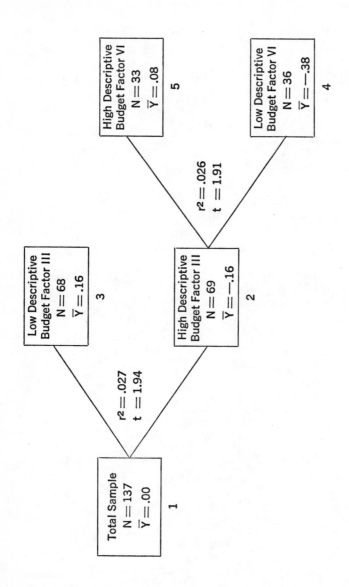

Figure 9-5
Descriptive Position Factor V:
Job-Related Satisfaction

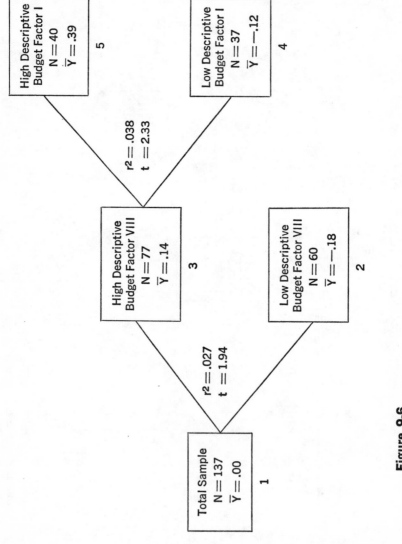

Figure 9-6
Normative Position Factor I:
Job-Related Influence

tively less influential in this process (Group 2). Moreover, of the managers who are less influential in budget setting, those who use the budget as an evaluative device more often (Group 5) think that their positions should give them these characteristics and opportunities more often than those who use the budget as an evaluative device less often.

The results of our analysis of this factor are not particularly strong. However, these results suggest that managers' attitudes about how influential they should be because of their position may be related to how influential they are in budget setting and whether they use the budget as an evaluative device.

Normative Position Factor II:
Job-Related Ambiguity and Self-Actualization

Managers with higher scores on this factor think that they should experience job-related ambiguity less often; that is, they think that they should know when they are doing well more often, should have opportunities more often to do the things they are best at, should know more often what is expected of them, and should be more clear about the tasks they are to perform.

As presented in Figure 9-7, our analysis of this factor indicates that managers who express their opinions on budget matters more often (Group 3) also think that they should experience less job-related ambiguity. Of the managers who tend to express their opinions on budget matters less often (Group 2), those who are less often shown comparisons of actual and budgeted results for other units and who pay more attention to details, personally investigate variances, and work with their subordinates in preparing the budget for their units think that they should experience less job-related ambiguity (Group 6).

These results suggest that the extent to which managers think they should experience job-related ambiguity may be related to the extent to which they are expressive about budgeting and perform various budget-oriented activities.

Normative Position Factor III:
Job-Related Tension

Managers who have higher scores on this factor think that their management positions should more often conflict with their family life and that their positions should more often give them more to do than they are best at. Figure 9-8 presents the results of our analysis of this factor.

Managers who more often are shown comparisons of actual and budgeted performance for other units (Group 3) think that they should experience higher job-related tension. Of the managers who less often are shown comparative reports for other units (Group 2), those whose

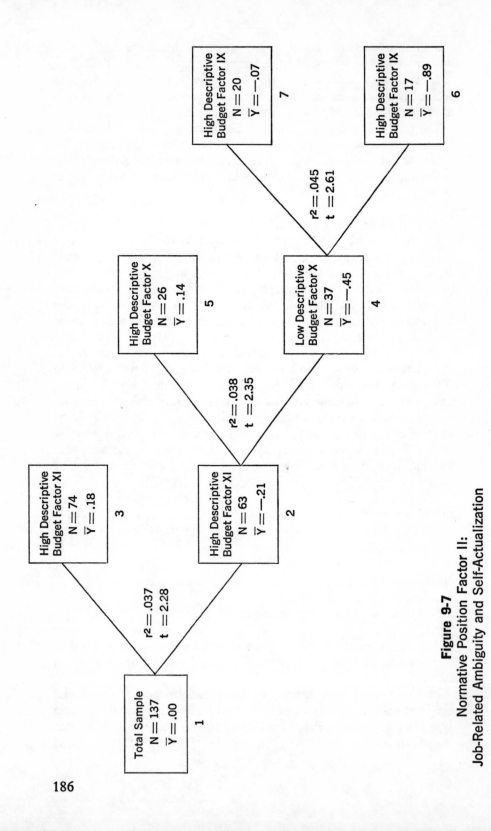

Figure 9-7
Normative Position Factor II:
Job-Related Ambiguity and Self-Actualization

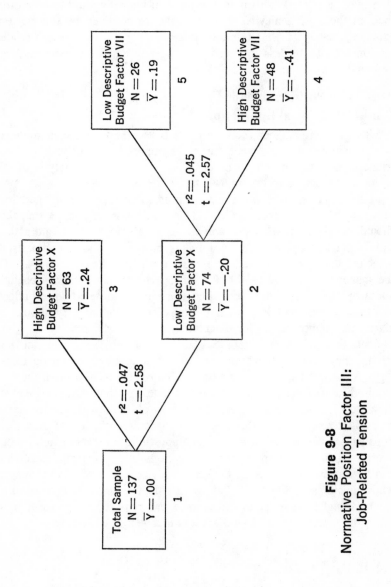

Figure 9-8
Normative Position Factor III:
Job-Related Tension

methods of achieving budget targets are accepted more often by their superiors and subordinates (Group 4) think they should experience less job-related tension than those whose methods are accepted by these persons less often (Group 5).

These results suggest that managers' attitudes about job-related tension may be related to their involvement in budgeting and to how often their methods of achieving their budgets are accepted by others. For example, managers who think they should experience less job-related tension tend to be less involved in budgeting and have their methods accepted more often.

Normative Position Factor IV: Job-Related Social Interaction

Managers with higher scores on this factor think that their management positions should give them more opportunities to develop close friendships and give help to others. The results of our analysis of this factor are presented in Figure 9-9.

Managers who more often are required to perform various activities brought about by budget variances (Group 2) less often think that they should be given more opportunities for meaningful social interaction. This is particularly true for those managers who are shown comparisons of actual and budgeted results for other units less often (Group 4). Of the managers who are required to engage in certain activities brought about by budget variances less often (Group 3), those who use budgets as evaluative devices less often (Group 7) think that they should be given more opportunities for meaningful social interaction.

Even though the results of our analysis of this factor are not very strong, they suggest that managers' attitudes about experiencing meaningful job-related social interaction may be related to how often they are required to perform various budget-oriented activities, how involved they are in the budgeting process, and how often they use the budget as an evaluative device. For example, managers who think that their positions should provide them with more opportunities for meaningful social interaction are required to perform various budget-oriented behaviors and to use the budget as an evaluative device less often than managers who think their positions should provide them with fewer opportunities for meaningful social interaction, who are required to perform these behaviors more often, and who are less involved in budgeting.

Normative Position Factor V: Job-Related Tension

Managers with higher scores on this factor think their position should give them more to do than they can accomplish within a working day. Figure 9-10 presents the results of our analysis of this factor.

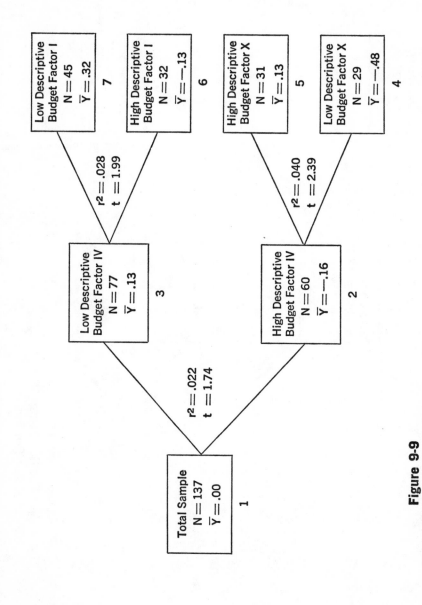

Figure 9-9
Normative Position Factor IV:
Job-Related Social Interaction

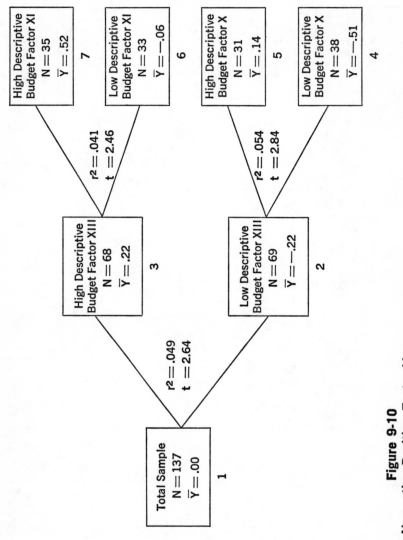

Figure 9-10
Normative Position Factor V:
Job-Related Tension

Managers who less often are able to spend as much time as they would like preparing the budget for their units (Group 3) think they should experience more job-related tension. This is particularly true for those managers who, in addition, are more expressive about budgeting. Managers who more often are able to spend as much time as they would like preparing the budgets for their units and who are less often shown comparisons of actual and budgeted results for other units (Group 4) think that they should experience less job-related tension.

These results suggest that managers' attitudes about job-related tension may be related to the time pressures they experience because of budgeting, how expressive they are about budgeting, and how involved they are in budgeting.

Discussion

Altogether, the results of our analysis of the relationships between the descriptive measures of managers' budget-oriented behavior and the descriptive and normative measures of managers' attitudes about their positions can be characterized as being both encouraging and disappointing. They are encouraging in that they reveal that some significant relationships exist between measures of this behavior, combinations of these measures, and measures of these attitudes. They also are encouraging in that even though they reveal that some relationships may not be significant, they generally are in the expected direction. These results are somewhat disappointing in that we had hoped that these measures of budget-oriented behavior and combinations of them would have accounted for a more substantial proportion of the variance on the measures of their attitudes about their positions. The budget-oriented behavior measures which are the most important predictors of the position measures account for between 2 and 10 percent, or an average of about 5 percent, of the total variance on these position measures. Moreover, combinations of these budget-oriented behavior measures account for between 5 and 22 percent, or an average of about 11 percent, of the total variance of these position measures.

Although the overall predictive power of these budget-oriented behavior measures is lower than we had hoped for, many of the predictions are above the chance level, and it becomes necessary for us to examine those relationships which appear to be significant and to try to arrive at an understanding of their underlying nature. The descriptive budget factors which are the most important predictors of the descriptive position factors account for between 3 and 10 percent, or an average of about 7 percent, of the total variance on these position factors. The most significant relationships exist between descriptive budget factors XIII, VIII, and VI and descriptive position factors III, IV, and II, respectively. These relationships suggest that how often managers tend to experience job-related tension may be related to how often they tend to experience time pressure from budgeting, that how often they tend to experience job-related self-actualization may be related to how often they tend to be influential in budgeting, and that how often they tend to experience job-related ambiguity may be related to how often they tend to have positive attitudes about the usefulness of budgeting.

These results have a considerable amount of face validity. For example, we might expect that managers who tend to experience more time pressure from budgeting also would tend to experience more job-related tension. Not being able to spend as much time as they would like preparing their operating budgets and spending time outside of normal working hours preparing their budgets may represent potential sources of managers' job-related tension. Moreover, it is not too surprising to find that managers who have been consulted about special factors they would like to have included in their operating budgets, whose budgets include changes they have suggested, and whose budgets are not finalized until they are satisfied with them might be expected to think that they are less often forced to do things that are against their better judgment and that they are more often given opportunities for advancement and promotion and for personal growth and development. Finally, it is not too surprising to find that managers who think that the budget enables them to be more flexible and innovative, to keep track of their success as managers, and to be better managers might be expected to think that they are more clear about the tasks they must perform, that they know when they are doing well, and that they know when something is wanted or expected of them.

Even those relationships which are less significant tend to be in the expected direction and also have a considerable amount of face validity. For example, the relationship between descriptive budget factor I and descriptive position factor I reveals that how often managers tend to have job-related influence may be related to how often they use budgets as evaluative devices. This suggests that managers who use the budget to evaluate their subordinates and whose superiors use it to evaluate them think that they get more prestige, authority, and responsibility from their management positions. The relationship between descriptive budget factor III and descriptive position factor V reveals that how often managers engage in meaningful social interaction may be related to the extent to which budget-oriented behavior is evaluation-oriented. For example, managers who are reminded of the importance of the budget and evaluated on their ability to meet the budget less often think that they more often tend to engage in meaningful social interaction.

Combinations of the descriptive budget factors account for between 5 and 14 percent, or an average of about 11 percent, of the total variance on the descriptive position factors. The most significant combination of these budget factors is on descriptive position factor III. This suggests that how much job-related tension managers experience may be related not only to how much time pressure they experience from budgeting, but also to how involved they are in the budgeting process. Being more involved in budgeting also may represent a potential source of job-related tension. A manager who is more involved in budgeting may find that his position gives him more to do than he can do his best at and more than he can accomplish in a working day, and he may find that this involvement conflicts with his family life.

Those descriptive budget factors which are the most important predictors of the normative position factors account for between 2 and 5 percent, or an average of about 4 percent, of the total variance of these position factors. The most significant relationships exist between descriptive budget factors XIII and X and normative position factors V and III, respectively. These relationships suggest that managers' attitudes about how often they think they should experience job-related tension may be related to how much time pressure they experience from budgeting and how involved they are in the budgeting process.

Combinations of descriptive budget factors account for between 6 and 15 percent, or an average of about 11 percent, of the total variance on the normative budget factor V. This suggests that managers' attitudes about how much job-related tension they think they should experience may be related to how much time pressure they experience from budgeting, how expressive they are about budgeting, and how involved they are in the budgeting process.

In general, the descriptive budget factors are relatively poor predictors of the normative position factors. The only possible exceptions are the relationships between these budget factors and normative position factors V and III. These factors reflect managers' attitudes about the extent to which they think their positions should conflict with their family life, give them more to do than they can do their best at, give them more to do than they can accomplish within a working day, and force them to do things that are against their better judgment. The descriptive budget factors which are the most important predictors of these two position factors reflect the amount of time pressure a manager experiences from budgeting, how expressive he is about budgeting, how involved he is in the budgeting process, and the extent to which his methods tend to be accepted by others. The relationships between various descriptive budget factors and the other normative position factors are less significant.

Chapter 10

Analysis of Relationships Between Normative Measures of Managers' Budget-Oriented Behavior and Measures of Managers' Attitudes About Their Positions

In this chapter we report the results of our analysis of the relationships between the normative measures of managers' budget-oriented behavior described in Chapter 4 and the descriptive and normative measures of managers' attitudes about their positions described in Chapter 8. The next section reports the results of our analysis of these relationships.

These results suggest that how often managers think that they engage in meaningful social interaction may be related to how often they think that they should be influential in budgeting and that how often managers tend to experience job-related ambiguity may be related to how often they think that their methods of achieving their budgets should be accepted by others. The results also suggest that managers' attitudes about experiencing job-related ambiguity may be related to their attitudes about being influential in budgeting, that their attitudes about having job-related influence may be related to their attitudes about the usefulness of budgeting, and that their attitudes about experiencing job-related tension may be related to their attitudes about going to and working with their superiors. Finally, the results suggest that managers' attitudes about experiencing meaningful job-related social interaction may be related to their attitudes about being expressive about budgeting.

The chapter concludes with a brief discussion of some of the implications of our findings.

Analysis

Because we derived both the normative budget factors and the normative and descriptive position factors from our empirical data, we could not specify a priori what the nature of the relationships between these two sets of measures might be. Accordingly, we again used the Automatic Interaction Detector (AID) to determine which budget factors and combinations of them would produce the greatest discrimination in the group means of the position factor scores. The AID program requires that the independent or predictor variables be categorical. We recoded the normative budget factors into dichotomous high and low categories. We calculated an overall sample median for each budget factor and then assigned managers with factor scores above this median to the "high" category and managers with factor scores below this median to the "low" category.

The results of our analysis of each factor will be presented in the form of a "tree diagram" showing the various splits made by the budget factors and the resulting subgroups which are brought about by combinations of these factors. The size, N, and the average factor score, $\overline{Y}$, are reported for each subgroup. Also, the r^2 and t-value that occasion each split are entered at the vertex of the split. Finally, Appendix A, which presents an abbreviated dictionary of variables, provides the reader with a quick reference for the variables presented in the tables that follow.

Descriptive Position Factor I:
Job-Related Influence

Managers who have higher scores on this factor think that their management positions give them more prestige and authority. The results of our analysis of this factor are presented in Figure 10-1.

Managers who think that they should have more positive attitudes about budgeting (Group 3) think that their positions give them more prestige and authority. Managers who think that they should have less positive attitudes about budgeting (Group 2) think that these characteristics are less often given to them by their positions. This is particularly true of those managers who think they should less often find it necessary to charge some activities to other accounts or stop activities in their unit when budgeted funds have been used up (Group 4).

These results suggest that how much job-related influence managers think they get from their management positions may be related to their attitudes about the usefulness of budgeting and about budget-oriented coping behavior.

Descriptive Position Factor II:
Job-Related Ambiguity

This factor reflects how clear managers are about their jobs. Managers with higher scores on this factor experience less job-related ambiguity.

As presented in Figure 10-2, the results of our analysis reveal that managers who think their methods of achieving budgeted performance should be accepted more often by their subordinates and superiors

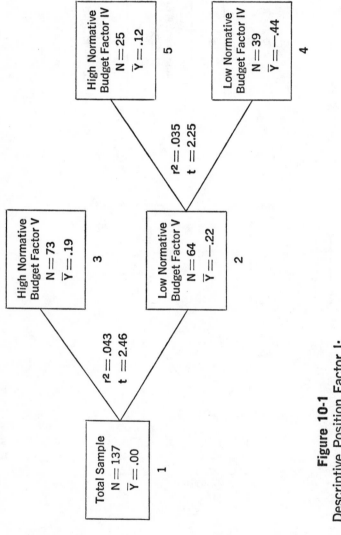

Figure 10-1
Descriptive Position Factor I:
Job-Related Influence

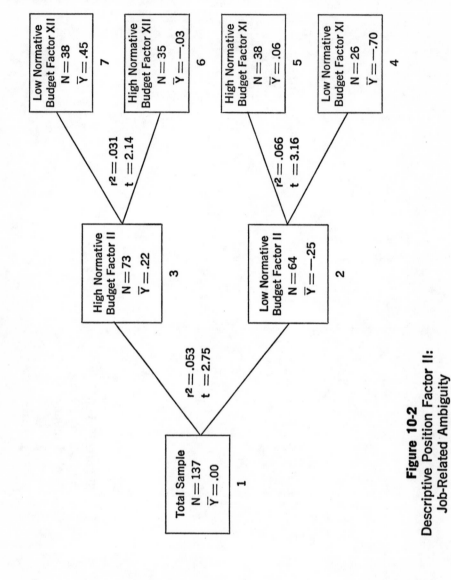

Figure 10-2
Descriptive Position Factor II:
Job-Related Ambiguity

(Group 3) experience less job-related ambiguity. This is particularly true for those managers who, in addition, think they should have less difficulty meeting their operating budgets (Group 7). Managers who think that their methods should be accepted less often, that they should be reminded of the importance of meeting the budget for their units less often, and that their superiors should less often express dissatisfaction to them when their budgets have not been met (Group 4) experience the most job-related ambiguity.

These results suggest that how much job-related ambiguity managers experience may be related to their attitudes about the acceptability of their methods for achieving their budgets and the use of the budget as an evaluative device. Managers who think that their methods should be accepted more often are more clear about the tasks they must perform, and this is particularly true for those managers who also think that they should have less difficulty meeting their budgets. Managers who think that their methods should be accepted less often are less clear about the tasks they must perform, and this is true for those managers who also think that the budget should less often be used as an evaluative device.

Descriptive Position Factor III:
Job-Related Tension

Managers who experience more job-related tension have higher scores on this factor. The results of our analysis are presented in Figure 10-3.

Managers who think they should more often engage in various budget-oriented coping behaviors (Group 3) experience more job-related tension. This is particularly true for managers who, in addition, have more positive attitudes about the budget (Group 7). Managers who think they should engage in these coping behaviors less often (Group 2) experience less job-related tension, and those managers who also think that they should go to and work with their superiors less often (Group 4) experience the least amount of job-related tension.

These results suggest that the extent to which managers experience job-related tension may be related to their attitudes about budget-oriented coping behavior, about the usefulness of budgeting, and about working with and going to their superiors. Managers who think they should engage in coping behaviors more often and have more positive attitudes about budgeting are subject to more job-related tension than those who think they should engage in coping behaviors less often and go to and work with their superiors less often.

Descriptive Position Factor IV:
Job-Related Self-Actualization

Managers who have higher scores on this factor experience more

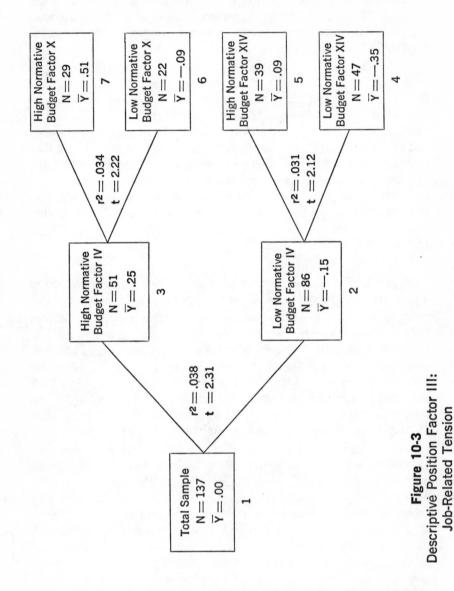

Figure 10-3
Descriptive Position Factor III:
Job-Related Tension

job-related self-actualization. As presented in Figure 10-4, the results of our analysis of this factor are not particularly strong.

Managers who think that they more often should be reminded of the importance of meeting their operating budgets and who think that their superiors should express dissatisfaction more often (Group 3) experience more job-related self-actualization. Those managers who think that these events should occur less often (Group 2) experience less self-actualization. Moreover, of the managers who think these events should occur less often, those who have less positive attitudes about budgeting (Group 4) experience less self-actualization.

These results suggest that the extent to which managers experience self-actualization because of their management positions may be somewhat related to their attitudes about using the budget as an evaluative device and about the usefulness of budgeting.

Descriptive Position Factor V:
Job-Related Satisfaction

Managers who have higher scores on this factor tend to experience more meaningful job-related social interaction. The results of our analysis of this factor are presented in Figure 10-5.

Managers who think that they should have a more influential role in the budgeting process (Group 3) experience more meaningful social interaction. Managers who think they should have a less influential role in the budgeting process and should less often take an active, expressive role in this process (Group 4) experience the least amount of meaningful social interaction.

These results suggest that the extent to which managers think that their management positions give them opportunities for meaningful social interaction may be related to their attitudes about being influential and expressive about budgeting. Managers who think that they should be more influential in budgeting are those who think that they experience more meaningful social interactions in their management positions.

Normative Position Factor I:
Job-Related Influence

Managers who have higher scores on this factor think that their management positions should give them more authority, prestige and opportunity to participate in goal setting. The results of our analysis of this factor are presented in Figure 10-6.

Managers who have more positive attitudes about budgeting (Group 3) think that more authority, prestige, and opportunity to participate should be associated with their positions. Of the managers who have less positive attitudes about budgeting (Group 2), those who also think that they should be involved in budgeting less often (Group 4)

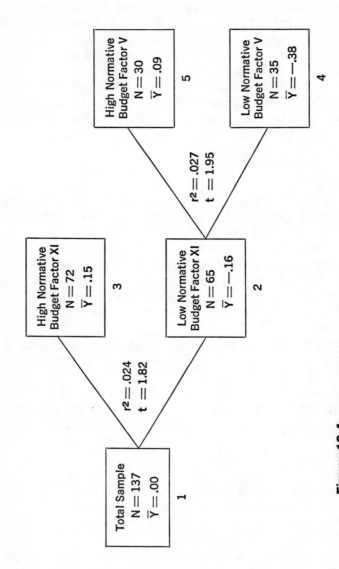

Figure 10-4
Descriptive Position Factor IV:
Job-Related Self-Actualization

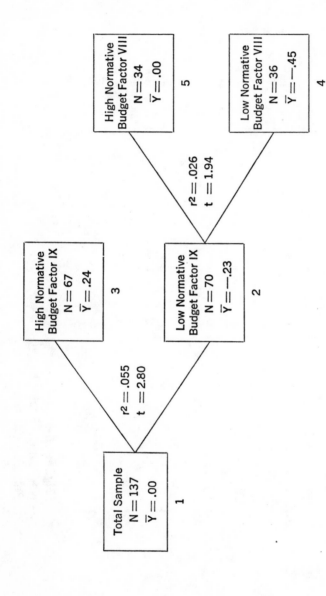

Figure 10-5
Descriptive Position Factor V:
Job-Related Satisfaction

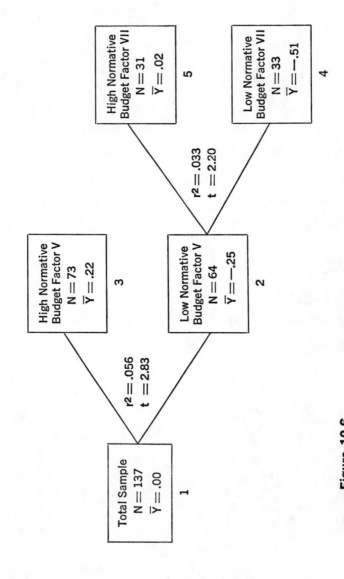

Figure 10-6
Normative Position Factor I:
Job-Related Influence

204

think that these attributes should be associated with their positions less often.

These results suggest that managers' attitudes about their job-related influence may be related to their attitudes about the usefulness of budgeting and about their involvement in budgeting.

Normative Position Factor II:
Job-Related Ambiguity and Self-Actualization

Managers who have higher scores on this factor think that they should experience less job-related ambiguity. The results of our analysis of this factor are presented in Figure 10-7.

Managers who think they should be more influential in the budgeting process (Group 3) think they should experience less job-related ambiguity. Of the managers who think they should be less influential in budgeting (Group 2), those who think they should be reminded of the importance of meeting the budget and their superiors should express dissatisfaction to them less often (Group 5) think they should experience more job-related ambiguity, and those who, in addition, think the budget should less often enable them to be innovative and flexible (Group 6) think that they should experience more job-related ambiguity.

These results suggest that managers' attitudes about the amount of job-related ambiguity they think they should experience because of their management positions may be related to their attitudes about how often they think they should be influential in budgeting, be reminded of the importance of their budgets, and have positive attitudes about the usefulness of budgeting.

Normative Position Factor III:
Job-Related Tension

Managers with higher scores on this factor think they should experience more job-related tension.

As presented in Figure 10-8, the results of our analysis of this factor reveal that those managers who think they should go to and work with their superiors more often (Group 3) think they should experience more job-related tension, and this is particularly true of those managers who, in addition, think they should more often engage in various budget-oriented coping behaviors (Group 7). Of the managers who think they should engage in these activities less often (Group 6), those who think they should more often have difficulty meeting their budgets (Group 9) think they should experience more job-related tension than those who think they should less often have difficulty meeting their budgets (Group 8). Of the managers who think they should go to and work with their superiors less often (Group 2), those who think their methods of reaching their budgets should more often be accepted by their

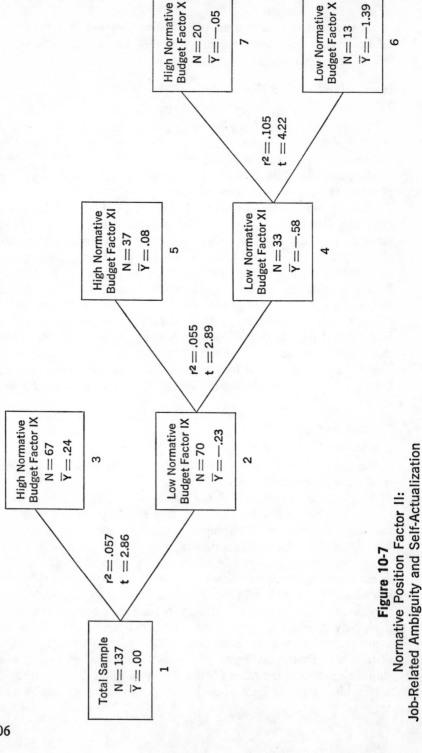

Figure 10-7
Normative Position Factor II:
Job-Related Ambiguity and Self-Actualization

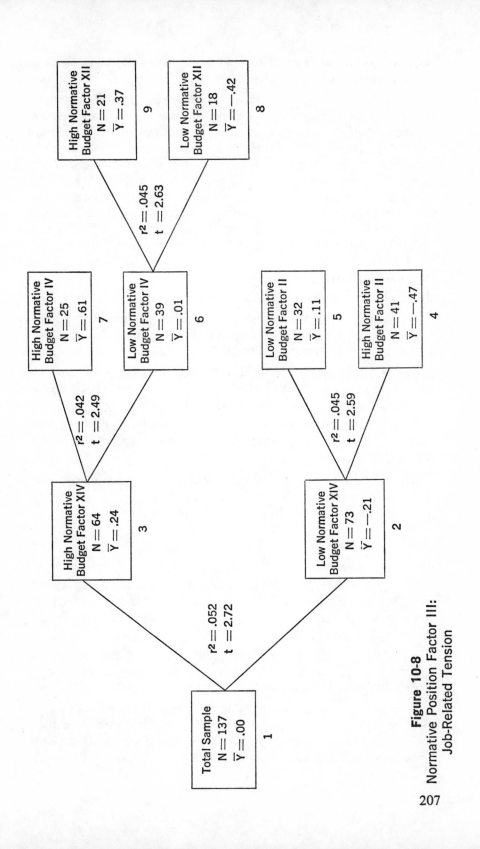

Figure 10-8
Normative Position Factor III:
Job-Related Tension

207

subordinates and superiors (Group 4) think they should experience less job-related tension.

These results suggest that managers' attitudes about the extent to which they think they should experience job-related tension may be related to their attitudes about interacting with their superiors, performing various budget-oriented coping behaviors, having difficulty meeting their budgets, and having their methods for achieving their budgets accepted by others. For example, managers who think they should interact with their superiors and should engage in various coping behaviors think they should experience more job-related tension than those who think they should less often interact with their superiors and should more often have their methods accepted by others.

Normative Position Factor IV:
Job-Related Social Interaction

Managers who have higher scores on this factor think they should have more opportunity for meaningful social interaction. The results of our analysis of this factor are presented in Figure 10-9.

The only normative budget factor that explains most of the variance on this factor is the extent to which managers think they should take a more active role in the budgeting process.

Managers who think they should more often express their opinions on budget matters (Group 3) think they should have more opportunity for social interaction.

These results suggest that managers' attitudes about having opportunities for meaningful social interaction because of their positions may be related to their attitudes about being expressive about budgeting.

Normative Position Factor V:
Job-Related Tension

Managers who have higher scores on this factor think they should experience more job-related tension, relative to managers who have lower scores on this factor. The results of our analysis of this factor are presented in Figure 10-10.

The only normative budget factor which explains differences on this factor reflects the extent to which managers think they should perform various budget-oriented coping behaviors.

Managers who think they should more often perform various budget-oriented coping behaviors (Group 3) think they should experience more job-related tension relative to those who think they should perform these activities less often (Group 2).

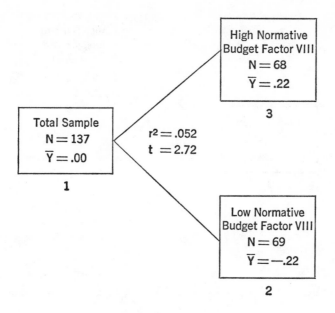

Figure 10-9
Normative Position Factor IV:
Job-Related Social Interaction

Discussion

The results of our analysis of the relationships between the normative measures of managers' budget-oriented behavior and the descriptive and normative measures of managers' attitudes about their positions also can be characterized as being both encouraging and disappointing. They are encouraging in that they reveal that some significant relationships exist between these measures of this behavior, combinations of these measures, and measures of these attitudes. However, they are somewhat disappointing in that we had hoped that these measures of budget-oriented behavior and combinations of them would have accounted for a more substantial proportion of the variance on the measures of their attitudes about their positions.

The normative budget factors which are the most important predictors of the descriptive position factors account for between 2 and 6 percent, or an average of about 5 percent, of the total variance on these position factors. The most significant relationships exist between normative budget factors IX and II and descriptive position factors V and II,

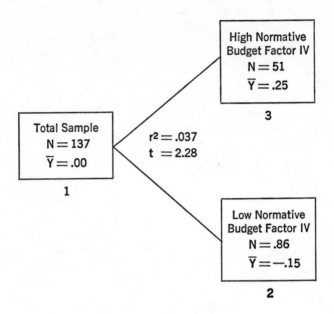

Figure 10-10
Normative Position Factor V:
Job-Related Tension

respectively. These relationships suggest that how often managers tend to think they should engage in meaningful social interaction may be related to how often they think they should be influential in budgeting and that how often managers experience job-related ambiguity may be related to how often they think their methods of achieving their budgets should be accepted by others.

Combinations of normative budget factors account for between 5 and 15 percent, or an average of about 9 percent, of the total variance on the descriptive position factors. The most significant combination of these budget factors is on normative position factor II. This suggests that how much job-related ambiguity managers experience may be related to managers' attitudes about the acceptability of their methods, the amount of difficulty they have meeting their budgets, and the use of budgets as evaluative devices.

With the exception of the relationships between normative budget factors IX and II and descriptive position factors V and II, respectively, the normative budget factors are relatively poor predictors of the descriptive position factors. We note, however, that the general direction of the predicted relationships is as we might expect. For example, the relationship between normative budget factor V and descriptive position factor I suggests that how much job-related influence managers get from their management positions may be related somewhat to their attitudes about the usefulness of budgeting. Similarly, the relationships between normative budget factors IV, X and XIV and descriptive position factor III suggest that how much job-related tension managers experience may be related to their attitudes about their performing various budget-oriented coping behaviors, the usefulness of budgeting, and their going to and working with their superiors.

Those normative budget factors which are the most important predictors of the normative position factors account for between 4 and 6 percent, or an average of about 5 percent, of the total variance on these position factors. The most significant relationships exist between normative budget factors IX, V, XIV and VIII, and relationships exist between normative budget factors IX, V, XIV and VIII and normative position factors II, I, III and IV, respectively. These relationships suggest that managers' attitudes about experiencing job-related ambiguity may be related to their attitudes about being influential in budgeting, that their attitudes about having job-related influence may be related to their attitudes about the usefulness of budgeting, that their attitudes about experiencing job-related tension may be related to their attitudes about going to and working with their superiors, and that their attitudes about experiencing meaningful job-related social interaction may be related to their attitudes about being expressive about budgeting.

Combinations of the normative budget factors account for between 4 and 22 percent, or an average of about 12 percent, of the total variance on these position factors. The most significant combinations of these budget factors exist on normative position factors II and III. These results suggest that managers' attitudes about job-related ambiguity may be related not only to their attitudes about being influential in budgeting, but also to their attitudes about the use of the budget as an evaluative device and the general usefulness of the budget. Similarly, they suggest that managers' attitudes about job-related tension may be related to their attitudes about going to and working with superiors and also to their attitudes about performing various coping behaviors, having difficulty meeting their budgets, and having their methods accepted by others.

Chapter 11

Implications, Limitations and Extensions
of the Research

In designing and redesigning budgeting systems, management accountants and others are often faced with the problem of choosing from among alternative amounts and forms of participation on the part of operating managers in the budget-setting process. In making these choices, it would be naive for these individuals to think that more participation is always to be preferred to less or vice versa. Rather, the choice of how much participation is appropriate for a given budgeting situation should be made on the basis of an evaluation of the consequences associated with alternative amounts and forms of participation. This choice will depend on the weights assigned to these consequences as well as on the likelihood that these consequences will obtain under each alternative. Because these weights and likelihoods are likely to vary from one situation to another, the choice of the appropriate amount and form of participation also is likely to vary.

It would seem safe to appraise as incomplete our present knowledge of the consequences associated with alternative amounts and forms of participation. We cannot attribute the incompleteness of our knowledge to a lack of concern; there are several studies and discussions that focus on these consequences. However, in part we can attribute this incompleteness to the manner in which these consequences have customarily been approached. In general, there has not been any systematic attempt to link a company's use of participative budgeting with the behavior of its managers and ultimately with any consequences or effects which may be associated with that behavior.

The previous chapters have reported the results of our exploratory investigation of some effects of participative budgeting on managerial behavior. This investigation included the development of a theoretical model that indicates some key variables and relationships among them that may be important in linking a company's use of participative budgeting with the behavior of its managers and with some effects which may be associated with that behavior (Chapter 2). It also included an empirical study designed to obtain measures of some of the variables contained in the model and to determine what gross relationships may exist among them (Chapter 3-10). Thus, our approach to investigating these effects was neither strictly theoretical nor purely empirical. Rather, we endeavored to bring to bear both theory and empirical data to provide insights into the nature and extent of these effects.

In this final chapter we discuss some implications, limitations and extensions of our research. In the first section we discuss the implications of our research for the development of a behavioral approach to participative budgeting. Although the formulation of prescriptions for practice was not a major stimulus for our research, some potential implications for practice do follow from it that seem to us to have special relevance for management accountants and others. In the second section we discuss some limitations and extensions of the research.

A Behavioral Approach to Participative Budgeting

Throughout this monograph, we have emphasized the importance of describing budgeting in behavioral terms. Budgeting usually is viewed as a basic financial planning and control procedure which encompasses (1) the preparation and adoption of a detailed operating plan, (2) the comparison of the actual results of operations with those set forth in the plan and (3) an analysis and evaluation of the reasons for deviations from the plan. Even though the objective of this procedure is to successfully influence managerial behavior — how managers plan, coordinate and control the activities of the company — there have been few, if any, attempts to describe how budgeting actually influences this behavior. Most budgeting and managerial accounting textbooks describe budgeting in terms of the set of technical methods and procedures budgeting usually encompasses. Similarly, many companies refer to these methods and procedures in describing their use of budgeting in procedure manuals, position and job descriptions, flow charts, memoranda and so forth. But how do these methods and procedures influence managerial behavior? What is the model or mechanism through which or by which budgeting is linked with this behavior?

Managers' Budget-Oriented Behavior

We have proposed "managers' budget-oriented behavior" as a key concept for describing budgeting in behavioral terms. Rather than view budgeting as a formal procedure and focus on the methods and techniques used by a company to implement this procedure, we have viewed budgeting as a behavior process and have focused on the actions and interactions that are brought about by a company's use of this process.

214

Many actions and interactions which occur as part of a manager's normal routine can be associated primarily, if not solely, with a company's use of budgeting. We have used the term "managers' budget-oriented behavior" to refer to these actions and interactions and have argued that from this concept stems a new view of budgeting, a fuller appreciation of its inherent structure, and a broader conception of its role and likely effects.

The primary focus of our theoretical model was on managers' budget-oriented behavior and the process through which it is defined. In order to describe how this behavior is brought about by a company's use of budgeting, we used a role model (Kahn *et al.*, 1964; Katz and Kahn, 1966; McGrath, 1966) to locate each manager within the total set of ongoing relationships and behaviors that comprise an organization. We viewed each manager as occupying a different position in the company, as performing the activities, and as engaging in the relationships associated with that position. We viewed a company's use of budgeting as, in effect, superimposing a set of potential budget-oriented behaviors on its management positions, and these behaviors as being reflected in the content of some of the activities and relationships associated with these positions.

A role episode model (Kahn *et al.*, 1964; Katz and Kahn, 1966) then was used to describe how these budget-oriented activities and relationships may be defined for a given manager. We viewed the actual budget-oriented behavior of a manager who occupies a given position as being a complex outcome of a definitional process between this manager and the managers who occupy other related positions. These Other Managers, including a manager's superiors, peers, subordinates and others, have expectations about what a manager should or should not do, observe and evaluate his actual performance, and exert pressure on him to influence him so that his actual performance will be congruent with their expectations. The manager experiences this pressure and acts or responds, showing some combination of compliance and noncompliance with the expectations of these Other Managers. The Other Managers again observe and evaluate the manager's performance, and the extent to which his performance conforms to the expectations they hold for him at one point in time will affect the state of those expectations at the next moment.

A major part of our empirical research was aimed at measuring managers' budget-oriented behavior and at identifying different dimensions of this behavior. To obtain measures of this behavior, we developed a set of 44 items which were representative of a broad range of actions, interactions and events which might be brought about by a company's use of budgeting. For each item, managers were asked three questions: (a) How frequently does it take place? (b) How frequently should it take place? (c) How important is it to me? Managers' responses to these questions for each item were used as different measures of their budget-oriented behavior. For example, managers' responses to the first question were used as *descriptive* measures of this behavior, their responses to the second question were used as *normative* measures of this behavior, and their responses to the third question were used as *evaluative* measures of this behavior.

Our analysis of the descriptive and normative measures of this behavior led us to posit the existence of several summary dimensions. For example, our analysis of the descriptive measures indicated that the extent to which managers perform budget-oriented activities and engage in budget-related interactions could be described along 13 separable dimensions. These dimensions were concerned with the extent to which managers tend to use the budget as an evaluative device, to perform various required activities because of budget variances, to engage in budget-related interactions with their superiors, subordinates and others, to be personally involved in budgeting, and so forth.

Similarly, our analysis of the normative measures indicated that the extent to which managers think they should perform these activities and engage in these interactions could be described along 14 dimensions. These dimensions were concerned with the extent to which managers tend to think they should perform various required activities because of budget variances, use the budget to evaluate their subordinates, take an influential role in budgeting, and so forth.

These descriptive and normative dimensions of managers' budget-oriented behavior provided us with considerable insight into the nature of this behavior. First, these dimensions provided us with an economical yet reasonably complete description of this behavior. They allowed us to focus on 13 and 14 summary dimensions while still preserving much of the variance in the original set of 44 items. Second, these dimensions provided us with new, fundamental and meaningful ways of describing this behavior. Our analysis was designed to seek out new dimensions of this behavior, and we found that the dimensions identified could be interpreted in natural and useful ways. Third, these dimensions revealed that this behavior may be very diverse and diffuse. What was striking about the dimensions identified was the extent to which they differed in both their scope and content. Fourth, these dimensions varied in the extent to which they were useful for explaining differences in this behavior. Where some dimensions accounted for more than 10 percent of the total variance, others accounted for less than 6 percent of this variance. Finally, these dimensions provided us with a set of summary measures of this behavior which we could use as a basis for our analysis of what variables may affect this behavior as well as for our analysis of what attitudinal effects may be associated with this behavior. These summary measures also had the advantages of being normally distributed and of being uncorrelated.

Four major areas of practical considerations are indicated by the concept of managers' budget-oriented behavior. The first concerns the basic defining characteristics of budgeting. In designing and redesigning budgeting systems, we think that while management accountants and others should continue to ask themselves the old questions of what is budgeting and wherein lies its structure, they should refuse to be satisfied with old answers to these questions. In the past, all too often the answers to these questions have been given in terms of the technical methods and procedures that budgeting typically encompasses. How many of these individuals when asked to describe a company's use of budgeting have done so by referring to the company's budget and procedure manuals, job descriptions, organization and flow charts, budget memoranda, and so forth?

Our research argues that answers to the questions of what is budgeting and wherein lies its structure should not be given only in terms of these formal representations of budgeting. At best, these documents provide a representation of how budgeting was intended to be used by managers rather than a description of how they, in fact, use budgeting. Instead, our research argues that answers to these questions should be given in terms of the behavior of managers that is brought about by budgeting. In short, a company's use of budgeting results in and is reflected in a pattern of managerial behavior that would not otherwise have occurred; it is in terms of this behavior that we think a company's use of budgeting should be described.

It is probably safe to say that many companies do not, in fact, really know what managerial behavior is brought about by their use of budgeting. On the basis of our research, we believe we are justified in emphasizing to management accountants and others the importance of focusing on this behavior and the desirability of obtaining data about this behavior. As part of our research, we developed a way of measuring this behavior. If companies actually used these methods to collect data about the budget-oriented behavior of their managers, it could be a very interesting and revealing experience. For example, if an analysis of these data indicated that relatively few inconsistencies and discrepancies exist between how managers use budgeting and how the company expects them to use budgeting, this would provide some evidence that a company's policies are being implemented effectively. However, if this analysis indicated that considerable discrepancies exist between how they use budgeting and how they are expected to use it, this would not necessarily mean that the company should change its policies. Rather, it might suggest that the company should consider whether its current policies and expectations are appropriate but not being implemented effectively or whether they are in need of reformulation. Thus, we think that obtaining systematic information about managers' budget-oriented behavior may constitute an essential step in gaining some insight into the effectiveness of a company's use of budgeting.

The second major area of practical consideration concerns the role of the formal documents of budgeting as a way of communicating the company's expectations about managers' budget-oriented behavior. A company's budget and procedure manuals, job descriptions, organization and flow charts, budget memoranda and so forth are usually prepared for the purpose of documenting its use of budgeting. However, these documents also represent repositories of the company's expectations about the budget-oriented behavior of its managers; they describe in a shorthand way the budget-oriented activities and relationships operating managers are expected to perform and engage in.

We think that companies may be able to improve the overall effectiveness of their use of budgeting simply by focusing greater attention on the use of these documents to communicate their expectations about managers' budget-oriented behavior. The more information that both operating managers and the company have about each other's expectations, the better. This information may help reduce any ambiguities that may be involved in evaluating the extent to which managers' performances meet these expectations. If it becomes clear to a manager that the company wants or expects certain kinds of behavior that he does not believe he can or should perform, then he has a more informed basis for deciding whether to change companies or positions within the company. Likewise, the company has a more informed basis for making promotion, transfer or separation decisions about this manager.

The third major area of practical consideration concerns the importance of determining to which other positions a manager is connected and what the nature of the connecting bonds is. We have viewed each manager as occupying a different position in a company and as being expected to perform and engage in the budget-oriented behaviors and relationships associated with that position. We also have viewed the actual budget-oriented behavior of the manager who occupies a given position as being a complex outcome of a definitional process between the manager and the managers who occupy other positions.

Because these Other Managers have expectations about a given manager's budget-oriented behavior and attempt to influence his behavior by exerting pressure on him, it is almost impossible to fully understand, describe or predict the manager's behavior without determining which other managers are attempting to influence him and without determining why and to what extent they are attempting to do so. Thus, in any process of evaluating a manager's budget-oriented behavior, the expectations of these other managers also must be considered.

A fourth area of practical consideration concerns the importance of recognizing that in order to change a manager's budget-oriented behavior, it may be necessary to bring about complementary changes on the parts of all the other managers to whom the manager is connected. As discussed, the budget-oriented behavior of a manager is of direct concern to Other Managers and is substantially determined by their behavior toward him. Any change in the manager's behavior will not only require complementary changes on their part, but also their acceptance and reinforcement of this change. Thus, the expectations of these Other Managers also must be taken into account in any process of attempting to change a manager's budget-oriented behavior.

Predictors of Managers' Budget-Oriented Behavior

Our theoretical model also focused on the broader context in which managers' budget-oriented behavior occurs. First, we linked a company's use of participative budgeting with the behavior of its managers by viewing the structural properties or characteristics of its use of participative budgeting as a potentially important antecedent of this behavior. We used the term "participative budgeting variables" to refer to alternative amounts and forms of participation by operating managers in the budget-setting process. Companies can differ dramatically in their use of participative budgeting, and these differences may be reflected in the content of the expectations Other Managers hold for a manager's budget-oriented behavior.

Second, we extended our analysis to include three additional sets of variables which, taken in combination, represent the broader context in which participative budgeting is used and in which managers' budget-oriented behavior occurs. These additional sets of variables, which we termed "mediating variables," include the more enduring states or characteristics of a company's organizational structure and operating environment, of the individual managers who perform budget-oriented behavior, and of the interpersonal relationships between these managers.

Another major part of our empirical research was designed to investigate the relationships between 17 predictor variables and managers' budget-oriented behavior. These predictor variables included several participative budgeting and mediating variables. Two of these variables reflected the fact that our total sample was drawn from four production companies that differed in their use of participative budgeting and from different management levels within each company. The other predictor variables included four demographic variables relating to age, experience and time spent on budgeting; three attitudinal variables relating to leadership style, machiavellianism and internal versus external feelings of locus of control; and eight personality variables relating to cautiousness, original thinking, personal relations, vigor, ascendency, responsibility, emotional stability and sociability.

Our analysis was designed to reveal which predictor variables and combinations of them were most important for explaining differences in measures of managers' budget-oriented behavior. The most important result of our analysis was the potential importance of the structural properties of a company's use of participative budgeting and of the organizational context within which it is used for explaining differences in measures of managers' budget-oriented behavior. For example, these results revealed that these variables were the most important predictors of the extent to which managers tend to engage in various budget-related coping behaviors, to be personally involved in budgeting, to be shown comparisons of actual and budgeted performance and to experience intensive time demands from budgeting. These results also revealed that these variables were the most important predictors of managers' attitudes about the extent to which they think they should perform certain budget-related activities, work with their superiors and others, suggest changes or improvements in budgeting, be expressive about budgeting, and have positive attitudes about the usefulness of budgeting.

The structural properties of a company's use of budgeting have received very little consideration in the literature. The human relations emphasis of the past 20 years has tended to emphasize the importance of personality and attitudinal variables and to de-emphasize the importance of structural and contextual variables. However, the results of our analysis suggest that these structural variables may be important for explaining differences in measures of managers' budget-oriented behavior, especially those measures which are descriptive of the performance of specific activities and interactions.

Another important result of our analysis was that personality and attitudinal variables also may be important for explaining differences in measures of managers' budget-oriented behavior. As indicated above, the literature on the behavioral effects of budgeting suggests that these variables may be important predictors of how managers use budgeting and what they think about their use of budgeting. The results of our analysis reveal that the personality variables of emotional stability and ascendency and the attitudinal variable of internal-external feelings of locus of control were the most important predictors of the extent to which managers' methods of achieving their budgets tend to be accepted by others and the extent to which managers tend to be influential in the budgeting process, expressive about budgeting, and have positive attitudes about budgeting. In addition, these results reveal that the personality variables of emotional stability and cautiousness are the most important predictors of managers' attitudes about the extent to which they think they should work with others in preparing their budgets, perform various budget-oriented activities, have positive attitudes about the usefulness of budgeting, and be influential in budgeting. Our analysis suggests, however, that these personality and attitudinal variables, as well as several demographic and organizational variables, may be important only in a context which begins with the structural characteristics of a company's use of participative budgeting and of the organizational context within which it is used.

The major implication of our analysis for practice is the potential importance of other variables and combinations of them for understanding managers' budget-oriented behavior. This suggests that it is necessary for management accountants and others to focus on the broader context in which this behavior occurs. The participative budgeting and mediating variables, taken in combination, represent this broader context and illustrate the importance of surrounding conditions for understanding this behavior. These conditions inhere in the structural properties of a company's use of participative budgeting, in the organizational setting in which it is used, in the personalities of the managers performing this behavior, and in the nature of the interpersonal relationships between these managers and other managers.

Effects of Managers' Budget-Oriented Behavior

When other managers are generally supportive of a manager's present budget-oriented behavior, we expect that fact to be so perceived by the manager and expect that his response is likely to be primarily one of satisfaction and confidence. However, when pressures from other managers are particularly strong and are directed toward changes in a manager's budget-oriented behavior, or when these pressures are contradictory with one another, we expect that a manager's experience may be fraught with conflict and ambiguity and may evoke responses of tension, anger, or indecision.

Another major part of our empirical research was designed to investigate the relationships between managers' budget-oriented behavior and managers' attitudes about their positions. A set of 20 attitudinal items was used to measure their attitudes about their positions. These items were drawn from questionnaires developed and used by Porter (1964), Haire, Ghiselli and Porter (1966), and Porter and Lawler (1968) to measure managers' job attitudes and by Kahn et al. (1964) to measure job-related tension, satisfaction and ambiguity. For each item, managers were asked three questions: (a) How frequently does it take place? (b) How frequently should it take place? (c) How important is it to me? Managers' responses to these questions were used as different measures of their attitudes about their positions: their responses to the first question were used as *descriptive* measures, their responses to the second question were used as *normative* measures, and their responses to the third question were used as *evaluative* measures.

221

Our analysis of the descriptive and normative measures resulted in the identification and description of five descriptive and five normative dimensions. The descriptive dimensions were concerned with the extent to which managers think they experience job-related influence or power, ambiguity, tension, self-actualization, and satisfaction. The normative dimensions were concerned with the extent to which managers think they should experience job-related influence, ambiguity and tension and engage in meaningful job-related social interaction.

Our analysis was designed to reveal which measures of managers' budget-oriented behavior may be important for explaining differences in measures of managers' attitudes about their positions. This analysis revealed that both positive and negative attitudinal effects may be associated with managers' budget-oriented behavior.

On the positive side, our analysis revealed that the extent to which managers tend to experience greater job-related self-actualization may be associated with the extent to which they tend to experience greater involvement and participation in budgeting. For example, managers who think they are less often forced to do things that are against their better judgment and think they are more often given opportunities for advancement and promotion and for personal growth and development think that they are more often consulted about special factors they would like to have included in their operating budgets, that their budgets more often include changes they have suggested, and that their budgets more often are not finalized until they are satisfied with them.

On the negative side, our analysis revealed that the extent to which managers experience job-related tension may be related to the extent to which they experience more felt-pressure from budgeting. For example, managers who think they experience more job-related tension also think they are not able to spend as much time and effort as they would like preparing their operating budgets and think they spend more time and effort outside of normal working hours preparing their operating budgets.

The finding that both positive and negative consequences may be associated with dimensions of managers' budget-oriented behavior is an important one for practice. In designing and redesigning budgeting systems, management accountants and others are effectively attempting to modify some of these dimensions for some managers. However, these individuals should recognize that there is no way to eliminate the negative effects that may be associated with these dimensions. Job-related tension and ambiguity are seemingly facts of organizational life. However, they should be sensitive to the possibility that a company's use of participative budgeting may require or bring about behavior that may increase or decrease the amount of tension and ambiguity experienced by some managers without producing corresponding benefits.

Conversely, these individuals should recognize that there is no way to realize completely the positive effects that may be associated with some of these dimensions. The extent to which managers may experience meaningful job-related social interaction and job-related self-actualization may be affected by factors other than a company's use of participative budgeting. A company's use of participative budgeting may require or bring about behavior that may increase the likelihood of managers experiencing more meaningful social interaction or experiencing higher self-actualization; however, given the complex nature of the organizational context within which it is used, management accountants and others should be sensitive to the extent to which its use can effectively realize these effects.

Limitations and Extensions of the Research

Our research has both some obvious limitations as well as some natural extensions which should be noted. First, some limitations are associated with the theoretical model we developed to help us identify some important variables and to hypothesize some general relationships between them. There was little in the way of empirical and theoretical work that could help us in developing this model. This placed severe limitations on our ability to formulate specific hypotheses about the relationships between these variables and led us to make general rather than specific assertions about these relationships. Given the paucity of previous work, it would have been pretentious for us to do otherwise.

Taken as a whole, our empirical findings tend to confirm the general pattern of relationships implied by the theoretical model. The participative budgeting and mediating variables presumed to affect managers' budget-oriented behavior turned out to be related to this behavior, and those effects presumed to be associated with this behavior also turned out to be related somewhat to this behavior. To this extent, our findings tend to validate the model.

A natural extension of the research reported here is the further elaboration of the variables contained in our model and the positing of specific hypotheses about the relationships between them. The crucial aspect of the model which remains to be validated in future research is the direction of the relationships depicted in the model. The model not only hypothesizes the existence of certain general patterns of relationships among the variables, but it also hypothesizes the direction of these relationships. For this feature of the model, our findings are only indirectly relevant because they are essentially of an associative nature. Nevertheless, it is sufficient to conclude at this point that the theoretical model has passed its first rough screening and that we are optimistic about its promise for indicating the direction of the relationships depicted in the model.

Some limitations also are associated with our overall research design. The field study research design has the distinct advantage of allowing data to be obtained from managers operating in real, existing organizations of the kind to which the results are intended to apply. However, this advantage is gained at the cost of less precision, less control, and less freedom to manipulate variables whose effects may be of central concern.

For example, we attempted to build some controls into our field study research design by drawing our total sample from production companies that were in the same general industry and by drawing one sub-sample of managers from the same level in each company. Moreover, we attempted to experimentally manipulate the participative budgeting variables by selecting companies that differed in their use of participative budgeting. However, these attempts at control and experimental manipulation were somewhat confounded by our lack of control over other variables which were allowed to vary freely and were not measured, a result of conducting our research in natural rather than contrived settings.

An appropriate extension of our research would be an investigation of the relationships depicted in our model in more controlled and experimentally manipulated settings. As indicated above, probably the most important research need for the future, in connection with the model, is to collect data that will provide evidence about the direction of these relationships. While it is relatively easy to state this aim, it is more difficult to generate this evidence. Because of the difficulties involved in controlling extraneous variables, it is almost impossible to successfully use true experimental research designs in field settings. A study by Stedry and Kay (1966) provides a ready example of some of the problems which can be encountered in conducting field experiments.

One alternative to using true experimental designs in these settings may be to use a quasi-experimental research design (Campbell and Stanley, 1963). These designs attempt to approximate true experimental designs by the deliberate introduction of certain changes in organizations or by the before-and-after observations of natural changes taking place in them. For example, instances in which companies are making definite changes in their use of participative budgeting may provide ideal situations for the collection of data relevant to obtaining evidence about the direction of the relationships depicted in the model.

A second alternative may be to use a longitudinal research design. The major problems associated with this type of design are the relatively long waiting periods before results are available and the necessity of specifying in advance what variables are to be measured. However, our model may be helpful in providing some definite leads about what variables should be measured and what kinds of research methods may be appropriate.

A third alternative may be to conduct true experimental designs in laboratory rather than field settings. The major problem with using these settings is the difficulty of generalizing results to field settings. Yet, by using laboratory settings, extraneous variables can be controlled and the relationships depicted in the model can be altered in systematic ways.

Finally, some limitations are associated with our research methods. We used questionnaires to obtain data from our sample of managers about their budget-oriented behavior, their attitudes about their positions, and about selected demographic, attitudinal, and personality variables, and we made extensive use of the multivariate techniques of factor analysis and the Automatic Interaction Detector (AID) in our analysis of these data. The limitations associated with the use of questionnaires were noted in Chapter 4, and the limitations associated with the use of factor analysis and the AID technique were discussed in Chapters 4 and 5, respectively. Natural extensions of our research include the use of alternative ways of obtaining data about some of the variables included in our research, the development of improved measures of these variables, and the use of alternative methods of analysis.

In many respects, our research not only generates more questions than it resolves, but it generates a new set of questions to be resolved in future research. First, we have identified managers' budget-oriented behavior as a potentially important concept which can be used to link a company's use of participative budgeting with the behavior of its managers. We have tried to describe this behavior, the process through which and by which it is defined for a given manager, and the context in which it occurs. We have derived measures of this behavior based on data obtained from a relatively large sample of managers, identified some variables which may be important for explaining differences in this behavior, and identified some effects which may be associated with this behavior.

Yet, we must conclude that our understanding of this behavior is still limited and that much remains to be done before we can fully appraise the potential implications of this approach for studying some effects of participative budgeting. Our measures of this behavior were relatively crude and require improvement. In addition, even though we identified several dimensions of this behavior and indicated their relative importance for explaining differences in how managers use budgeting and what they think about their use of budgeting, subsequent research should focus on cross-validating these dimensions and developing better descriptions and measures of these dimensions as well as on seeking out additional dimensions of this behavior.

Second, we have identified some of the variables which may affect this behavior. The finding that the structural characteristics of a company's use of participative budgeting and of the organizational context in which it is used may be important for explaining differences in this behavior is a very significant finding. Further research into the nature of these characteristics is an important and natural extension of this research. We encourage both practitioners and researchers alike to focus their attention on the structural characteristics and properties of a company's use of participative budgeting. Even though this has been a neglected area of behavioral research in budgeting, our research suggests that this area may hold considerable promise for a better understanding of the effects of participative budgeting on managerial behavior.

The finding that personality and attitudinal variables may be relatively less important in explaining differences in this behavior is also an important result. We obtained relatively complete measures of these variables as part of our research. The fact that these variables were relatively less important than expected suggests that our understanding of the effects of these variables may be more limited than we thought generally.

Finally, we have identified some effects which may be associated with this behavior. The findings that job-related tension may be related to felt-pressure from budgeting and that job-related self-actualization may be related to involvement and participation in budgeting are important results. They reflect the highly contingent and highly complex nature of the effects of this behavior. More research must be undertaken to determine what effects may be associated with this behavior. We have focused only on a few attitudinal effects of this behavior. Identification and measurement of other effects which may be associated with this behavior would seem to be a natural extension of our research.

From all that we have said in this chapter, it is obvious that future research in connection with refining and improving our behavioral approach to participative budgeting is both possible and necessary. We have emphasized the importance of attempting to describe budgeting in behavioral terms, and we have proposed managers' budget-oriented behavior as a key concept for doing this. We have argued that from this concept stems a new view of budgeting, a fuller appreciation of its inherent structure, and a broader concept of its role and likely effects.

We believe that this approach, even in its present form, can serve a useful function by providing clues about the kinds of information that may be required to gain a greater comprehension of the effects of participative budgeting on managerial behavior. We are aware that our knowledge of the dimensions, predictors, and effects of this behavior still is fragmentary and that our knowledge can be advanced best by research based on this more general view. This is a difficult task, and the outcome is not likely to be uniformly satisfactory. Our hope is that the effort and its product may contribute to our understanding of these effects. We know of no more urgent or exciting problem.

APPENDIX A
ABBREVIATED VARIABLE DICTIONARY

A. Measures of Managers' Budget-Oriented Behavior

  1. Descriptive Budget Factors

      I. Evaluation by Superiors and of Subordinates

      II. Actions Brought About by Expected Budget Overruns

      III. Responsibility for Meeting Budget

      IV. Required Explanations of Budget Variances

      V. Interactions with Superiors

      VI. Usefulness of Budgeting

      VII. Acceptability of Methods

      VIII. Influence in Budget Setting

      IX. Personal Attention to Budgeting

      X. Involvement in Budgeting

      XI. Expressive about Budgeting

      XII. Interactions with Peers and Financial Staff

      XIII. Time Demands of Budgeting

  2. Normative Budget Factors

      I. Required Explanations of Budget Variances

      II. Acceptability of Methods

      III. Interactions with Peers and Financial Staff

      IV. Actions Brought About by Expected Budget Overruns

      V. Usefulness of Budgeting

      VI. Suggestions about Budgeting

      VII. Involvement in Budgeting

      VIII. Expressive about Budgeting

      IX. Influence in Budget Setting

      X. Influence on Flexibility and Innovation

      XI. Evaluation by Superiors

      XII. Difficulty Meeting Budget

      XIII. Anticipatory Budget Preparation

      XIV. Interactions with Superiors

B. The Predictor Variables

1. Company
2. Sample Selected
3. Time out of School
4. Time in Company
5. Time in Position
6. Time Spent Budgeting
7. LPC (Least Preferred Co-worker)
8. Mach (Machiavellianism)
9. I/E Control (Internal versus External Feelings of Locus of Control)
10. Cautiousness
11. Original Thinking
12. Personal Relations
13. Vigor
14. Ascendency
15. Responsibility
16. Emotional Stability
17. Sociability

C. Measures of Managers' Attitudes about Their Positions

1. Descriptive Position Factors
    I.   Job-Related Influence
    II. Job-Related Ambiguity
    III. Job-Related Tension
    IV. Job-Related Self-Actualization
    V.   Job-Related Satisfaction

2. Normative Position Factors
    I.   Job-Related Influence
    II. Job-Related Ambiguity and Self-Actualization
    III. Job-Related Tension
    IV. Job-Related Social Interaction
    V.   Job-Related Tension

RESEARCH ON BUDGETING IN INDUSTRY

PART I

1. For how long have you worked:

   a. Since leaving school? _____years
   b. For this company? _____years
   c. In your present position? _____years

2. Consider last month; what percentage of your time was spent on budget-related activities? _____%

PART II

Several characteristics or qualities relating to your use of budgeting are listed below. For each characteristic you are asked to give three ratings:

   a. How frequently does the characteristic take place?
   b. How frequently do you think the characteristic should take place?
   c. How important is the characteristic to you?

Each rating will be made on a line which looks like this:

   minimum_____maximum

Please put a mark (X) on the lines at a point that approximates how frequently the characteristic takes place, how frequently it should take place, and how important it is to you. For example, if you think the characteristic "never" takes place, you should place an X at the "minimum" end of the line. Alternatively, if you think the characteristic "always" takes place, you should place an X at the "maximum" end of the line.

Please do not omit any scales.

1. I start preparing the budget for my unit before I am asked to.

    a. How often does it take place? (min)_____(max)
    b. How often should it take place?   _____
    c. How important is it to me?   _____

2. I spend time outside of normal working hours preparing the budget for my unit.

    a. How often does it take place? (min)_____(max)
    b. How often should it take place?   _____
    c. Ilow important is it to me?   _____

3. I am not able to spend as much time as I would like preparing the budget for my unit.

    a. How often does it take place? (min)_____(max)
    b. How often should it take place?   _____
    c. How important is it to me?   _____

4. I work with my superior in preparing the budget for my unit.

    a. How often does it take place? (min)_____(max)
    b. How often should it take place?   _____
    c. How important is it to me?   _____

5. I work with my subordinates in preparing the budget for my unit.

    a. How often does it take place? (min)_____(max)
    b. How often should it take place?   _____
    c. How important is it to me?   _____

6. I work with other unit heads in preparing the budget for my unit.

    a. How often does it take place? (min)_____(max)
    b. How often should it take place?   _____
    c. How important is it to me?   _____

7. I work with financial staff people in preparing the budget for my unit.

    a. How often does it take place? (min)_____(max)
    b. How often should it take place?   _____
    c. How important is it to me?   _____

8. I am consulted about special factors I would like to have included in the budget being prepared.

    a. How often does it take place? (min)_____(max)
    b. How often should it take place?   _____
    c. How important is it to me?   _____

9. New budgets include changes I have suggested.

    a. How often does it take place? (min)_____(max)
    b. How often should it take place?   _____
    c. How important is it to me?   _____

10. The budget is not finalized until I am satisfied with it.

    a. How often does it take place? (min)_____(max)
    b. How often should it take place?   _____
    c. How important is it to me?   _____

11. Preparing the budget for my unit requires my attention to a great number of details.

    a. How often does it take place? (min)_____(max)
    b. How often should it take place?   _____
    c. How important is it to me?   _____

12. I am reminded of the importance of meeting the budget for my unit.

    a. How often does it take place? (min)_____(max)
    b. How often should it take place?   _____
    c. How important is it to me?   _____

13. I am evaluated on my ability to meet the budget for my unit.

    a. How often does it take place? (min)_____(max)
    b. How often should it take place?   _____
    c. How important is it to me?   _____

14. I have difficulty meeting the budget for my unit.

    a. How often does it take place? (min)_____(max)
    b. How often should it take place?   _____
    c. How important is it to me?   _____

15. I am shown comparisons of actual and budgeted performance for other units.

    a. How often does it take place? (min)_____(max)
    b. How often should it take place? _____
    c. How important is it to me? _____

16. My explanation of budget variances is included in performance reports.

    a. How often does it take place? (min)_____(max)
    b. How often should it take place? _____
    c. How important is it to me? _____

17. I investigate favorable as well as unfavorable budget variances for my unit.

    a. How often does it take place? (min)_____(max)
    b. How often should it take place? _____
    c. How important is it to me? _____

18. I go to my superior for advice on how to achieve my budget.

    a. How often does it take place? (min)_____(max)
    b. How often should it take place? _____
    c. How important is it to me? _____

19. I am required to prepare reports comparing actual results with budget.

    a. How often does it take place? (min)_____(max)
    b. How often should it take place? _____
    c. How important is it to me? _____

20. My methods of reaching budgeted performance are accepted without question by my superior.

    a. How often does it take place? (min)_____(max)
    b. How often should it take place? _____
    c. How important is it to me? _____

21. My methods of reaching budgeted performance are accepted without question by my subordinates.

    a. How often does it take place? (min)_____(max)
    b. How often should it take place? _____
    c. How important is it to me? _____

22. My superior calls me in to discuss variations from the budget.

    a. How often does it take place? (min)_____(max)
    b. How often should it take place?   _____
    c. How important is it to me?   _____

23. My superior accepts my explanation of budget variances in my unit.

    a. How often does it take place? (min)_____(max)
    b. How often should it take place?   _____
    c. How important is it to me?   _____

24. My superior expresses dissatisfaction to me about results in my unit when the budget has not been met.

    a. How often does it take place? (min)_____(max)
    b. How often should it take place?   _____
    c. How important is it to me?   _____

25. My superior mentions budgets when talking to me about my efficiency as a manager.

    a. How often does it take place? (min)_____(max)
    b. How often should it take place?   _____
    c. How important is it to me?   _____

26. I ask for assistance from staff departments concerned with budgeting.

    a. How often does it take place? (min)_____(max)
    b. How often should it take place?   _____
    c. How important is it to me?   _____

27. I am required to submit an explanation in writing about causes of large budget variances.

    a. How often does it take place? (min)_____(max)
    b. How often should it take place?   _____
    c. How important is it to me?   _____

28. I use the budget to plan activities in my unit.

    a. How often does it take place? (min)_____(max)
    b. How often should it take place?   _____
    c. How important is it to me?   _____

29. I am required to trace the cause of budget variances to groups or individuals within my unit.

  a. How often does it take place? (min)_____(max)
  b. How often should it take place?   _____
  c. How important is it to me?   _____

30. I personally investigate budget variances in my unit.

  a. How often does it take place? (min)_____(max)
  b. How often should it take place?   _____
  c. How important is it to me?   _____

31. I evaluate my subordinates by means of the budget.

  a. How often does it take place? (min)_____(max)
  b. How often should it take place?   _____
  c. How important is it to me?   _____

32. I am required to report actions I take to correct causes of budget variance.

  a. How often does it take place? (min)_____(max)
  b. How often should it take place?   _____
  c. How important is it to me?   _____

33. I find it necessary to stop some activities in my unit when budgeted funds are used up.

  a. How often does it take place? (min)_____(max)
  b. How often should it take place?   _____
  c. How important is it to me?   _____

34. I find it necessary to charge some activities to other accounts when budgeted funds for these activities have been used up.

  a. How often does it take place? (min)_____(max)
  b. How often should it take place?   _____
  c. How important is it to me?   _____

35. I have to shift figures relating to operations to reduce budget variances.

  a. How often does it take place? (min)_____(max)
  b. How often should it take place?   _____
  c. How important is it to me?   _____

36. Budget matters are mentioned in informal conversations.

    a. How often does it take place? (min)_____(max)
    b. How often should it take place?   _____
    c. How important is it to me?   _____

37. I express my opinions on budget matters.

    a. How often does it take place? (min)_____(max)
    b. How often should it take place?   _____
    c. How important is it to me?   _____

38. I offer suggestions for the improvement of budget systems.

    a. How often does it take place? (min)_____(max)
    b. How often should it take place?   _____
    c. How important is it to me?   _____

39. The budgeting system is changed in accordance with my suggestions.

    a. How often does it take place? (min)_____(max)
    b. How often should it take place?   _____
    c. How important is it to me?   _____

40. I discuss budget items when problems occur.

    a. How often does it take place? (min)_____(max)
    b. How often should it take place?   _____
    c. How important is it to me?   _____

41. The budget enables me to be more flexible.

    a. How often does it take place? (min)_____(max)
    b. How often should it take place?   _____
    c. How important is it to me?   _____

42. The budget enables me to be more innovative.

    a. How often does it take place? (min)_____(max)
    b. How often should it take place?   _____
    c. How important is it to me?   _____

43. The budget enables me to keep track of my success as a manager.

   a. How often does it take place? (min)_____(max)
   b. How often should it take place?   _____
   c. How important is it to me?   _____

44. The budget enables me to be a better manager.

   a. How often does it take place? (min)_____(max)
   b. How often should it take place?   _____
   c. How important is it to me?   _____

PART III

Several characteristics or qualities relating to your management position in your firm are listed below. As in Part II, put a mark (X) on the lines at a point that approximates (a) how frequently the characteristic takes place, (b) how frequently it should take place, and (c) how important it is to you.

Please do not omit any scales.

1. My management position gives me the opportunity to give help to others.

   a. How often does it take place? (min)_____(max)
   b. How often should it take place?   _____
   c. How important is it to me?   _____

2. My management position gives me the opportunity to develop close friendships.

   a. How often does it take place? (min)_____(max)
   b. How often should it take place?   _____
   c. How important is it to me?   _____

3. My management position forces me to decide things that affect the lives of people that I know.

   a. How often does it take place? (min)_____(max)
   b. How often should it take place?   _____
   c. How important is it to me?   _____

4. My management position forces me to resolve conflicting demands that people make on me.

    a. How often does it take place? (min)_____(max)
    b. How often should it take place?   _____
    c. How important is it to me?   _____

5. My management position gives me prestige within the company.

    a. How often does it take place? (min)_____(max)
    b. How often should it take place?   _____
    c. How important is it to me?   _____

6. My management position gives me prestige outside the company.

    a. How often does it take place? (min)_____(max)
    b. How often should it take place?   _____
    c. How important is it to me?   _____

7. My management position gives me authority.

    a. How often does it take place? (min)_____(max)
    b. How often should it take place?   _____
    c. How important is it to me?   _____

8. My management position forces me to do things that are against my better judgment.

    a. How often does it take place? (min)_____(max)
    b. How often should it take place?   _____
    c. How important is it to me?   _____

9. My management position gives me opportunities for independent thought and action.

    a. How often does it take place? (min)_____(max)
    b. How often should it take place?   _____
    c. How important is it to me?   _____

10. My management position gives me opportunities for participation in the setting of goals.

    a. How often does it take place? (min)_____(max)
    b. How often should it take place?   _____
    c. How important is it to me?   _____

11. My management position gives me opportunities for participation in determining methods and procedures.

    a. How often does it take place? (min)_____(max)
    b. How often should it take place?   _____
    c. How important is it to me?   _____

12. My management position gives me more to do than I can accomplish within a working day.

    a. How often does it take place? (min)_____(max)
    b. How often should it take place?   _____
    c. How important is it to me?   _____

13. My management position gives me opportunities for personal growth and development.

    a. How often does it take place? (min)_____(max)
    b. How often should it take place?   _____
    c. How important is it to me?   _____

14. My management position gives me opportunities for advancement and promotion.

    a. How often does it take place? (min)_____(max)
    b. How often should it take place?   _____
    c. How important is it to me?   _____

15. My management position gives me more to do than I can do my best at.

    a. How often does it take place? (min)_____(max)
    b. How often should it take place?   _____
    c. How important is it to me?   _____

16. My management position conflicts with my family life.

    a. How often does it take place? (min)_____(max)
    b. How often should it take place?   _____
    c. How important is it to me?   _____

17. I am clear about the tasks I must perform in my management position.

    a. How often does it take place? (min)_____(max)
    b. How often should it take place?   _____
    c. How important is it to me?   _____

18. My management position gives me opportunities to do the things I am best at.
    a. How often does it take place? (min)_____(max)
    b. How often should it take place? _____
    c. How important is it to me? _____

19. I know when something is wanted or expected of me in my management position.
    a. How often does it take place? (min)_____(max)
    b. How often should it take place? _____
    c. How important is it to me? _____

20. I know when I am doing well in my management position.
    a. How often does it take place? (min)_____(max)
    b. How often should it take place? _____
    c. How important is it to me? _____

PART IV

People differ in the ways they think about those with whom they work and this may be important in working with others. Think of the person **with whom you can work least well.** He may be someone you work with now, or he may be someone you knew in the past. He does not have to be the person you like least well, but he should be the person with whom you had the most difficulty in getting a job done.

Below are listed pairs of words which are opposite in meaning. Please describe the person **with whom you can work least well** by putting a mark (X) on the line between the two words. For example, if the two words were Very Neat and Not Neat, and you ordinarily think of the person with whom you are able to work least well as being **very neat,** you should put an X at the **Very Neat** end of the line. Alternatively, if you ordinarily think of this person as being **very untidy,** you should put an X at the **Not Neat** end of the line.

Please remember that there are no right or wrong answers. Work rapidly; give your immediate, first reaction to each item. Please do not omit any items, and mark each item only once.

Pleasant	Unpleasant
Friendly	Unfriendly
Rejecting	Accepting
Helpful	Frustrating
Unenthusiastic	Enthusiastic
Tense	Relaxed
Open	Guarded
Distant	Close
Cold	Warm
Cooperative	Uncooperative
Supportive	Hostile
Boring	Interesting
Quarrelsome	Harmonious
Self-Assured	Hesitant
Efficient	Inefficient
Gloomy	Cheerful

PART V

Several statements are listed below. Please put a mark (X) on the line at a point that approximates the extent to which you agree or disagree with the statement.

1. The best way to handle people is to tell them what they want to hear.

   Agree_____Disagree

2. When you ask someone to do something for you, it is best to give the real reasons for wanting it rather than giving reasons which might carry more weight.

   Agree_____Disagree

3. Anyone who completely trusts anyone else is asking for trouble.

   Agree_____Disagree

4. It is hard to get ahead without cutting corners here and there.

   Agree_____Disagree

5. It is safest to assume that all people have a vicious streak and it will come out when they are given a chance.

   Agree_____Disagree

6. One should take action only when sure it is morally right.

   Agree_____Disagree

7. Most people are basically good and kind.

   Agree_____Disagree

8. There is no excuse for lying to someone else.

   Agree_____Disagree

9. Most men forget more easily the death of their father than the loss of their property.

   Agree_____Disagree

10. Generally speaking, men won't work hard unless they're forced to do so.

    Agree_____Disagree

PART VI

Certain important events in our society affect people in different ways. Each item presented below consists of a pair of alternatives lettered a or b. Please circle the letter which corresponds with the one statement of each pair **(and only one)** which you more strongly **believe** to be the case as far as you're concerned. Be sure to select the one which you actually **believe** to be more true rather than the one you think you should choose or the one you would like to be true. This is a measure of personal belief; obviously there are no right or wrong answers.

Please answer these items **carefully** but do not spend too much time on any one item. Be sure to find an answer for every choice. In some instances you may discover that you believe both statements or neither one. In such cases, be sure to select the **one** you more strongly believe to be the case as far as you're concerned. Also try to respond to each item **independently** when making your choice; do not be influenced by your previous choices.

1. a. Children get into trouble because their parents punish them too much.
   b. The trouble with most children nowadays is that their parents are too easy with them.

2. a. Many of the unhappy things in peoples' lives are partly due to bad luck.
   b. People's misfortunes result from the mistakes they make.

3. a. One of the major reasons why we have wars is because people don't take enough interest in politics.
   b. There will always be wars, no matter how hard people try to prevent them.

4. a. In the long run people get the respect they deserve in this world.
   b. Unfortunately, an individual's worth often passes unrecognized no matter how hard he tries.

5. a. The idea that teachers are unfair to students is nonsense.
   b. Most students don't realize the extent to which their grades are influenced by accidental happenings.

6. a. Without the right breaks one cannot be an effective leader.
   b. Capable people who fail to become leaders have not taken advantage of their opportunities.

7. a. No matter how hard you try some people just don't like you.
   b. People who can't get others to like them don't understand how to get along with others.

8. a. Heredity plays the major role in determining one's personality.
   b. It is one's experiences in life which determine what they're like.

9. a. I have often found that what is going to happen will happen.
   b. Trusting to fate has never turned out as well for me as making a decision to take a definite course of action.

242

10. a. In the case of the well prepared student there is rarely if ever such a thing as an unfair test.
    b. Many times exam questions tend to be so unrelated to course work that studying is really useless.

11. a. Becoming a success is a matter of hard work; luck has little or nothing to do with it.
    b. Getting a good job depends mainly on being in the right place at the right time.

12. a. The average citizen can have an influence in government decisions.
    b. This world is run by the few people in power, and there is not much the little guy can do about it.

13. a. When I make plans I am almost certain that I can make them work.
    b. It is not always wise to plan too far ahead because many things turn out to be a matter of good or bad fortune anyway.

14. a. There are certain people who are just no good.
    b. There is some good in everybody.

15. a. In my case getting what I want has little or nothing to do with luck.
    b. Many times we might just as well decide what to do by flipping a coin.

16. a. Who gets to be the boss often depends on who was lucky enough to be in the right place first.
    b. Getting people to do the right thing depends upon ability; luck has little or nothing to do with it.

17. a. As far as world affairs are concerned, most of us are the victims of forces we can neither understand, nor control.
    b. By taking an active part in political and social affairs the people can control world events.

18. a. Most people don't realize the extent to which their lives are controlled by accidental happenings.
    b. There really is no such thing as "luck."

19. a. One should always be willing to admit mistakes.
    b. It is usually best to cover up one's mistakes.

20. a. It is hard to know whether or not a person really likes you.
    b. How many friends you have depends upon how nice a person you are.

21. a. In the long run the bad things that happen to us are balanced by the good ones.
    b. Most misfortunes are the result of lack of ability, ignorance, laziness, or all three.

22. a. With enough effort we can wipe out political corruption.

   b. It is difficult for people to have much control over the things politicians do in office.

23. a. Sometimes I can't understand how teachers arrive at the grades they give.

   b. There is a direct connection between how hard I study and the grades I get.

24. a. A good leader expects people to decide for themselves what they should do.

   b. A good leader makes it clear to everybody what their jobs are.

25. a. Many times I feel that I have little influence over the things that happen to me.

   b. It is impossible for me to believe that chance or luck plays an important role in my life.

26. a. People are lonely because they don't try to be friendly.

   b. There's not much use in trying too hard to please people; if they like you, they like you.

27. a. There is too much emphasis on athletics in high school.

   b. Team sports are an excellent way to build character.

28. a. What happens to me is my own doing.

   b. Sometimes I feel that I don't have enough control over the direction my life is taking.

29. a. Most of the time I can't understand why politicians behave the way they do.

   b. In the long run the people are responsible for bad government on a national as well as on a local level.

PART VII

On the following pages are a number of descriptions of personal characteristics of people. These descriptions are grouped in sets of four. You are to examine each set and find the one description that is **most like you.** Then place an X on the line following that statement, in the column headed **M** (most).

Next examine the other three statements in the set and find the one description that is **least like you;** then place an X on the line following that statement, in the column headed **L** (least). Do **not** make any marks following the two remaining statements.

	M	L
Here is a sample set: prefers to get up early in the morning	___	X
doesn't care for popular music	___	___
has an excellent command of English	___	___
obtains a poorly balanced diet	X	___

Suppose that you have read the four descriptive statements in the sample and have decided that, although several of the statements may apply to you to some degree, "obtains a poorly balanced diet" is **more like you** than any of the others. You would place an X on the line following that statement in the column headed M (most), as shown in the sample.

You would then examine the other three statements to decide which one is **least like you.** Suppose that "prefers to get up early in the morning" is **less like you** than the other two. You would place an X on the line following that statement in the column headed L (least), as shown in the sample above.

For every set you should have one and only one mark in the M (most) column, and one and only one mark in the L (least) column. There should be no marks following two of the statements.

In some cases it may be difficult to decide which statements you should mark. Make the best decisions you can. Remember, this is not a test; there are no right or wrong answers. You are to mark certain statements in the way in which they most nearly apply to you. Be sure to mark one statement as being most like you and one as being least like you, leaving two statements unmarked. Do this for every set.

	M	L
a very original thinker		
a somewhat slow and leisurely person		
tends to be critical of others		
makes decisions only after a great deal of thought ..		

	M	L
believes that everyone is essentially honest		
likes to take it relatively easy at work or play ...		
has a very inquiring attitude		
tends to act on impulse		

	M	L
a very energetic person		
doesn't get angry at other people		
dislikes working on complex and difficult problems ..		
prefers gay parties to quiet gatherings		

	M	L
enjoys philosophical discussion		
gets tired somewhat easily		
considers matters very carefully before acting		
does not have a great deal of confidence in people ..		

	M	L
likes to work primarily with ideas		
does things at a rather slow pace		
very careful when making a decision		
finds a number of people hard to get along with		

	M	L
a great person for taking chances		
becomes irritated at other people quite readily		
can get a great deal done in a short time		
spends considerable time thinking of new ideas		

	M	L
a very patient person		
seeks thrills and excitement		
able to keep working for long stretches		
would rather carry out a project than plan it		

	M	L
feels very tired and weary at the end of the day ...		
inclined to make hurried or snap judgments		
doesn't get resentful toward other people		
has a great thirst for knowledge		

	M	L
does not act on the spur of the moment		
becomes irritated by faults in others		
lacks interest in doing critical thinking		
prefers to work rapidly		

	M	L
inclined to become very annoyed at people	____	____
likes to keep "on the go" all the time	____	____
would rather not take chances or run risks	____	____
prefers work requiring little or no original thought	____	____

	M	L
a very cautious person	____	____
prefers to work rather slowly	____	____
very tactful and diplomatic	____	____
would rather not occupy the mind with deep thoughts	____	____

	M	L
loses patience readily with people	____	____
has somewhat less endurance than most people	____	____
tends to be creative and original	____	____
doesn't care much for excitement	____	____

	M	L
tends to act on hunches	____	____
has a great deal of vigor and drive	____	____
doesn't trust people until they prove themselves	____	____
enjoys questions involving considerable thought	____	____

	M	L
doesn't like to work at a fast pace	____	____
has great faith in people	____	____
tends to give in to the wishes of the moment	____	____
enjoys working out complicated problems	____	____

	M	L
a very energetic worker	____	____
accepts criticism with very good grace	____	____
dislikes problems requiring a great deal of reasoning	____	____
inclined to act first and think afterward	____	____

	M	L
speaks nothing but the best about other people	____	____
very cautious before proceeding	____	____
not interested in thought-provoking discussions	____	____
does not hurry in going from place to place	____	____

	M	L
doesn't have an inquiring mind	____	____
doesn't act on impulse	____	____
generally bursting with energy	____	____
becomes irritated by weaknesses in other people	____	____

	M	L
able to get more things done than other people	____	____
enjoys taking chances just for the excitement	____	____
takes offense when subjected to criticism	____	____
would rather work with ideas than things	____	____

	M	L
very trustful of other people	___	___
prefers work that is routine and simple	___	___
does things on the spur of the moment	___	___
full of vigor and vitality	___	___

	M	L
makes decisions much too quickly	___	___
has a great liking for everybody	___	___
maintains a lively pace at work or play	___	___
does not have a great interest in acquiring knowledge	___	___

	M	L
a good mixer socially	___	___
lacking in self-confidence	___	___
thorough in any work undertaken	___	___
tends to be somewhat emotional	___	___

	M	L
not interested in being with other people	___	___
free from anxieties or tensions	___	___
quite an unreliable person	___	___
takes the lead in group discussion	___	___

	M	L
acts somewhat jumpy and nervous	___	___
a strong influence on others	___	___
does not like social gatherings	___	___
a very persistent and steady worker	___	___

	M	L
finds it easy to make new acquaintances	___	___
cannot stick to the same task for long	___	___
easily managed by other people	___	___
maintains self-control even when frustrated	___	___

	M	L
able to make important decisions without help	___	___
does not mix easily with new people	___	___
inclined to be tense or high-strung	___	___
sees a job through despite difficulties	___	___

	M	L
not too interested in mixing socially with people	___	___
doesn't take responsibilities seriously	___	___
steady and composed at all times	___	___
takes the lead in group activities	___	___

	M	L
a person who can be relied upon	___	___
easily upset when things go wrong	___	___
not too sure of own opinions	___	___
prefers to be around other people	___	___

	M	L
finds it easy to influence other people	___	___
gets the job done in the face of any obstacle	___	___
limits social relations to a select few	___	___
tends to be a rather nervous person	___	___

	M	L
doesn't make friends very readily	___	___
takes an active part in group affairs	___	___
keeps at routine duties until completed	___	___
not too well-balanced emotionally	___	___

	M	L
assured in relationships with others	___	___
feelings are rather easily hurt	___	___
follows well-developed work habits	___	___
would rather keep to a small group of friends	___	___

	M	L
becomes irritated somewhat readily	___	___
capable of handling any situation	___	___
does not like to converse with strangers	___	___
thorough in any work performed	___	___

	M	L
prefers not to argue with other people	___	___
unable to keep to a fixed schedule	___	___
a calm and unexcitable person	___	___
inclined to be highly sociable	___	___

	M	L
free from worry or care	___	___
lacks a sense of responsibility	___	___
not interested in mixing with the opposite sex	___	___
skillful in handling other people	___	___

	M	L
finds it easy to be friendly with others	___	___
prefers to let others take the lead in group activity	___	___
seems to have a worrying nature	___	___
sticks to a job despite any difficulty	___	___

	M	L
able to sway other people's opinions	___	___
lacks interest in joining group activities	___	___
quite a nervous person	___	___
very persistent in any task undertaken	___	___

	M	L
calm and easygoing in manner	___	___
cannot stick to the task at hand	___	___
enjoys having lots of people around	___	___
not too confident of own abilities	___	___

	M	L
can be relied upon entirely	____	____
doesn't care for the company of most people	____	____
finds it rather difficult to relax	____	____
takes an active part in group discussion	____	____

	M	L
doesn't give up easily on a problem	____	____
inclined to be somewhat nervous in manner	____	____
lacking in self assurance	____	____
prefers to pass the time in the company of others	____	____

PART VIII

Drafting and using budgets brings you into contact with a number of people. Please list below the names of members of this company **with whom you have spent the most time in drafting and using budgets.** Please list them in order (from most to least) according to the amount of time you have spent with them. List first the people under your supervision, if any. List second the people you do not supervise. The second list may include your supervisor and peers, as well as subordinates in other units that you do not supervise. The brackets before each entry are explained later.

Members You Supervise. Please list here only your subordinates (those persons who work under you in the unit which you supervise). With which ones do you spend the most time in drafting and using budgets?

( ) Most time _____ _____
                                Name   Title

( ) Second _____ _____

( ) Third _____ _____

( ) Fourth _____ _____

( ) Fifth _____ _____

( ) Sixth _____ _____

Members You Do Not Supervise. Please list here members who are not under your supervision. This may include members in positions above your own, those at the same level, and those in positions below your own. With whom do you spend the most time in drafting and using budgets?

( ) Most time _____ _____
                                Name   Title

( ) Second _____ _____

( ) Third _____ _____

( ) Fourth _____ _____

( ) Fifth _____ _____

Now considering all the names in both of the above lists, write a number in the bracket ( ) before each name to show its rank order in the total list. If eleven names are listed, rank them in order from (1) to (11) according to amount of time spent with them.

PART IX

TEST OF IMAGINATION

An important asset in the world is imagination — the capacity to think on your feet. This test gives you an opportunity to use your imagination, to show how you can create ideas and situations by yourself. In other words, instead of presenting you with answers already made up, from which you have to pick one, it gives you the chance to show how you can think things up on your own.

On the following pages you are to write out some brief stories that you make up on your own. In order to help you get started there is a series of pictures that you can look at and around which you can build your stories. When you have finished reading these instructions, you should turn the page, look at the first picture briefly, then turn the page again and write a story suggested by the picture. To help you cover all the elements of a story plot in the time allowed, you will find four questions spaced out over the page. They are:

1. What is happening? Who are the people?
2. What has led up to this situation? That is, what happened in the past?
3. What is being thought? What is wanted? By whom?
4. What will happen? What will be done?

Please remember that the questions are only guides for your thinking, and need not be answered specifically in so many words. That is, your story should be continuous and not just a set of answers to these questions. Do not take over 5 minutes per story. You should complete the whole test 25 minutes after you get started, although you may finish in less time if you like.

There are no right or wrong stories. In fact, any kind of story is quite all right. You have a chance to show how quickly you can imagine and write a story on your own. Don't just describe the pictures, but write a story about them. They are vague and suggestive of many things on purpose, and are just to help give you an idea to write about.

Try to make your stories interesting and dramatic. Show that you have an understanding of people and can make up stories about human relationships.

If you have read these instructions carefully and understood them, turn the page, look at the picture. Turn the page again and write the story suggested to you by the picture. Don't take more than 5 minutes. Then turn the page, look at the next picture briefly, write out the story it suggests, and so on through the booklet.

Just look at the picture briefly (10-15 seconds), turn the page and write out the story it suggests.

Work rapidly. Don't spend over 5 minutes on this story.

1. What is happening? Who are the people?

2. What has led up to this situation? That is, what has happened in the past?

3. What is being thought? What is wanted? By whom?

4. What will happen? What will be done?

When you have finished your story or your time is up, turn to the next picture. If you haven't quite finished, go on anyway. You may return at the end to complete this story.

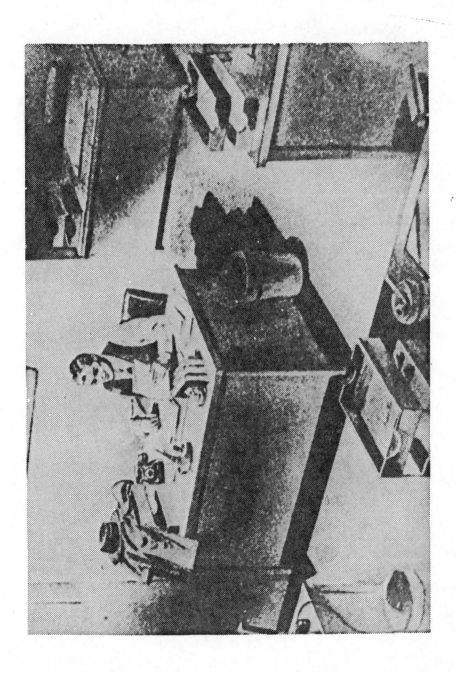

Just look at the picture briefly (10-15 seconds), turn the page and write out the story it suggests.

Work rapidly. Don't spend over 5 minutes on this story.

1. What is happening? Who are the people?

2. What has led up to this situation? That is, what has happened in the past?

3. What is being thought? What is wanted? By whom?

4. What will happen? What will be done?

When you have finished your story or your time is up, turn to the next picture. If you haven't quite finished, go on anyway. You may return at the end to complete this story.

Just look at the picture briefly (10-15 seconds), turn the page and write out
the story it suggests.

Work rapidly. Don't spend over 5 minutes on this story.

1. What is happening? Who are the people?

2. What has led up to this situation? That is, what has happened in the past?

3. What is being thought? What is wanted? By whom?

4. What will happen? What will be done?

When you have finished your story or your time is up, turn to the next picture. If you haven't quite finished, go on anyway. You may return at the end to complete this story.

REFERENCES

ARGYRIS, CHRIS

1952　*The Impact of Budgets on People.* Ithaca: The Controllership Foundation, Inc., Cornell University.

1957　*Personality and Organisation; the Conflict Between System and the Individual.* New York: Harper.

1964　*Integrating the Individual and the Organization.* New York: Wiley.

BACON, JEREMY

1970　*Managing the Budget Function, Business Policy Study No. 131.* New York: National Industrial Conference Board, Inc.

BATTLE, ESTER, AND J. B. ROTTER

1963　"Children's Feelings of Personal Control as Related to Social Class and Ethnic Group," *Journal of Personality*, 31: 482-490.

BECKER, SELWYN, AND DAVID GREEN, JR.

1962　"Budgeting and Employee Behavior," *The Journal of Business*, 35: 392-402.

CAMPBELL, JOHN P., MARVIN D. DUNNETTE, EDWARD E. LAWLER, III, AND KARL E. WEICK, JR.

1970　*Managerial Behavior, Performance and Effectiveness.* New York, McGraw-Hill.

CAPLAN, EDWIN H.

1971　*Management Accounting and Behavioral Science.* Reading: Addison-Wesley.

CHRISTIE, RICHARD

1970　"The Machiavellis Among Us," *Psychology Today*, 3: 82-86.

CHRISTIE, RICHARD, AND FLORENCE GEIS

1970　*Studies in Machiavellianism.* New York: Academic Press.

CYERT, RICHARD M., J. G. MARCH, AND W. H. STARBUCK

1961　"Two Experiments on Bias and Conflict in Organizational Estimation," *Management Science*, 7: 254-264.

FERTAKIS, JOHN P.

1967　*Budget-Induced Pressure and Its Relationship to Supervisory Behavior in Selected Organizations.* Doctoral dissertation, University of Washington.

FIEDLER, FRED E.

1967　*A Theory of Leadership Effectiveness.* New York: McGraw-Hill.

GEIS, FLORENCE

1964　"Machiavellianism and the Manipulation of One's Fellow Man." Report presented at the Annual Meeting of the American Psychological Association, Los Angeles.

GEIS, FLORENCE, AND RICHARD CHRISTIE

1965 "Machiavellianism and the Tactics of Manipulation." Paper presented at the Annual Meeting of the American Psychological Association, Chicago.

GORDON, LEONARD V.

1963 *Gordon Personal Inventory: Manual.* Revised. New York: Harcourt, Brace and World.

1963 *Gordon Personal Profile: Manual.* Revised. New York: Harcourt, Brace and World.

HAIRE, H., E. E. GHISELLI, AND L. W. PORTER

1966 *Managerial Thinking: An International Study.* New York: Wiley.

HALPIN, ANDREW W.

1957 *Manual for the Leadership Behavior Description Questionnaire.* Columbus: Bureau of Business Research, The Ohio State University.

HARMAN, HARRY H.

1967 *Modern Factor Analysis* (2nd edition, Revised). Chicago: University of Chicago Press.

HOFSTEDE, G. H.

1967 *The Game of Budget Control.* New York: Van Nostrum.

HOPWOOD, ANTHONY G.

1972 "An Empirical Study of the Role of Accounting Data in Performance Evaluation," *Empirical Research in Accounting: Selected Studies, 1972,* Supplement to the *Journal of Accounting Research:* 156-182.

HORNGREN, CHARLES T.

1970 *Accounting for Managerial Control: An Introduction* (2nd edition). Englewood Cliffs: Prentice-Hall.

1972 *Cost Accounting: A Managerial Emphasis* (3rd edition). Englewood Cliffs: Prentice-Hall.

HUGHES, CHARLES L.

1965 "Why Budgets Go Wrong," *Personnel,* 43: 19-26.

KAHN, ROBERT L., DONALD M. WOLFE, ROBERT P. QUINN, J. DIEDRICK SNOEK, AND ROBERT A. ROSENTHAL

1964 *Organizational Stress: Studies in Role Conflict and Ambiguity.* New York: Wiley.

KAISER, H. F.

1960 "Comments on Communalities and the Number of Factors." Paper read at an informal conference, "The Communality Problem in Factor Analysis," Washington University, St. Louis.

KATZ, DANIEL, AND ROBERT L. KAHN

1966 *The Social Psychology of Organizations.* New York: Wiley.

KOONTZ, HAROLD, AND CYRIL O'DONNELL
1964 *Principles of Management; an Analysis of Managerial Functions* (3rd edition). New York: McGraw-Hill.

LIKERT, RENSIS
1961 *New Patterns of Management.* New York: McGraw-Hill.
1967 *Human Organization: Its Management and Value.* New York: McGraw-Hill.

MASLOW, A. H.
1954 *Motivation and Personality.* New York: Harper.

MAYO, E.
1945 *The Social Problems of an Industrial Civilization.* Cambridge: Harvard University Press.

MCGRATH, JOSEPH E.
1966 *Social Psychology: A Brief Introduction.* New York: Holt, Rinehart and Winston.

MCGREGOR, D.
1960 *The Human Side of Enterprise.* New York: McGraw-Hill.

MONCUR, ROBERT H., AND ROBERT J. SWIERINGA
1973 "A Study of Participative Budgeting Systems and Managers' Budget-Oriented Behavior," Unpublished Manuscript, Stanford University.

MONCUR, ROBERT H.
1975 *The Effects of Individual Differences on the Efficacy of Participative Budgeting Systems.* Doctoral dissertation, Stanford University.

ONSI, MOHAMED
1973 "Factor Analysis of Behavioral Variables Affecting Budgetary Slack," *Accounting Review,* XLVIII: 535-548.

OSGOOD, CHARLES E., GEORGE J. SUCI, AND PERCY H. TANNENBAUM
1957 *The Measurement of Meaning.* Champaign: The University of Illinois Press.

PONDY, LOUIS R., AND JACOB L. BIRNBERG
1969 "An Experimental Study of the Allocation of Financial Resources within Small Hierarchical Task Groups," *Administrative Science Quarterly,* 14: 192-201.

PORTER, L. W.
1964 *Organizational Patterns of Managerial Job Attitudes.* New York: American Foundation for Management Research, Inc.

PORTER, L. W., AND E. E. LAWLER, III
1968 *Managerial Attitudes and Performance.* Homewood: Richard D. Irwin, Inc.

ROTTER, JULIAN B.

1966 "Generalized Expectancies for Internal versus External Control of Reinforcement," *Psychological Monographs: General and Applied,* Volume 80: 1-21.

1971 "External and Internal Control," *Psychology Today,* 4: 36-42, 58-59.

ROTTER, JULIAN B., M. B. SEEMAN, AND S. LIVERANT

1962 "Internal versus External Control of Reinforcements: A Major Variable in Behavior Theory," in N. F. Washburn (ed.) *Decisions, Values, and Groups.* Volume 2: 473-516. New York: Pergamon.

SCHIFF, MICHAEL, AND ARIE Y. LEWIN

1968 "Where Traditional Budgeting Fails," *Financial Executive,* 36: 50-52, 55-56, 61-62.

1970 "The Impact of People on Budgets," *Accounting Review,* 45: 259-268.

SONQUIST, J. A., AND J. N. MORGAN

1964 *The Detection of Interaction Effects.* Ann Arbor: Institute for Social Research, The University of Michigan.

SONQUIST, JOHN A., ELIZABETH LAUH BAKER, AND JAMES N. MORGAN

1971 *Searching for Structure* (ALIAS, AID-III). Ann Arbor: Institute for Social Research, The University of Michigan.

STEDRY, ANDREW C.

1960 *Budget Control and Cost Behavior.* Englewood Cliffs: Prentice-Hall.

STEDRY, ANDREW C., AND E. KAY

1966 "The Effects of Goal Difficulty on Performance: A Field Experiment," *Behavioral Science,* 11: 459-470.

STOGDILL, RALPH M., AND CARROLL L. SHARTLE

1955 *Methods in the Study of Administrative Leadership.* Columbus: Bureau of Business Research, The Ohio State University.

SWIERINGA, ROBERT J.

1974 "A Cooperative Formulation of the Choice of an Optimal Participative Budgeting System." Paper presented at the Annual Meeting of the Operations Research Society of America and The Institute of Management Sciences, Boston.

SWIERINGA, ROBERT J., AND ROBERT H. MONCUR

1972 "The Relationship Between Managers' Budget-Oriented Behavior and Selected Attitude, Position, Size, and Performance Measures," *Empirical Research in Accounting: Selected Studies,* 1972, Supplement to the *Journal of Accounting Research:* 194-205.

VATTER, WILLIAM J.

1969 *Operating Budgets.* Belmont: Wadsworth.

VROOM, VICTOR H.
    1969   "Industrial Social Psychology," in Gardner Lindzey and Elliot Aronson (eds.) *The Handbook of Social Psychology:* 2nd ed., Volume Five: 196-268. Reading: Addison-Wesley.

WALLACE, MICHAEL E.
    1966   "Behavioral Considerations in Budgeting," *Management Accounting,* 47: 3-8.

WELSCH, GLEN A.
    1971   *Budget Profit Planning and Control* (3rd edition). Englewood Cliffs: Prentice-Hall.

No. 7475 - RRD - 2.5M - 1/75